Better Homes and Gardens®

NEW DECORATING BOOK

© Copyright 1990 by Meredith Corporation, Des Moines, Iowa.
All Rights Reserved. Printed in the United States of America.
Sixth Edition. First Printing.
Library of Congress Catalog Card Number: 89-82444
ISBN: 0-696-00093-8

BETTER HOMES AND GARDENS® BOOKS
Editor: Gerald M. Knox
Art Director: Ernest Shelton
Managing Editor: David A. Kirchner
Project Editors: James D. Blume, Marsha Jahns
Project Managers: Liz Anderson, Jennifer Speer Ramundt,
Angela Renkoski

Associate Art Directors: Neoma Thomas, Linda Ford Vermie,
Randall Yontz
Assistant Art Directors: Lynda Haupert, Harijs Priekulis,
Tom Wegner
Graphic Designers: Mary Schlueter Bendgen, Mike Burns,
Brenda Drake Lesch
Art Production: Director, John Berg; Associate, Joe Heuer;
Office Manager, Michaela Lester

President, Book Group: Jeramy Lanigan
Vice President, Retail Marketing: Jamie L. Martin
Vice President, Administrative Services: Rick Rundall

BETTER HOMES AND GARDENS® MAGAZINE
President, Magazine Group: James A. Autry
Editorial Director: Doris Eby
Furnishings and Design Editor: Denise L. Caringer

MEREDITH CORPORATION OFFICERS
Chairman of the Executive Committee: E. T. Meredith III
Chairman of the Board: Robert A. Burnett
President and Chief Executive Officer: Jack D. Rehm

NEW DECORATING BOOK
Editor: Pamela Wilson
Project Editor: Marsha Jahns
Graphic Designer: Brenda Drake Lesch
Writers: Sharon Novotne O'Keefe, Sandra Soria,
Gayle Butler, Heather Paper, Rosemary Rennicke,
Liz Seymour, Rebecca Jerdee, Jim Hufnagel
Electronic Text Processor: Paula Forest
Indexer: Barbara Klein

Special thanks to Shirley Van Zante, Geraldine Wilson,
Jill Mead, Rosa Snyder, and Kathy Stevens

INTRODUCTION

Welcome to the latest, all-new edition of the Better Homes and Gardens® **New Decorating Book.** Its 384 pages are packed with ideas—and hundreds of color photographs—to help you create a beautiful, comfortable, truly personal home.

The book covers all you need to know about decorating: furniture selection; color schemes; fabrics; room arranging; lighting; window, wall, and floor treatments; and more. Five chapters focus on specific areas of the house—living spaces, dining rooms, kitchens, bedrooms, and baths. Another chapter takes you on a tour of five lovely, highly individual homes.

Whether your seeking practical information or inspiration, you're sure to find it in the **New Decorating Book.**

CONTENTS

BEGINNINGS

Decorating a home is a rewarding experience, and not necessarily a costly one. However, few of us embark on a decorating project with total and absolute confidence. We may know in our mind's eye what we want our home (or a specific room) to look like, but turning this vision into a reality is often easier said than done. The difficulty, usually, is simply not knowing where to begin. Sometimes it's not being sure how to best express our tastes in a personal way. With so many options and so many directions to go, it's easy to get confused. This chapter is written to help you over the initial hurdles and show you how to create a home that not only looks good, but is truly right for you.

The process of decorating a home begins long before the first piece of furniture is purchased, or the first stroke of a paintbrush touches the wall. Actually, the process begins in childhood. Consciously or subconsciously, we take note of our own and other people's surroundings, and form an image of what for us constitutes beauty and comfort in a home. If our fondest memories include curling up with a good book in an overstuffed easy chair, it's likely we'll want or have a similar chair in our own homes. We can know and appreciate only the things we've been exposed to.

To expand our awareness of good design, it's necessary for most of us to study and observe. We can do this by making a concerted effort to expose ourselves to as many design influences as possible (books, magazines, museums, high-quality furniture stores, decorator showhouses), and by learning what we can about basic design principles, such as scale, balance, and contrast. One of the most important things to be learned from an increased awareness and sensitivity to good design is that good taste is not dependent on the size of one's bankbook. Quite the contrary. What matters most is expressing a sense of personal style—something that money can't buy. Here's another tenet of good design: Don't overdecorate. The secret of success is knowing when to stop.

Not only do personal concepts of design influence how we decorate our homes; much also depends on what's happening to society as a whole. Changing social patterns and economic trends invariably are reflected in our attitudes toward our homes. Consider the continued rise of women in the work force. It is now the exception—not the rule—for a woman to be a full-time homemaker. It wasn't that long ago that women—theoretically at least—could devote most of their time and energies to domestic activities. Now that this is no longer the case, one might think that interest in decorating would have decreased. But it hasn't. If anything, the interest is stronger. What has changed is our attitude toward furnishings. Most people today simply won't tolerate products that demand excessive time and effort to keep them looking and functioning well. It is no longer enough for, say, a floor covering to be merely beautiful. Now it must be beautiful, well-made, and most of all, easy to maintain. These demands extend to virtually all home furnishings products available today.

The space inside your home is your own little slice of the universe. It's where you do what you want, where you shut out the rest of the world if

BEGINNINGS

you choose, or invite others in to share your surroundings and hospitality. When you think of it like this, the space that is your home takes on new meaning and importance. How you use this space should, too.

To best use the space you have—both aesthetically and functionally—try to visualize a room totally empty. The space itself should dictate how you approach a decorating plan. Study the light in the room, the architecture that surrounds the space, the view out the window. Decide what elements you want to play up and the ones you'd like to minimize. Add furnishings to the space little by little so you don't obscure its character.

It isn't necessary—or even wise—to decorate an entire room all at once. To do so is hard on the budget. More importantly, additions to a room need to "settle in" before you can accurately assess what other furnishings are necessary. Only when several pieces are assimilated into the space around them should you think about adding more.

Be open-minded about your space. No longer should you allow a floor plan to dictate how you put various rooms to work. Forget labels. If you'd rather the dining room be a living room or vice versa, then by all means make the switch. The important thing is to make your space function in a way that will best suit you and your family's needs. If this means turning an extra bedroom into a den or a dining room, then so be it.

Don't overlook the possibilities that remodeling changes offer. Add divider "walls" where you want them, or, where structurally practical, consider removing unneeded walls that confine space in small-room cubicles. Open up these tightly strictured areas into one larger space and you immediately increase the options for function, comfort, and livability.

BEGINNINGS

Remember, too, that it isn't the size of the space you have but how you use it that counts. Don't let small space intimidate you. Even the smallest home can be given the illusion of spaciousness. Start by paring down. Many people feel compelled to fill every square inch with things and more things. All too often the end effect is downright claustrophobic. Any room can be made to look considerably larger than it is simply by stripping it of unnecessary furniture and extraneous accessories.

In the pages that follow we'll demonstrate just how easily some sound decorating principles can help you visually expand your space. You'll see how low furniture arrangements tend to give a room an open, uncrowded feeling, and how small-scale furniture creates a light, open effect in a room. There's the illusion that more space exists for people and activities when less of the space is taken up by furniture.

Color can visually alter how large an area appears. To make a room look larger than it is, use a light color on the walls and ceiling. Reflective surfaces such as lacquered or mirrored walls make the illusion of spaciousness still greater, as do dimensional effects such as scenic murals and *trompe l'oeil* creations.

And to make the space you have work even harder, do not settle for furniture that performs only a single function. Choose versatile dual-purpose pieces. And try to build more than one function into each room. Combine day and night uses for bedrooms so they are sleeping quarters by night, but when the sun comes up, they easily convert to office, playroom, or den.

BEGINNINGS

Before a decorating dream can become a reality, certain practicalities must be attended to. First, you must be honest with yourself. Is the project you have in mind realistic? Have you figured out approximately how much it's going to cost and whether your pocketbook can afford it? Is it a project you can do yourself, or will outside help be required? Is it a project you are willing to do yourself? If not, you might consider hiring the services of an interior designer. If you're not sure of your talents, paying for professional help might well save you money in the long run. Once you've established whether your dream is within the realm of possibility, develop a game plan that will see the project through to completion. You'll want to do this whether your project involves a total redo, or simply sprucing up an existing scheme. The objective is to work out your plan in attainable increments of both time and money. Begin by listing your priorities in terms of needs and wants. Some expenditures should take precedence. For instance, a comfortable bed is a must, but the bedroom wallpaper can wait. Once you've established priorities, you can determine how quickly you can afford to proceed. Don't be discouraged if your decorating plan is going to take longer than you'd hoped. The best decorating schemes develop slowly over a period of time.

You'll get a lot more mileage from your decorating dollar if you spend the most on what has to last the longest and will get the hardest wear. For instance, if your budget is tight, invest in good hall carpet and cut back on the quality of the bedroom floor covering. Similarly, spend money on a good sofa, even if it means dining at a makeshift, skirted table until you can afford dining furniture.

BEGINNINGS

In the long run you'll find that buying a few good pieces over a period of time is a wiser investment than filling a space with less-costly and less-well-designed furnishings. One special piece of furniture, an elegant area rug, or a piece or two of original art can set the mood for an entire room and—more importantly—give you pleasure for years to come. Besides being a decorative bonus, one fine furniture piece or art object is an investment in the future—something that will reward you with many years of classic beauty and function.

This doesn't mean, however, that you must settle for a half-empty room while you work to complete your decorating plan. On the contrary. Today, you do not have to look very far to find exceptionally well-designed "interim" furnishings and accessories to suit every budget and style preference. Examples of interim furnishings include inexpensive wicker pieces, sofas, tables, chairs, and wall systems from life-style stores and mail order outlets; and unfinished pieces from specialty stores.

And, of course, there are always "finds" to be unearthed at garage sales, flea markets, secondhand shops, and auctions. By all means, fill in with these pieces now; later, when you can afford to replace them, you can move these good-looking standbys to less-public rooms, or sell them at your own garage sale.

But remember, furnishing a room with budget pieces requires an eye for good value. In addition to beauty and comfort, you'll want to look for pieces that are flexible, functional, and durable. Also, the more basic the lines, the more easily they'll mix with other furnishings.

AMBIENCE

Memorable rooms, like memorable people, have distinct personalities. In decorating parlance, "personality" means the overall statement a room makes, the feelings it evokes when you enter, and what it says to you about the people who live there. This overriding ambience is the heart of a successful room scheme. And because ambience is a matter of personal expression, not specific style, you can select from the entire spectrum of furnishings, fabrics, lighting, and accessories to create the mood you want. Here, to inspire you, is a selection of rooms—some of them romantic, some casual, some contemporary, but all highly individual.

AMBIENCE
TRADITIONAL

A respect for the gracious past and its time-honored furnishings inspires the traditional room. On the design spectrum, it may be elegantly formal, simply lighthearted, or somewhere in between, but it's always wonderfully comfortable. Impervious to fleeting fads, traditional decorating embraces yesterday's best, a genteel blend of furnishings and accents that deservedly have earned a classic cachet. The traditional room, today, is lovely and appealing, wrapped in rich colors and fabrics and reflecting the highly personal style of its creator.

Whether they are 18th- and 19th-century antiques or the meticulous line-for-line reproductions crafted today, traditional pieces imbue a room with timeless beauty. They adapt easily to change, so you can mix periods and styles to match the room's formal or informal mood. The traditional category includes classic French furniture, pieces by Thomas Chippendale, George Hepplewhite, Thomas Sheraton, and Robert Adam of England, plus selected American styles, French provincial, Oriental, art nouveau and deco, and fine examples of Victoriana.

Traditional design offers an exciting range of interpretations for the contemporary home. Furnished more sparsely than their English counterparts, American traditional interiors play up the importance of each well-chosen piece and often mix mellow woods with fresh elements, such as elegant painted wall finishes, serene pastels, and updated versions of classic fabrics. But, no matter how formal the furniture arrangement or how prized the pieces and collectibles, the room's overall mood must be one of welcoming hospitality, not a museumlike setting with invisible velvet ropes.

*Its sunny outlook inspired ▶
by the window's softly pleated
floral chintz, the gracious living
room celebrates tradition with
classic seating, rich fabrics, and
antique accents. A wood screen
and fresh lacquer finish for the
old coffee table add a touch of
Oriental spice.*

AMBIENCE
TRADITIONAL

To put your room in a traditional mood, choose design elements appropriate for your classic furniture.

- Set the stage with antique Oriental rugs, classic French designs, or new carpets inspired by the historic designs of Colonial Williamsburg or the Victorian era.
- Emphasize collectibles. Accessories and mementos lovingly accumulated over the years add personality.
- Imbue character with architectural details—crown moldings, raised wood paneling, neoclassical cornices.
- Treat windows to flowing draperies, shirred valances, shutters, fabric-covered cornices, and swags and jabots.
- Consider historic reproduction wall coverings in stripes, Oriental motifs, or crewelwork designs. Or "age" walls with a sponge-painting or glazing technique.
- Finish up with exquisite details, such as elegant fringe, braids, tassels, and finely woven cord on draperies, upholstery, pillows, and table coverings.

▲
Restfully elegant, the bedroom surrounds heirloom Irish brass beds with fitting accents: antique prints, handwoven spreads, and damask draperies.

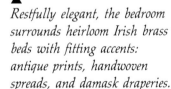

◀ *Classic furnishings and cozy-up colors grant this inviting living room timeless appeal. Cinnabar paint warms the walls, and checked fabric on the wing chair and swags recalls yesterday's homespun.*

Old and new make a lively ▶ mix in this dining room. Against a creamy backdrop, mahogany Hepplewhite-style chairs wear floral chintz and ring a glass-topped table with a bamboo base.

AMBIENCE
CASUAL

Settle back, put your feet up, relax, and recharge your spirits. That's the house rule in easygoing living spaces, designed informally to serve and soothe. At the heart of get-casual decorating is individual comfort—physical and psychological. So let your personal definition of it guide your furnishings choices. Pass up chairs with a straight-laced Victorian attitude, or a perch-on-the-edge contemporary bent. Ditto for fragile fabrics, don't-touch antiques, complicated window treatments, too-bright backdrops, and accessories that demand a lot of upkeep. Establish a light, serene mood with simply-functional, undemanding furnishings.

Although it looks nonchalant, the well-designed casual room doesn't just happen. It requires as much thoughtful planning as the most formal scheme to avoid appearing merely decoratively disheveled or indifferent. In selecting furnishings, consider these criteria:

• Is it comfortable? Does it feel good to sit on, to walk over, and to touch? Is it visually pleasing?

• Does it fit in naturally, or look contrived and self-conscious in the room's mix?

• Is it easy-care, or does it need special maintenance?

Relax your room with proven at-ease elements. Set a restful backdrop with creamy white, earthy neutrals, or soft colors. Choose inherently pleasing natural materials— mellow woods for exposed beams, paneled walls and floors with durable protective finishes, and also slate, tile, brick, or stone. Hand-loomed rugs, old quilts, and fabrics in nubby textures, robust plaids, ticking, and crisp canvas are casual warm-ups. Soil-resistant finishes add care-free appeal to fabrics and carpeting. Treat windows to shutters or pleated shades to make the most of natural light.

The take-it-easy attitude of ▶ the living room builds beautifully upon no-fuss fabrics, fresh colors, settle-back comfort, and convenience. In crisp slipcovers, old modular seating faces off by the alcove, where sleek storage stows entertainment gear.

AMBIENCE
CASUAL

▲
Though its architecture soars to dazzling heights, this relaxed living room is naturally down-to-earth. Wicker, a wooden settee, and a contemporary sofa mingle congenially in separately defined conversation areas.

Once a porch, this casual ▶ off-the-kitchen dining spot retains its outdoor feel with a woody backdrop and wrap of windows. Spicy red chairs season the setting.

◀ *A simply set-for-comfort bedroom calls on an antique star-patterned quilt to deliver soft color and a new storage wall to corral books and treasures.*

Carefree living space succeeds on a comfy furnishings mix and wise use of your room's natural resources.

• In furniture, consider versatile modular seating that adapts to any floor plan, durable laminate-clad tables, friendly wicker, and timeworn woods that don't fret over today's scratches. Personality pieces are welcome, and antiques, too, as long as they don't assume formal airs. Upholstered in a bright cotton print, a Louis XIV armchair would be right at home.

• Comfort also means convenience, so plan for an entertainment center, game table, storage, and the right light for reading, casual dining, and other family activities.

• Capitalize on the room's architectural amenities—built-in bookcases, a fireplace, a sitting-spot alcove, or a view—to give the room singular charm and focus.

• Edit accents and collectibles to an artful few, in keeping with the room's no-fuss, clutter-free attitude.

AMBIENCE
CONTEMPORARY

Spare, sculptural, and serene, today's contemporary room remains, in essence, true to the practical credo of 1920s Bauhaus designers: Form follows function. Body-soothing seating, understated background colors, exciting textures, and an emphasis on the natural, the uncomplicated, and the personal combine to create a mood that's sophisticated, yet appealingly warm. Although technology continues to redefine "state-of-the-art" in materials, and subsequent 20th-century movements have added classic pieces of their own, contemporary furnishings are unrivaled in the comfort and honest design they bring to a scheme.

Rejecting extraneous embellishments and clutter, contemporary settings succeed on simplicity, so each element receives its due of attention. Furniture is judiciously chosen for its flawless proportions, wonderful angles, and smooth planes. This basic beauty makes it versatile enough to go from the elegant to more relaxed settings. Counted among the classics are pieces by Marcel Breuer, Mies van der Rohe, Le Corbusier, and Charles Eames. Today's clean-lined upholstered seating, especially modulars, enhances comfort, adds textural interest, and fits the functional criteria.

Essential to the contemporary room is an intriguing mix of textures to contrast with hallmark sleek surfaces: marble, glass, lacquer finishes, metals, and acrylics. Upholstery and accent fabrics, such as leathers, buttery suedes, raw silks, wools, crisp linens, and nubby weaves, can provide the requisite counterpoint. Parquet floors, brick walls, and even a simply crafted antique piece or two are natural warm-up elements. In art and collectibles, the less-is-more philosophy prevails, with favorites well-edited for the drama, color, or sculptural appeal.

◀ *Pared to an elegant minimum, this Southwest-flavored living room tempers sleek surfaces with warm handcrafted woods and natural textures in seating wraps and rug. Art delivers color punch in the modern mix.*

AMBIENCE
CONTEMPORARY

From the flowing lines of a modern chair to the scheme's mood-setting palette, each design element must enhance the contemporary room's sense of harmony and ease.

• Light-touch backdrops—whites, neutrals, and bright pastels—play to the style's understated premise. Bold colors in contemporary art, accessories, or fabrics enliven the mood and add a dash of drama.

• Invite in the sun, but, if windows must be adorned, choose low-profile treatments, such as slim minislat blinds, elegant vertical blinds, or pleated or Roman shades, to give the room airy appeal.

• To supplement natural light, consider subtle recessed lighting, track lighting, or graceful torchères.

• Emphasize architectural details. Whitewashing beams imparts a sculptural quality. Or warm a wall with soft color, or the ceiling with sky-blue paint.

▲
Vibrant hues and intriguing textures warm the comfy conversation area in this sun-room. Tubular-frame chairs are 20th-century classics, upholstered in mohair and leather.

◀ *Beneath a blue "sky," this contemporary bedroom enjoys fresh fabrics and an interplay of colors. Antiques nestle in sleek shelving.*

Dramatic in black and ▶ off-white, this elegant dining room keeps the setting simple to show off slick-and-shine furnishings. The marble-topped table's base has an ebony satin finish, as do clean-lined Andover chairs.

AMBIENCE
ECLECTIC

Variety is the spice of exciting and uniquely personal eclectic living spaces. Waging gentle rebellion against decorating's past dicta, these warm one-of-a-kind rooms reject a matched-set furnishings philosophy and static arrangements, and chart a new and comfortable interiors course. Strictly speaking, eclectic design blends the best in furniture styles, regardless of period or pedigree, and, quite subjectively, the best in disparate accessories. Bringing pleasing harmony to a mix of elements demands a sophisticated design sense, creativity, and confidence.

To weave favorite furnishings and beloved collections into an eclectic scheme, find a strong design thread, a common denominator such as color, pattern, or the mood of each piece because each element must stand on its own appealing merits. Otherwise, your well-intentioned eclectic room will end up a catchall for the good, but the mismatched.

Color is an artful ally, and in backdrops, fabrics, and accessories, smoothly blends different elements. Keep the palette simple, working with a few colors and repeating those colors throughout the room for a well-balanced effect. For example, against a white backdrop, a medley of aged Chippendale chairs and classic modern seating—both upholstered in neutrals—contemporary art, and archaeological column-based tables share a sculptural quality. In an old-and-new amalgam, let color and pattern make the marriage of styles work. Freshen older period furniture with decidedly contemporary patterned fabrics, or use old tapestry pillows to soften a sweep of modern seating. Let the muted tones of a prized Oriental rug, or another major accessory, cue the room's unifying palette, choosing accent fabrics and paints that echo those colors.

Delightfully unexpected jux- ▶
taposition of elements imbues an
aerie with eclectic spirit. A
Louis XVI armchair and tall
chest mix with classic
contemporary seating. Wood,
stone, leather, and tapestry
fabrics add textural excitement.

AMBIENCE
ECLECTIC

Eclectic design appeals to collectors because such schemes warmly embrace the objects of their affections: the dramatic, the venerable, the rustic, the sleek, or the just-plain offbeat. But, to create a masterpiece, be selective, and apply basic criteria to each element.

• Is it well-designed and in good taste?

• Is the piece appropriate to the overall formal or informal mood you're striving for, decoratively?

For example, an antique quilt plays to informality, an elegant Persian rug to a more-formal attitude. Classic French armchairs, a Chippendale camelback sofa, and contemporary vertical blinds share a formal quality. On the other hand, modern modular seating, country-auction folk art, a sisal floor covering, and a glass-topped wicker-basket coffee table play to informality. Furnishings should be comfortable and functional to ensure that the eclectic room's livability is on a par with its visual appeal.

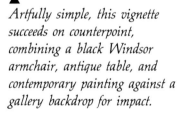

▲
Artfully simple, this vignette succeeds on counterpoint, combining a black Windsor armchair, antique table, and contemporary painting against a gallery backdrop for impact.

◄ *Traditional armchairs and casual woven-seat side chairs around an English pine table keep the eyes on an earthly plane in the dining room of an old church-turned-home.*

Colors picked from a soft and ► neutral palette unify disparate furnishings and accents in this living room. Sparkling white-on-white upholstery and silk patterned pillows soften the bamboo-trimmed sofa.

AMBIENCE
COUNTRY

Inherently comfortable and exceedingly warm, today's country-style room is, by design, an appealing touchstone of simpler times. Yesterday's handcrafted furniture, homespun textiles, natural motifs and textures, and charming collectibles deliver a special sense of heritage and easygoing hospitality to a room scheme. In this technology-intensive age, it's no wonder country's friendly face has become an enduring favorite, not only as a decorating style, but also as an expression of a casual, uncomplicated life-style.

Enchanting in its many moods, country is a versatile and truly satisfying choice for personalizing your decor. Furnishings can be farmhouse spare or softly sentimental, cabin rustic or refined New England Colonial. Regional styles, such as American Southwest with its rough-hewn furniture and textiles in bold sun-baked colors, spice country's repertoire. Or pick country in a European flavor—the pine-and-chintz of an English cottage, the fresh colors and painted woods of Scandinavia, or the rich prints and provincial antiques of the French countryside.

Handcrafted antique furniture is a hallmark of the country room. These sturdy, straightforward pieces, early renditions of aristocratic designs, fit well in today's homes because they are highly functional and comfortable. Country furniture ranges from classics (Shaker and adaptations of Queen Anne and Windsor) to primitive pieces (scrubbed pine, painted wood, and golden oak). Twig and wicker also add natural appeal. Today, line-for-line reproductions and varied adaptations of timeless furniture designs easily put any room in a delightful country mood.

Brimming with the fanciful ▶
finds of antiques lovers, this
welcoming living room was
"aged" with new rough-hewn
beams and fireplace paneling.
An 1800s German haywagon
serves as coffee table.
Americana treasures include
quilts, carousel horses, old toys,
and latter-day Amish dolls.

AMBIENCE
COUNTRY

For country personality, think homey and natural when choosing design elements and finishing touches.

• Calico, chintz, ticking, sporty plaids, and fabrics with a hand-loomed look fit the casual criteria. Antique linens add heirloom appeal.

• Well-edited collectibles accent country character, so show off favorites: folk art, farm tools, quilts, kitchenware, baskets, old toys, or weather vanes.

• Underfoot, consider natural wood, flagstone, or painted floors, topped with rustic rag, hooked, or folkish dhurrie rugs, or stenciled floorcloths.

• Palette options range from muted buttermilk hues and earth tones to bold quilt-inspired primaries and garden-fresh pastels.

• Set a rustic backdrop with exposed beams, mellow pine paneling, barn boards, or brick walls. Or, paint walls crisp white for a contemporary country look.

▲

Naturally kindred spirits, country woods warm this casual dining room. New chairs and an old French settee edge the library-dining table, beneath a rustic baker's-rack chandelier.

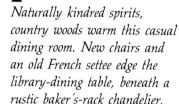

◄ *Versatile country meets contemporary in a spirited living room. Plump pillows, quilts, and paisley shawls softly wrap casual seating and echo the bold hues of the antique kilim.*

Tailored to country comfort, ► this cozy bedroom lets a subtle-hued backdrop showcase the bed, crisply dressed in a French cotton coverlet and antique Solomon's Puzzle quilt.

AMBIENCE
COUNTRY

As country decorating embraces European influences, one of the most captivating looks to emerge is English country. Its essence is comfort, with plenty of irresistible seating: oversize, down-filled, deeply skirted, and draped with old paisley throws or plumped with embroidered pillows. Its charming cachet is flowers, fragrant just-picked bouquets of the real thing and romantic chintz fabrics, crewelwork upholstery, and needlepoint rugs festooned with garden-cued motifs. Treasures, such as porcelain collections, gilt-edged mirrors, and framed botanical prints, add essential accents. Simple scrubbed pine pieces set a cozy cottage mood, and a mélange of antique burnished woods create an amiable country-house attitude. Rooms with an English accent exude an air of acquired luxury without pretension by blending rustic elements, such as plank floors and timeworn beams, with richly layered fabrics and fresh backdrop colors for counterpoint.

▲
With garden-fresh prints, soft pastels, and a grand canopy topper for the bed, this rustic retreat exudes English cottage charm without pretension.

◀ *Against a lettuce-green backdrop beribboned in grosgrain at the ceiling, heirlooms mix with auction finds, such as the newly painted tea table. The plank floor's diamond design is comb-painted.*

In an enchantingly English ▶ *mood, an airy living room blends classic elements—floral motifs, overstuffed seating, treasured collectibles, and gentle chintz-inspired colors.*

AMBIENCE
ROMANTIC

Lighthearted romantic rooms challenge your imagination and coax you to indulge your design passions. Perhaps you love crisp antique linens, or the ruffles and flourishes of Victoriana. Perhaps your fantasy is a garden-inspired wickery, or an inn-style bedroom bedecked in handmade lace. Or, maybe you'd like to cozy up a contemporary living space with a bit of nostalgia. Romantic decorating invites you to turn daydreams into reality—warm, intimate, soul-soothing rooms that are one of a kind.

Eschew the ordinary, the predictable, and the heavy-handed in selecting design elements. Instead, use a light touch, a free-spirited mix, and sentimental details in abundance. The mood-setting key? Simply surround yourself with things you love—fanciful accents, collectible treasures, soft colors, pretty fabrics, and era-evoking furnishings.

To keep the mood light, avoid weighty, dark-colored furniture; opt, instead, for pale woods, wicker, gracefully carved chairs, cheery painted armoires, and sink-in sofas and chaises. Manufacturers have noted the return to romance with new adaptations of 19th-century pieces such as hall trees, skirted sofas, and brass daybeds. Heirlooms fit perfectly here, not only grandmother's eccentric little tea table, but also her antimacassars and whimsical lamps.

Colors should be pretty: pastels or crisp white. Fabrics, such as flowered chintz, moiré, and linen, should play to the pampering mood. Today's washable laces and easy-care fabric finishes add to the romantic advantage. Glazed or sponged-on wall finishes create an elegant backdrop. If you mix patterns in wall coverings, upholstery, and accents, link them with a common-denominator color.

Lavishly flowered fabrics, ▶ crisp lattice on built-ins, and a generous bayfull of blooms and collectibles grant the garden-inspired living room sentimental appeal. Aged furnishings and soft touches—ruffles and ribbon-hung botanical prints— keep the mood captivating.

AMBIENCE
ROMANTIC

Sentimental attention to detail enhances the romantic mood and lets you personalize your room schemes.

• Cluster collectibles in charming vignettes, such as silver-framed family photos atop a lace-draped table, a lineup of old porcelain on the mantel, or botanical prints hung on ribbons. Dolls, ceramic animals, and Victorian birdcages are among the heartwarming treasures that charm any room. Scent the setting with fresh flowers and potpourris.

• Dress the windows in plisse, Priscillas, Austrian shades, or generous balloon shades of linen. Lavish laces in panels and cafés make a delicate treatment, as do swags and jabots in ninon and taffeta.

• Accent softly, using ruffled lampshades and table-covers, needlepoint carpets, tapestry pillows, or antique lace tablecloths as bedcovers.

• Illuminate this romantic stage with nonglare lighting, and include a dimmer switch to control the mood.

▲
A sun-filled summer's fantasy awash in pastels and old lace, the airy living room beckons with European country furnishings and artful accents, such as a sculptural birdcage and hand-painted floral ceiling.

White-on-white fabrics spark ▶ old-fashioned romance and link disparate elements in this elegant dining spot. Gauzy floor-to-ceiling draperies are festooned and tied with tasseled gold braid.

◀ *Nostalgia reigns in a charming guest room, its antique iron beds luxuriously dressed in yesterday's paperwhite eyelet and lace. Sponged-on peach paint creates a soft contrast to the burnished oak floors.*

AMBIENCE
INTERNATIONAL

Highly sophisticated and supremely confident in its approach to personal style, the living space with a world view celebrates exquisite design, regardless of period or national origin. It is a singular look strongly influenced by varied European movements, past and present, from classic pieces such as those of the Bauhaus to the sculptural furnishings of modern-day Italian and Scandinavian designers. But, it also can embrace any one of a range of timelessly distinctive moods, such as Oriental style with its exotic-blossomed motifs, intricately carved fretwork, and lacquered-wood finishes.

Decided elegance and luxurious comfort are inherent in the worldly scheme, and an artistic eye and an understanding of good design are imperative in setting the decorative stage. With its emphasis on cultured antiques or the artful new in furnishings, it is a look that appeals to those who can afford to indulge their taste preferences.

More than merely eclectic, the internationally inspired room achieves its high-style approach by putting its finest in context. Create a room around an especially beautiful antique piece or exotic collection, but design elements should match the richness of the mood. Such schemes are rounded out with noncompetitive furniture and accessories. Often expressions of the less-is-more design philosophy, furnishings are simple, yet not spare, and colors are understated and cool to foster a spacious feeling. With the focus on classic pieces of fine design, these worldly settings avoid clutter and the contrived, opting for distinctive accessories with integrity of form and function.

Home to world travelers, this ▶ polished living room is a trove of well-edited treasures. The gallerylike niche displays eclectic art and a French Empire desk, laden with antique jades. Chinese masks, carved in ivory, top the 19th-century armchair.

AMBIENCE
INTERNATIONAL

Interiors with a world view are well-suited to urban living and reflect a city-style urbanity in the fine furnishings, museum-quality art, and prized collections that grant them striking personality.

• Creamy color offers a dramatic gallerylike backdrop for simple compositions of objets d'art and paintings, hallmarks of such schemes. If accents share exquisite design, juxtapose them for interest, regardless of age or origin.

• Underfoot warm-ups include lustrous hardwood and parquet floors topped by antique Oriental carpets, or colorful dhurrie or nubby-wool Berber rugs.

• Artful lighting adds drama and spotlights treasures. Consider cove, recessed, and track lighting instead of conventional-style lamps, unless they are of the authentic Tiffany or antique variety or contemporary classics.

• If privacy is a considereation, opt for tailored vertical or minislat blinds or unobtrusive pleated shades.

▲
Elegantly Old World, this living room sets a beautiful stage—cappuccino walls and glittery Japanese tea paper ceiling—for its sumptuous seating and dramatic collections.

◀ *Sans cushion, a sleek Le Corbusier chaise longue creates striking contemporary contrast to antique collectibles and ornately framed artwork in a library that doubles as guest sleep space.*

In this sophisticated retreat, ▶ *luxurious linens of custom Egyptian design and antique shams seem to float atop the bed's black base. Architectural drawings and antiques accent with timeless appeal.*

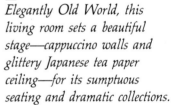

FURNITURE

Furniture is the essence of what makes a livable, likable home. Strip a room of its furnishings and all that remains is an empty shell, a space devoid of comfort, convenience, and visual appeal. Comfort and convenience mean different things to different people, however. It's up to you to define the terms. Once done, proceed with care, and never in haste. Take time to consider your present and future needs, your space, and your way of life. Be tempted not by looks alone, but by the promise that the furnishings you select will be truly at home, in terms of style, size, and function. This chapter is designed to help you fulfill that promise.

FURNITURE
ENGLISH AMERICAN CLASSICS

Styles and forms of furniture that have endured through the centuries earn the distinction of being called classic. This time-honored furniture continues to serve our needs today as handsomely as it served the needs of the people at the time it was created. It is also furniture with a design that looks fresh and fashionable in any period: Good furniture design is indeed timeless.

Furniture that is considered classic today had its roots primarily in England. When the first permanent settlers to America left their 17th-century homeland, they brought with them a taste for the prevailing furniture fashion, a somewhat heavy style named for period rulers William and Mary. This furniture, made primarily of oak, is characterized by lathe-turned parts. The gateleg tables and banister-back chairs that proliferated in this period are usually made with legs, stretchers, and posts featuring vase-and-ring or ball-and-ring turnings.

Although based on English design, the earliest furniture in the New World was also tempered by the immigrants' needs and the available materials. The primitive, "survival" furniture during this era of settlement includes bulky trestle tables made simply of a wood-slab top slid over I-shaped supports; the top could be removed and the table set aside to make more space in small homes.

A more elegant style replaced William and Mary in the 1720s. Named for William's successor, Queen Anne, this furniture is characterized by its graceful, delicate proportions. No longer a mere necessity, furniture began paying greater attention to comfort and aesthetics: curving cabriole legs ending in dainty pad feet appeared, and seating furniture, especially the roomy wing chair, received thick animal-hair cushioning under fabric upholstery.

Queen Anne pieces are made primarily of walnut, and sometimes decorated with japanning, a paint technique imitating Oriental lacquerwork. A number of new furniture forms were introduced, reflecting the more established life-style of the early 18th century. Tea tables and game tables make their debut, along with elegant lowboys used as dressing tables.

Trestle table
This circa-1650 oak table is adapted from a simple medieval form of a slab top on supports.

Queen Anne lowboy
Ladies and gentlemen used the lowboy to store their powders and pomades. This example was made in New England around 1720.

▲ Banister-back armchair

This circa-1700 New England chair features "banisters" or baluster-shaped buck slats, and a rush seat, a carved crest, and curled "Spanish" feet.

▲ Queen Anne vase-splat side chair

With its gently curving back, scalloped skirts, and cabriole legs, the vase-splat chair is a classic example of the period's restrained, elegant look.

▲ Queen Anne card table

Evidence of growing leisure time in the mid-1700s, this table is fitted with corner wells for game chips and an embroidered top.

▲ Queen Anne tea table

As the custom of drinking tea became common, so did the tea table. This piece has a tray top.

William and Mary ▼ gateleg table

The gateleg table, like this circa-1720 oak and maple example, was a popular space-saver. Two of the legs pivot out like a gate to support the open drop leaves.

Queen Anne ▶ wing chair

This type of easy chair was named for its protruding side wings, which helped shield the sitter from drafts. This 1758 example features its original flame-stitch embroidery.

51

FURNITURE
ENGLISH AMERICAN CLASSICS

The mid-18th century ushered in the era of the great furniture designer: English furniture was no longer associated with a monarch, but with a cabinetmaker. Thomas Chippendale, a London craftsman, is the name that dominates this period. A major influence on design from its first publication in 1754 through the 1780s, Chippendale's pattern book of furniture, *The Gentleman and Cabinet-Maker's Director*, was widely read and consulted in Europe and America. Furniture made in the style represented in his guide is generally called Chippendale, even if it is not an exact copy or was not made by him.

Because the 18th century was an era of some prosperity, especially in America's East Coast settlements, homeowners developed a taste for elaborate, elegant furniture. Chippendale complied with sophisticated designs for every furniture form, and called for fine-grained, imported mahogany to replace native walnut as the preferred wood.

The principal pieces of the Chippendale period include graceful chairs with pierced back splats, camelback sofas, block-front chests, and tilt-top tea tables. Chippendale furniture is instantly recognizable for distinctive elements: ball-and-claw feet, for example, and carved scallop-shell motifs, broken pediments, and flame finials.

Although Chippendale was greatly influenced by the prevailing rococo style, which called for fussy ornamentation, the cabinetmaker also introduced Oriental design to Western furniture. His "chinoiserie" style resulted in chairs and other seating pieces with "pagoda" backs, intricate fretwork, and straight legs ending in block, or Marlborough, feet.

Concurrent with the Chippendale style was another classic furniture form: the Windsor chair. Originally English seating pieces, Windsor chairs, along with rockers, settees, and benches, were made in America primarily between the 1730s and 1830s. These simple yet popular pieces are characterized by turned legs and stretchers, saddle-shaped seats, and spindle backs. Windsor seating is designed with a number of different back styles, including the arched bow-back and tall comb-back.

▲
Pembroke table
Named for an English noblewoman, this table was introduced in the mid-1700s and features drop leaves.

◄ **Tall-case clock**
Tall-case clocks like this pine and mahogany piece became common in the mid-1700s.

▲
Tilt-top tea table
This circa-1760 table features a tilting "piecrust" top, ball-and-claw feet, and a "birdcage" support.

Windsor settee
Elements of the Windsor style, such as the spindled back, were also used on this rocking settee.

Comb-back Windsor
This circa-1760 chair is named for the high "comb" surmounting its back.

Bow-back Windsor
The bow-back or hoop-back Windsor chair is one of the most common styles.

Chippendale side chair
This classic Chippendale chair has ball-and-claw feet, a pierced splat, and carved "ears."

Chinese ▶
Chippendale settee
With its carved "pagoda" back, this circa-1760 mahogany settee reflects Chinese style.

◀ Chest-on-chest
Made around 1765, this chest-on-chest is decorated with carved shells.

Camelback sofa ▼
Sofas with arched backs, like this circa-1770 example with straight block legs, are commonly called camelbacks.

FURNITURE
FRENCH CLASSICS

The classic periods of French furniture fell under the reigns of two kings, Louis XV and Louis XVI. Royal cabinetmakers filled their courts with the most lavish furniture of the 18th century, and set the standard for European fashion.

Louis XV, great-grandson of the famous Sun King, Louis XIV, perpetuated his ancestor's love of luxury and extravagance. The monarch ruled between 1723 and 1774, which coincided with the romantic, frivolous rococo period. Furniture followed suit, bearing curvy lines, intricate marquetry with exotic woods, lacquerwork, and much-applied gilt ornamentation. The bombé commode, a chest of drawers with bulging front, exemplifies this fancy style. Yet Louis XV furniture is also noted for its attention to comfort. The bergère, one of the first upholstered armchairs, features graceful proportions geared to the human form, comfortably padded arms, and thick cushioning. Related to the bergère is the fauteuil, which has open, rather than closed, arms.

Louis XV's grandson, Louis XVI, ruled between 1774 and the French Revolution in 1789. Unlike his grandfather, Louis XVI was a shy, dull man who let his wife, Marie Antoinette, preside over court. Furniture gradually changed from playful and sinuous to staid and straight. Influenced by neoclassicism, a return to the design values of ancient civilizations, cabinetmakers produced angular versions of the forms popular earlier in the century. Commodes, chairs, and desks boast squarish silhouettes, tapered and fluted legs, and small spade or ball feet.

Not all French furniture was intended for courtiers. Country craftsmen produced simplified versions of Louis XV and XVI pieces for commoners, creating handsome provincial designs with native materials. The most common forms are ladder-back chairs, often carved and turned, and fitted with rush seats; and armoires, or wardrobes, generally carved on doors, skirt, and curved legs.

▲
Louis XVI armchair
Armchairs in the symmetrical Louis XVI style, like this example, were scaled down to fit the intimate salons popular under Marie Antoinette.

▲
Bombé commode
Gilt mounts on the sides of the circa-1750 commode emphasize its bulbous "bombé" form.

Bergère

The bergère is distinguished by "closed" arms, made by extending upholstery from the arm to the seat rail.

Fauteuil

Sumptuous silk or brocade upholstery covered fauteuils, as on this example, which features comfortable cushioning.

Armoire

This late-1700s Louis XV-style walnut armoire from Provence features cabriole legs, daintily scrolled feet, and a carved skirt.

Provincial armchair ▶

This provincial armchair, made of oak and beechwood around 1775, has a rush seat, typical of French country pieces.

Guéridon ▼

A guéridon is a small table. These pieces are of steel and gilt bronze, with lapis lazuli tops, reeded legs, and ball feet.

Lady's desk ▶

Made in the mid-1700s, this desk has a pull-up mirror that swivels to a leather writing pad.

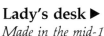

FURNITURE
NEOCLASSICAL

Neoclassical furniture dates from the late 1700s to the mid-1800s, and includes both the Federal and Empire styles. The rage for a classicism mimicking ancient Greek and Roman design was inspired by the excavation of Pompeii. Also, America's Founding Fathers turned to early democracies as models for their new republic and believed classical design should represent the new United States; Americans soon expressed their pride by filling Greek Revival buildings with neoclassical furniture. This peaceful era saw the rise of nationalism in several European countries as well, and the furniture generally reflects the introspective mood of the period.

Federal furniture is noted for delicate, geometric shapes: columnar legs, square backs, and block feet. The style was popularized by two English cabinetmakers, George Hepplewhite and Thomas Sheraton, who published pattern books of their designs. Typical Federal pieces are made of mahogany and include square-back sofas and shield-back chairs—often decorated with such patriotic symbols as eagles—and lolling chairs, also known as Martha Washington chairs. Desks and secretaries proliferated, indicating the country's new thirst for reading and writing, and the sideboard debuted to furnish the new dining rooms.

Empire furniture is also grounded in the ancient world, but takes its cue from the French empire of Napoleon. Its major proponent in America was Duncan Phyfe, whose designs are a bit heavier and more curving than those of the Federal era. Favorite forms include the Grecian couch, a daybed often set on flared legs and hairy-paw feet. A standard Empire motif is the lyre, used for chair backs and table bases. Dark mahogany and rosewood were popular, and deep carving and gilding were common.

The national movement in early 19th-century Germany resulted in the Biedermeier style. The term "Biedermeier" derives from a cartoon satirizing the domesticity of German burghers. Biedermeier furniture, which came to America with German settlers, retained the classical lines of the period, but was simplified for middle-class consumption. Made primarily of light, figured woods, it features geometric shapes, architectural motifs like columns and pediments, and little decoration except inlay.

▲ **Hepplewhite sideboard**
Inlaid bellflowers and other designs adorn this mahogany-veneer sideboard made in Rhode Island around 1785 to 1795.

◄ **Tambour desk**
This mahogany and pine desk was made at the turn of the 19th century. It features a glazed bookcase and a sliding tambour over the writing surface.

▲ Shield-back chair

Light, easy-to-move side chairs like this example were often fitted with a "shield" back, a favorite classical motif.

▲ Biedermeier chair

The classical silhouette, light carving, and pale, figured wood used on this chair are typical elements of Biedermeier style.

▲ Lolling chair

A high back and open arms typify the lolling chair, an American innovation of the Federal period.

▲ Bow-front chest of drawers

This Sheraton chest of drawers, with a characteristic bow front, is decorated with fine mahogany veneer over the drawer fronts.

Lyre-base table ▶

This circa-1810 mahogany card table is built with a base shaped like a lyre, a favorite motif of the Empire period.

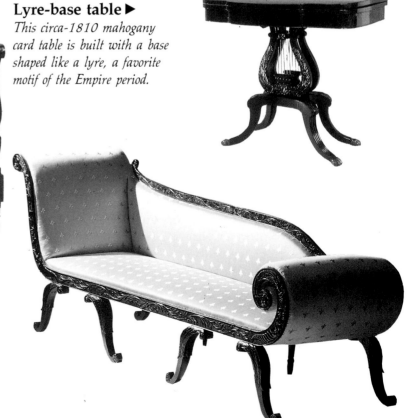

▲ Square-back sofa

This sofa is typically decorated with carving along its top rail. The piece was made by Samuel McIntire, a noted Federal-era craftsman from Massachusetts.

Grecian couch ▶

Used as a recliner, the Grecian couch, like this example, usually features deep carving, a curving partial back, and scrolled ends.

FURNITURE
AMERICAN COUNTRY

Country furniture is defined not by a period or cabinet-maker, but by the life-style of the common folk. This simple furniture was made throughout America from the earliest colonial days until the advent of machine-made furniture in the mid-19th century. Unlike "high-style" furniture made by skilled craftsmen, however, country pieces were usually built by untrained or self-taught woodworkers. They turned their limited talents and the materials at hand to providing a rural populace with needed furnishings in every form.

Consequently, country furniture is functional, sturdy, and one-of-a-kind. Although this furniture is recognizable for its handmade look, it also offers a range of styles—from the very "primitive" pieces hastily constructed by the pioneers to the relatively sophisticated objects made by more experienced country woodworkers.

This diversity reflects the influences affecting country craftsmen. Many tried to copy the fashions popular in urban style centers. Yet, because they often worked from memory instead of pattern books, they might naively combine elements from several style periods into one piece. Country craftsmen also imitated the look of fine materials like mahogany by decorating pine and other common woods with painted "grain." Paint also was used to add color and stenciled patterns to otherwise plain pieces. Other craftsmen shunned fashion and built furniture especially geared to the needs of country homes. The ingenious chair-table, for instance, was meant for cramped quarters: The tabletop could be flipped back from its base to form a chair.

Although country furniture is distinctively American, many pieces betray the immigrants' diverse cultural and religious heritages. English, French, German, Scandinavian, and Hispanic settlers all contributed native woodworking and decorative techniques to the melting pot of American country furniture. Pieces made by the Shakers, for example, a religious sect that emigrated from England in the late 1700s, reflect the fundamentalist tenets of the group with its functional, unadorned style. Germans in Pennsylvania created unique pieces lavishly decorated with painted and inlaid old-world motifs.

Dower chest ▼
German settlers in Pennsylvania painted pine chests with favorite motifs. This late-1700s piece depicts Adam and Eve in Eden.

▲
Chair-table
The chair-table was conceived as a space-saver for small country homes. This pine piece dates from the 1800s.

▲ Hitchcock-style chair

This chair is an example of the "fancy" painted and stencil-decorated chairs first manufactured by Lambert Hitchcock in the early 1800s.

▲ Shaker rocker

This circa-1850 rocking chair exemplifies the severe, utilitarian furniture style created by the Shakers.

◄ Cupboard

Open-top cupboards, or dressers, like this painted piece, were common in country homes for storing kitchen wares.

Federal ▼ drop-leaf table

Country craftsmen often tried to copy "high-style" furniture. This drop-leaf table imitates furniture design of the early 19th-century Federal period.

◄ Schrank

This 1779 Pennsylvania-German wardrobe, or schrank, is inlaid with a sulphur compound.

Grain-painted ▶ blanket chest

This Hepplewhite-style chest is painted to mimic the wood grain and inlay of fancy furniture.

FURNITURE
VICTORIAN CLASSICS

Furniture from the middle to late 19th century is commonly grouped under the heading "Victorian," but the Victorian era was really an age of diversity and eclecticism. For the first time, no one style predominated. Furniture was shaped by three very different influences: revival of past styles, reaction against the encroaching machine age, and innovations in materials and techniques.

Throughout the period, furniture makers delved into history to find inspiration. In rapid succession there appeared revivals of traditional styles, such as Gothic, renaissance, and rococo. This interest in the past resulted in massive, richly ornamented mahogany or rosewood furniture to suit the large and excessively decorated rooms of the period. John Belter is the furniture maker associated with the revival era; his ornate pierced and carved chairs, settees, and tables are typical of mid-19th-century style.

In reaction to revival furniture, which critics denounced as shoddily made goods hidden beneath elaborate surfaces, several craftsmen proposed a return to "honest" furniture around the 1860s. Champions of this reform included English architect Charles Eastlake, who advocated simple, geometric furniture with high-quality construction and minimal decoration. In the 1890s, Gustav Stickley embodied the new look in his mission furniture: plain, angular oak pieces that bore visible joints and other signs of handwork. Aesthetic or art furniture, such as pieces made by Herter Brothers, combined simple forms with rich, naturalistic ornamentation. This paved the way at the turn of the century for the sensuous, organic lines of art nouveau furniture, which was translated throughout Europe and America into unique national styles.

The 19th century was also the age of innovation. The innerspring mattress arrived in the 1850s, making beds more comfortable. Michael Thonet discovered how to shape wood with steam in 1840, turning out bentwood chairs and sofas at an Austrian factory. Wicker, cast iron, and such unusual objects as animal horn debuted as furniture material. The Industrial Revolution gave rise to factories that could mass-produce attractive, inexpensive "cottage" furniture for modest homes.

▲
Thonet bentwood armchair
Thonet turned his bentwood technique to settees, rockers, and armchairs, like this piece.

▲
Wiener Werkstätte chair
The Wiener Werkstätte (Viennese Workshop) brought art nouveau style to Austria. This curvy "Fledermaus" chair was designed in 1907.

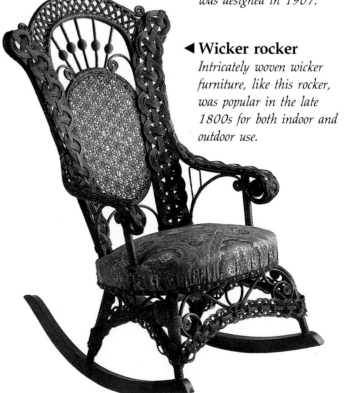

◀ ### Wicker rocker
Intricately woven wicker furniture, like this rocker, was popular in the late 1800s for both indoor and outdoor use.

Rococo Revival armchair

This ornate armchair was made around 1860 of ebonized walnut with gilt-bronze ornamentation.

Eastlake settee

This angular settee was popularized by Charles Eastlake in the late 1800s as a reaction to excessive Victorian adornment.

▲
Belter center table

Laminated rosewood was used to create fancy furniture, such as this pierced and carved table.

▲
Cottage chest of drawers

Painted "cottage" furniture, like this chest of drawers, was mass produced for modest homes.

Herter secretary ▶

Following Eastlake's reform, Herter Brothers crafted this circa-1877 angular secretary of ebonized cherry and marquetry.

▲
Stickley side chair

Simple rectilinear oak furniture, like this side chair, marked a return to handcraftsmanship.

FURNITURE
CONTEMPORARY

Like its predecessors, contemporary style began with a few talented individuals setting the tone. Instead of cabinetmakers and woodworkers, however, 20th-century furniture makers were architects and designers. This new wave of craftsmen was trained at the Bauhaus, a German art school founded in 1919. Under the credo "Form follows function," they were taught to apply the precepts of good design to the demands of commercial mass production and the needs of postindustrial homes. The resulting furniture is simple, geometric, and unafraid to show its machined materials.

The leaders of this style include Marcel Breuer, Ludwig Mies van der Rohe, and Charles Edouard Jeanneret, who called himself Le Corbusier. Breuer launched the new age in 1925 with his "Wassily" chair, a light steel-tube frame fitted with flexible, body-hugging canvas slings. He followed with the "Cesca" chair, which replaced conventional four-legged design with a shaped ribbon of steel tubing for support. Other designers were quick to embrace the potential of tubular steel. Le Corbusier created his angular chaise in 1927, and Mies van der Rohe introduced his "Barcelona" series—a chair, stool, and table designed around a steel "X"—at the 1929 international arts exhibition in Barcelona; a sofa was added in 1931.

The 1920s and '30s marked the era of art deco style, named for the Paris exposition of decorative arts held in 1925, when this *"style moderne"* was introduced. The Bauhaus principles of spare geometry were combined with other contemporary influences—including Cubist art and colorful Russian ballet theater design—to produce dramatic, exotic, sophisticated furniture. A period classic is the club chair, an overstuffed seat with a steamlined look.

Furniture makers in Scandinavia and America also contributed to the trend. In the 1930s, Finnish architect Alvar Aalto replaced the cold steel of his predecessors with pale woods while retaining the same fluid look. His birch plywood chairs are noted for their elastic, sculpted quality. Another important figure at mid-century was Charles Eames, who created a lounge chair and ottoman of molded rosewood with removable tufted-leather cushions.

▲
Noguchi coffee table
American sculptor Isamu Noguchi designed this table in 1947, using a plate-glass top over a free-form wooden base.

▲
Paimio armchair
Alvar Aalto's circa-1931 armchair is made of laminated birch plywood: two loops for the sides and a sheet for the seat.

Cesca armchair ▶
Marcel Breuer's "Cesca" chair, introduced in 1928, features a cantilever design: a steel double-"S" frame, instead of the customary four legs, supports the caned seat.

▲ Wassily chair

The 1925 "Wassily" chair was the first to be made from steel tubes. Breuer reportedly was inspired by bicycle handlebars.

▲ Barcelona chair

The "Barcelona" chair is based on X-shaped seats used in ancient Greece and Rome.

▲ Art deco club chair

The art deco club chair, designed by French architect Pierre Chareau around 1924, reflects the era's streamlined, yet decorative, style.

Barcelona sofa ▼

Ludwig Mies van der Rohe designed this sofa in 1931 to complement his "Barcelona" series. The sofa shares the spare, clean look of the series, but not the X-shaped legs.

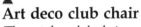

Eames lounge ▼ and ottoman

This 1956 lounge and ottoman, designed by Charles Eames, is made of molded plywood with a rosewood veneer.

▲ Le Corbusier chaise

Le Corbusier's chaise longue, designed in 1927, adjusts from upright to reclining positions on its steel runners.

FURNITURE
FURNISHING YOUR HOME

Furnishing a home is an evolutionary process. Although you may dream of "doing" your home and being done forever, in fact, you probably will be buying things for it all your life. And why not. You and your family are constantly changing, and your home changes with you. Even if it is fully furnished, it's wise to take a periodic inventory to see if the things you own are truly meeting your needs.

PLANNING YOUR PURCHASES

The furniture you will love the most and keep the longest will be chosen with three considerations in mind: your family, your way of life, and your tastes.

Your family: Family size and composition dictate a great deal about the furniture you buy. Each family has certain basic needs: a place to sleep, storage, and a place to eat. You can't really begin to address other decorating questions until you've met those fundamental needs.

Your way of life: Life-style, not convention, should play the major role in setting your priorities. Don't spend thousands of dollars on a dining room set, for example, if you hate to entertain. Instead, choose furniture that will make the most sense for the space and money you have. Double-duty furnishings—a coffee table that rises to dining height or a console that hides a fold-out bed—often are economical problem-solvers; you may have to special-order them, but they can be worth the wait.

Would you describe your family as formal or casual? Neat or disorganized? Do you spend a lot of time at home, or are you gone most of the day? How do you entertain? All these factors help to determine the furniture you need.

Your taste: Sometimes, it's hard to define one's own tastes. If you are unsure of what you like, begin by looking around your own house: The pieces that please you most will tell you a lot about yourself and your taste.

Save magazine pictures of room settings and furniture pieces that you like. Think of rooms you have loved and analyze what you liked about them. If you find yourself torn between several "looks," post photographs of each on a wall for a few days; time will help clarify your thinking.

Once you've assessed your needs and established prior-ities, you're ready to shop. Remember that *every* piece of furniture you own doesn't have to be bought new: Antiques, secondhand furnishings, and handcrafted pieces add character to a home. Similarly, don't be afraid to mix styles and finishes. Just keep in mind that when the elements are disparate, they should have a unifying mood—whether it is formal, informal, sophisticated, or cozy.

A few other practical considerations:

Will it fit—and fit in? Never buy a major piece of furniture without knowing where it is going in your home. Shop armed with accurate measurements of your floor space, a tape measure, and samples of your wall colors and fabrics.

Can you afford it? Decide before you shop how much you can afford to spend, and stick to it. Don't feel you need to buy top-quality furniture all at once. You may be able to afford the special pieces you want if you are willing to acquire furniture slowly, filling in with lower-cost pieces or accessories.

Will it last? Don't waste money on poorly made furniture that will wear out or "ugly out" in a couple of years. The next few pages will help you evaluate quality.

WORKING WITH DESIGNERS

Professional interior design services aren't just for those with a huge budget. A good designer often can help you get the most value from limited resources—and help you avoid costly mistakes.

An interior designer can advise you on decorating treatments, room arrangements, furnishings, and wise use of space. If you're able to splurge, a designer also can provide access to merchandise sold only "to the trade"—top-quality, well-designed furnishings sold exclusively to and through designers.

Interior designers may charge an hourly fee, or cover their services by marking up the price of furnishings they purchase for you at wholesale.

FURNITURE
BUYING ANTIQUES

Buying antique furniture is one of the most exciting ways to personalize your home. Part of the fun is the thrill of the hunt: Antiques lovers seek out special shops and shows, flea markets, and auctions for that one-of-a-kind piece. Wherever you shop, it's important to be well prepared. Educate yourself by visiting shops, museums, and shows, talking with dealers and collectors, and reading books and magazines on the subject. The more informed you are, the better equipped you'll be to evaluate quality, rarity, condition, authenticity, joinery techniques, and price.

Although an antique is generally defined as any object more than 100 years old, not every old piece is valuable. A piece with a known maker and date, fine design, original hardware and surface finish, and no damage or repairs will be more valuable and expensive than a piece without such desirable features. Buyers should also be wary of cleverly "aged" reproductions being sold as originals, and "marriages" between two separate pieces that did not belong together, such as a chest surmounted by a bookcase to create a secretary.

One way to make sure you acquire high-quality antique furniture is to buy from reputable shops run by professionals. Even experts make honest mistakes, but you may be more comfortable initially dealing with a reliable shop. Prices are sometimes a bit higher at shops than at other outlets because you're also paying for the discrimination of the dealer in providing an authentic piece. Consequently, spend wisely by taking full advantage of a dealer's experience and inquire about your prospective purchase.

Antiques shows are another dependable source of antique furniture. Shows afford buyers the opportunity to meet many dealers at once and expose them to dealers' finest wares. As with shops, feel free to ask questions and expect competitive prices.

Flea markets and garage sales are a casual, inexpensive way to pick up furnishings. Although there are few "undiscovered" treasures hiding in barns and attics anymore—antiques are too popular for that—you may be able to obtain a piece that suits your needs at reasonable cost. Prices are generally low, because you are not buying from dealers with guaranteed standards.

Sooner or later, every antiques shopper attends an auction. Besides being a diverse source for furniture, auctions are entertaining—there is nothing as exciting to an antiques buff as waiting for the first bid. Auctions can be dangerous for the unprepared, however. Auction-goers can become hypnotized by the fast pace and act carelessly.

When you attend an auction, first, thoroughly examine the pieces during the preview, usually held the evening or a few hours before bidding begins. Obtain a catalog if one is available, choose the "lots" (the number of units of an article or a parcel of articles offered as one item) that interest you, and spend as much time as you need inspecting the pieces for quality, condition, and attribution. Establish a firm limit on the amount you are willing to pay for a particular piece. Also be sure to note whether a particular lot is a single piece, a pair, or a set.

Once bidding begins, find a comfortable position where you can see the auctioneer and other bidders. There are many strategies for gaining an advantage at auction, but most bidders simply wait to hear the auctioneer's lowest bid before indicating interest—by a nod or a raised hand. Propelled by the auctioneer's rapid-fire speech, the bidding will be feverish, so keep your maximum figure in mind. Don't be tempted to bid "just another $10" until you have exceeded your limit by hundreds. Part of the auction experience is learning to let a piece you love go to the highest bidder.

Although you may see some pricey showstoppers—you will often be bidding against experienced collectors for top-quality items—you also may find some unbelievable bargains. You might be interested in a Victorian piece, for example, when most of the other bidders are buying Chippendale—and you can be pleasantly surprised when your low bid is rewarded with a resounding "Sold."

After you successfully bid on a piece, you'll have to show the number assigned to you when you entered, which helps the house keep track of buyers. It's wise to jot down your final bids for items you've purchased, so you can compare figures with the house's total. Once you pay for your piece—there may be sales tax and a seller's premium, as well—all that remains is to take it home.

FURNITURE
SMART SHOPPING

Buying new furniture should be one of life's pleasures, but for too many shoppers it's an anxiety-producing experience. It doesn't have to be.

The next few pages will help you learn how to evaluate furniture quality. One of the most valuable ways to build your shopping skills is to browse widely, in stores and through catalogs, magazines, and books. Explore available options and look at furniture in *all* price ranges, even pieces that exceed your budget. It's the best way to get a feel for differences in quality, features, and price ranges.

By the time you embark on a serious buying trip, you should have firm ideas about what you want. Otherwise, it's easy to be overly influenced by the tastes and interests of the salesperson assisting you. In addition, what you *really* want might not even be on display; you may have to ask for it to be special-ordered.

When you shop, think in pieces, not groups. Furniture is often displayed in sets simply because that's how manufacturers market it. That doesn't mean you have to buy it that way. Only buy matched sets when you want matched sets. If you want to mix styles or finishes, a talented salesperson can help you do so.

A few other sound shopping strategies:

• **Evaluate your salesperson with care.** Many of the people who sell furniture are quite knowledgeable, and some have degrees in interior design. But many do not. Ask about your salesperson's background before you accept too much free advice. On the other hand, if you find a good salesperson, take advantage of his or her expertise.

• **Ask questions.** Inquire about price, construction, and anything you don't understand. And when you're ready to make a decision, don't be afraid to bargain. Furniture retailers may make you a deal, especially if you are a frequent customer or are making a large purchase.

• **Plan ahead.** Buying furniture can be a waiting game, especially if you are special-ordering or have custom upholstery. Case goods (wooden furniture) are made in "cuttings"—that is, a factory will wait until it has several orders on a piece before it cuts the lumber for it. It can take eight or even 12 weeks to receive the pieces you order.

WHERE TO SHOP

Today, you have many options for buying furniture. Full-service furniture stores offer two very important advantages: service and selection. Most carry furniture from a number of manufacturers and can special-order pieces not on display. Full-service stores also usually offer a choice of fabrics for upholstered furniture.

Just as important, a good furniture store and some department stores will have well-informed salespersons, and—sometimes—in-store interior designers. Don't let a limited budget prevent you from shopping in a full-service store; salespersons often are able to guide you to economical pieces.

TERMS TO KNOW:

Collection: A manufacturer's grouping of related furniture pieces. Although furniture usually is displayed in collections, you needn't buy it that way.

Reproductions: Exact copies of fine antiques, usually made with the same materials and detail as the originals. "Visual reproductions" use modern shortcuts to hold down costs or add modern convenience.

Adaptations: Loosely based on originals. Tags may say "based on," "adapted from," or "in the style of."

Sectionals: Upholstered pieces made in sections that fit together in a set configuration.

Modulars: Fully upholstered seating components such as armless chairs, one-arm chairs, and corner pieces that may be used in many configurations.

COM: Custom-Ordered Material. Manufacturers may offer you a choice of COM fabrics when you buy an upholstered piece or let you supply your own.

Apartment-size furniture: Smaller-size upholstered pieces and case goods.

RTA: Affordable, ready-to-assemble furniture that can be carried home immediately.

Other options include:

- **Galleries.** These stores, or sections of stores, feature furniture from one manufacturer in complete room settings. Galleries help you picture the pieces in your own home, and provide ideas on design treatments.

- **Custom sofa stores.** These stores specialize in affordable, custom-designed seating pieces. They offer several basic sofa and chair frame styles and allow you to choose the fabric and tailoring you prefer. Some promise delivery in 30 to 45 days—speedy for a custom order.

- **Mail order.** Catalogs from direct-mail companies and furniture stores can be a convenient way to shop, especially if you live in an area with few furniture retailers. Be sure to check shipping costs, which can add hundreds of dollars to the price of a piece.

- **Discount stores.** These stores usually are bare-bones operations with minimal services. Their advantage is price, with discounts of 30 to 50 percent off list price. Discount stock may include close-outs, seconds, and overruns.

- **Trans-shippers.** These no-frills furniture discounters often are based in the furniture-manufacturing regions of North Carolina. These companies fulfill orders for specific pieces of furniture, often at incredible savings. Because you are dealing at long distances, it's especially important to check credentials with the Better Business Bureau and to inquire about delivery schedules and return policies.

FURNITURE
PURCHASING PRIMER: CASE GOODS

In the furniture industry, the term "case goods" has come to denote a broad array of hard furniture, rather than soft upholstered furniture. In evaluating case goods, it's important to check out materials, construction, and finishes.

MATERIALS AND LABELS

Hangtags and labels will tell you a lot about the materials used in a piece of furniture. Labeling terms have explicit meanings, regulated by the Federal Trade Commission:
- **Solid wood** ("solid oak") means that exposed surfaces should be made of the wood named, without any veneer or plywood. Other woods may be used on drawer sides, unfinished backs, and other hidden areas.
- **Genuine** used with the name of a wood means that all exposed parts of the piece are made of veneer of the named wood, over hardwood plywood.
- **Wood** means that a piece has no major components of plastic, metal, or other materials.
- **Man-made materials** refer to plastic laminate panels printed to mimic wood. Case pieces also may include plastic molded to look like wood carving or trim. Simulated woods and molded plastic are sometimes used in top-quality pieces. Color laminates are gaining popularity as a good-quality surface material for furnishings.

If you choose a piece that includes laminated components, check to see that the laminate is securely and smoothly bonded to the material underneath. High-pressure laminates resist damage better than other types.

ABOUT WOODS

Keep in mind that, when you evaluate labels like "all wood," there can be quite a difference among woods.

Furniture may be constructed of hardwood, of softwood, or of composition materials. Hardwoods are woods from slow-growing deciduous trees, such as mahogany, walnut, cherry, maple, and oak. These woods are often preferred for case goods because they have more strength for their weight than softwoods. Softwoods come from faster-growing evergreens, such as pine, cedar, and redwood. Well-seasoned and kiln-dried softwoods are fine, but unseasoned or poor-quality softwoods split and splinter easily.

Hardwoods have richer grains and often are used in the form of veneers, thin sheets of wood bonded to less-expensive wood. Years ago, veneers were associated with poor quality, but today they're used on most wood furniture in all price ranges. Veneered woods may be stronger than solid wood, and they permit dramatically grained rare woods to be used beautifully and economically.

Composition boards such as plywood and particleboard are included in the "all wood" label, but tags seldom mention them specifically. Manufacturers like these products because they cost less than solid wood or plywood. In medium-priced furniture, composition boards may be used in hidden places like dresser backs or bottoms; they may be used extensively in budget pieces. Particleboard is more vulnerable to chips and breaks than hardboard.

JOINERY TECHNIQUES

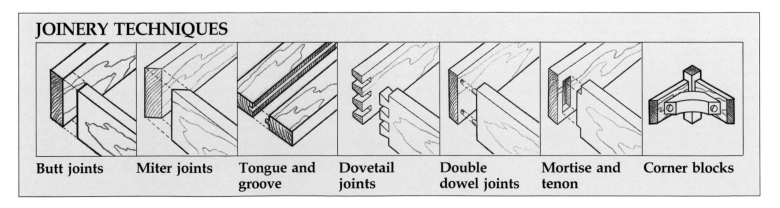

Butt joints   Miter joints   Tongue and groove   Dovetail joints   Double dowel joints   Mortise and tenon   Corner blocks

JOINING METHODS

There are five principal methods of putting furniture together: staples, nails, screws, joints, and glue. Most pieces use more than one method. Look for the strongest construction where a piece will bear the most weight or receive the most stress (legs, shelf braces, drawers).

Joints are the places where one component in a piece of furniture fits into another. These joints are often reinforced by glue; synthetic glues are the most durable.

Where joints are impractical, screws are the best fasteners; they should be secure and screwed in all the way. Staples are used only on budget furniture and are inappropriate for joining pieces that bear weight or undergo stress. Nails are stronger than staples, but not as strong as other joining methods.

A good joint can make all the difference in the life span of your furniture. The illustrations *opposite* will help you become familiar with the basic types of joints.

- **Butt joints,** in which two pieces are simply joined together where they abut, are weak joints. They can work in some places (where a bureau top meets a frame, for example), but not in places subject to stress or weight.
- **Miter joints** are used at the corners of tables. Look for reinforcements such as dowels, nails, screws, or a spline.
- **Tongue-and-groove** joinery is used to join two boards together side by side, as in a tabletop.
- **Dovetail joints** are found joining drawer sides. Dovetails should fit together smoothly. Avoid pieces in which the dovetails are cracked or seem too small.
- **Double-dowel joints** use two dowels to peg the joint together. A sturdy joint, it is used to create the framing for case goods or to attach legs to side rails of chairs.
- **Mortise and tenon** is the strongest method of joining pieces of wood at right angles. The end of one piece of wood is shaped to fit into a hole in the other. This construction distributes stress over a wide area.

At points of special strain—like the corner of chairs or tables—look underneath for *corner blocks* that are screwed in place. They provide extra support.

FACTS ABOUT FINISHES

Furniture may be stained, painted, or lacquered to add color, and most pieces are treated with a final protective finish. The gloss and depth of a finish is a matter of personal preference, but the finish should always be strong enough to resist moisture.

The best way to learn about finishes is to compare the look and feel of budget and upper-end pieces. Inexpensive furniture will simply be coated with a layer of polyurethane. Fine furniture goes through a series of finishing steps (often more than 20) that include sanding, glazing, waxing, and hand buffing. Whatever the finish, check to make sure the surface is hard, smooth, and even; beware of uneven coloration, bubbles, pockmarks, or cracks.

QUICK CHECKS FOR QUALITY

Different standards of quality apply at different price levels. No matter what your budget, you'll learn a lot about a piece through these quick checks:

Cabinet doors: Check the edges to see if veneers or laminates have been used, and how well laminates are joined to the base material. Operate the doors to make sure they work smoothly; push down firmly on the open door: The hinges should be strong enough to prevent sagging.

Drawers: Drawers should fit well, with no more than 1/4 inch of "play" from side to side. Better pieces have center or side glides and drawer stops, and the bottoms are held by grooves, not staples or nails. The insides of drawers are smooth and sealed.

Better pieces also have dovetail joints at all four corners. Examine the fit of these joints carefully; dovetails are a good measure of overall quality.

Back panels: In better furniture, the back panel is finished and inset and screwed into the frame.

FURNITURE
PURCHASING PRIMER: UPHOLSTERY

Sofas, chairs, and other upholstered pieces provide the "bones" for most room arrangements. So, select your pieces with care, keeping in mind your seating needs, your space limitations, and the flexibility of each piece.

In upholstered furniture, it's what's inside that counts. Because you can't *see* inside, you'll have to garner information from tags, salespeople, and manufacturers' catalogs.

THE INSIDE STORY

Most upholstered furniture begins with a wooden frame (although some European manufacturers use metal or molded plastic frames). A good-quality wood frame is made of seasoned hardwood, kiln-dried to prevent warping. It's joined by dowels and interlocking pieces, rather than butted together. Corner blocks are cut to fit, and screwed and glued into position.

Legs should be a continuation of the back or front frame, or should be locked into the frame with heavy-duty joining techniques. Be wary of legs screwed into the frame or screwed into metal plates joined to the frame.

Attached to the frame are the springs. Springs support the sitter and help give a piece shape; saggy springs make sorry-looking furniture. Springs may be coil or sagless; both types are made of tempered steel.

In high-quality coil-spring systems, the funnel-shaped coils are spaced closely and hand-tied eight ways. In this construction, the coils are securely anchored to the frame with a strong network of cords; springs tied four or six ways are not nearly as supportive. Coil springs usually are undergirded by webbing. The webbing should be tight and smooth, without big gaps between straps. Webbing may be reinforced by steel straps under each row of springs.

Some furniture is made with double sagless springs, flat wavy lines of high-grade steel. These wavy bands should be connected with spiral springs for greater stability. Sagless springs offer a firmer, less resilient feel than coil springs.

THE SOFT SIDE OF QUALITY

Strong and resilient, polyurethane foam is now the most widely used filling for lift-out seat and back cushions. Because it is fairly firm, it's most comfortable when wrapped with another material, such as down or polyester batting. To test the quality of a polyurethane-foam cushion, pick it up. If it is very light, it may be made of poor-quality material. As a rule of thumb, a 6-inch cushion that measures 2x2 feet shouldn't weigh less than two pounds.

SUPPORT SYSTEMS

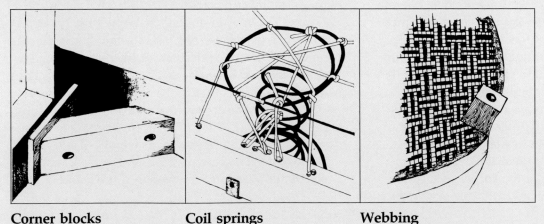

Corner blocks   Coil springs   Webbing

Strong support systems make for high-quality upholstery. A few benchmarks: Where the legs meet the frame, there should be well-fit corner blocks screwed and glued—not stapled or nailed—in place. Coils should be hand-tied to the frame in eight places. T webbing below the coils should be closely spaced.

This type of furniture will last longest if it is made of a "layer cake" of foam, with softer foam on top.

Down is a luxury filling material, renowned for softness. Today, it's usually reserved for very expensive furniture, or is combined with other materials. Polyester fiber filling has become a popular alternative, both in cushions and in chair and sofa backs. Fiber filling is sold in a range of grades and under a variety of brand names; ask your salesperson about the pros and cons of different types.

COVERINGS

The "Fabrics" chapter of this book will help you choose the right fabric for your upholstery. But it's helpful to know that, when you buy an upholstered piece, you often can choose among several price levels of fabrics, called "grades." Fabric grades run from A at the high end to D at the low end. Grading is influenced by several factors: the expense of the raw material, the quality of its weave, the amount of fabric needed to achieve a good match, and the origin of the pattern (a pattern authorized by a museum or designed by a famous designer costs more).

Leather is an alternative to a fabric covering. Strong and durable, leather—with reasonable care—can last up to four times as long as fabric. Leather, which comes in a whole range of colors, has become much more affordable in recent years, and new soil-resistant finishes also make it more practical for everyday use.

Leather may be glazed or aniline dyed. Glazed, or coated, leather, the shiny, stiff leather sometimes seen on traditional furnishings, may crack with wear. Aniline-dyed leather is almost as soft as fabric, so it will not crack. However, it's more more susceptible to stains than coated leather.

Leather grading is based on such factors as softness, blemishes, and color. All leather is equally tough, although some grades are more porous than others. Top-grain leather is leather that's been treated only for color and stain resistance; it's not been split or sanded to remove blemishes.

WHAT YOU PAY FOR

Two chairs of comparable construction may bear very different prices. Cover material has the biggest influence on price, but other factors come into play as well.

- **Frame design:** As a general rule, curves are more expensive than straight lines. It takes more labor and materials to construct a curved frame—a wing chair, for example, or a Queen Anne leg. It also takes more fabric to cover a curve.
- **Cover design:** There is always some wasted fabric when an upholsterer must match a pattern; the larger or more complex the pattern, the harder it is to match.
- **"Dressmaker details"** such as pleats, welts, braids, and tassels add to the price of a piece.

TEST-DRIVE A CHAIR

Sit in it: Firmness or softness is a matter of personal taste, but no matter how cushy it is, a chair should give you support and feel good. You should not be able to feel individual springs or hard frame edges. The filling should be even and free of lumps.

Lean on it: It should feel solid, without wobbling or swaying. Lean back into the chair and bounce on the seat to be sure the frame feels secure.

Lift it: Pick up one end of the piece. Creaks or squeaks can tip you off to a frame made of wood that has been improperly dried, or corner joints that are merely nailed or screwed together. Pat the underside of the chair. A hollow drumlike sound indicates tight coils and webbing. Signs of poor quality include excess glue, raveled fabric edges, and rough lumber.

Look it over: Tailoring is telling. Look for straight, neatly sewn welts, with no puckering or loose threads. Pull the seams gently to see if the stitches are tight. Skirts should be lined, hang straight, and have crisp corners. Patterns should be carefully matched, and trims should be securely attached.

FURNITURE
PURCHASING PRIMER: FOR OUTDOORS

Porches, patios, and decks have become part of everyday living for many families. If you spend much of your time outside, you may want to put some extra thought—and money—into furnishing your outdoor "room."

The array of options in outdoor furniture is impressive, but it also can be confusing. Wood, aluminum, plastic, wrought iron—there are almost as many materials as there are styles. Several factors should influence your choice.

• **What is your climate?** You want your outdoor furniture to be able to take a beating, but materials react differently in different climates. Sea air corrodes iron, for instance; extreme cold can crack some plastics.

• **Will the furniture be around a pool?** Most outdoor furniture is designed to shed water, but some pieces—particularly cushions—are not designed for frequent prolonged wettings. On the other hand, you may not like the feel of straps on the back and legs.

• **Will you want to add to your set later?** Most people still buy outdoor furniture in sets; when they add pieces, they want them to match what they already own. If you hope to expand your set later, make sure that the group you choose has additional pieces and will be in stock a year from now.

• **Will you store your patio furniture for the winter?** If storage space is limited, consider folding or stacked furniture, or furniture that can be disassembled.

IRON

Iron (steel is actually used these days) comes in two forms, wrought and cast. Cast iron—iron that is poured into a mold—is often used for accent pieces, such as garden benches or chairs, usually in an antique style. Much more common is wrought iron, made by welding bent rods of steel together.

Wrought iron has several advantages. It's less expensive than aluminum of the same weight and quality, and comes in contemporary and traditional styles. Given reasonable care, wrought iron will last for years—you can repaint it yourself if it begins to show signs of age. Iron will weather eventually, but many people like this natural "antiquing."

Wrought iron is a heavy material, which can be an advantage in a windy location. It is not recommended for oceanside, however, where salt air will rust the metal. Wrought iron also can pose a problem on concrete decks, where unprotected feet can leave rust spots. This last problem can be alleviated with protective plastic cups.

ALUMINUM

Like iron, aluminum can be either cast or wrought, although wrought aluminum is more common for outdoor use. Aluminum (usually finished with a baked-on enamel) doesn't rust or corrode, and weighs less than iron.

Seats and backs on aluminum chairs are formed in several ways. The least expensive is plastic webbing, which has a tendency to fray. More practical is plastic strapping, which can be woven in several designs. It's tough and durable; if a strap should break, you usually can replace it yourself. (The exception is diagonal crisscross strapping, which must go back to the factory for repair).

Increasingly popular is the mesh sling, made of tightly stretched plastic-coated fabric. More comfortable than straps, it has a stylishly contemporary look. Both straps and mesh are often used in conjunction with cushions.

PLASTIC

Low-cost, low-maintenance plastic has become a popular material for outdoor furniture in recent years. The two most common types are *PVC* and resin furniture.

PVC furniture (also known as "pipe furniture") originally was made of industrial piping jointed together. Now, manufacturers use pipe designed especially for the furniture, but the material is still polyvinylchloride, or PVC. PVC furniture tends to be square in design, and usually is cushioned for comfort.

Resin furniture is molded, which allows a variety of shapes. Expensive resin furniture (usually imported from Europe) is lacquered, but less-expensive unlacquered furniture will hold up just as well. Resin comes in a variety of styles, from woodlike traditional to contemporary.

The biggest enemy of plastic is sunlight, which can cause the plastic to chalk, fade, and eventually deteriorate. However, most plastic outdoor furniture contains UV inhibitors that block out harmful ultraviolet rays and prolong the life of the plastic.

WOOD

By far the most durable wood for outdoor use is redwood, which naturally resists warping and decay. A good value because of its longevity, redwood nonetheless involves some initial expense. Redwood styles also tend to be bulky. Be wary of less costly redwood look-alikes that are actually made of stained pine. They will not last nearly as long as genuine redwood.

Teak, used for years in ship construction, is also a durable though pricey wood for outdoor furniture. Teak shows up most often in garden seats and benches, many of which are handsome enough to work indoors, too.

In recent years, old-fashioned wooden garden furniture has made a comeback. It comes in a variety of hardwoods, including oak, beech, and maple. Treated with stain or ordinary paint and left exposed to the elements, any wood furniture will weather. Many people like the soft look of weathered wood, but if you want your wooden furniture to keep looking new, take extra care in its maintenance. Start with furniture that has been treated with a wood preservative finish; keep the furniture out of the elements as much as possible (a sheltered deck, perhaps, instead of an open yard); and be prepared to repaint often.

CUSHIONS

A lot of outdoor furniture gets its stretch-out comfort from cushions. Canvas or cotton duck is a perennial favorite, particularly for printed pillows—most synthetic outdoor fabrics do not take prints well. Cotton cushions should be used only in a sheltered area such as a porch, or should be put away when not in use. Sun and rain will fade natural fabrics, and prolonged dampness can lead to mildew.

People looking for low-maintenance cushions can find several synthetic alternatives. The most common outdoor fabric is a mesh made of fibers that have been coated with plastic and then woven. This fabric shows up on cushions, slings, and even umbrellas. It needs very little care; a quick rinse with a hose will clean off most spots.

Some manufacturers offer cushions in an acrylic fabric that looks like cotton duck. Because it is made of acrylic, the fabric dries quickly and does not mildew. Long used in Europe, this fabric is just beginning to be widely used in this country.

For long-lasting cushions, be sure to get the inside story. The best cushioning for outdoor use is a polyester fiber filling, which will not absorb water. Cotton, kapok, and polyurethane foam all retain water, and should be used only on furniture that will not be exposed to the elements—or to dripping swimmers.

FURNITURE
PURCHASING PRIMER: OTHER GOODS

Today's rooms thrive on diversity. Though wood is still America's favorite furniture, wooden pieces now keep company with brass, wicker, plastic, and many other materials. Each material has its own personality—and its own measure of quality.

BRASS

From doorknobs to canopy beds, the glow of brass warms a room. Not all that glitters, however, is genuine brass. Check labels before you buy.

Brass is an alloy of copper and zinc, with small amounts of other metals added for strength. Its color largely depends on the proportion of copper. A piece of furniture labeled genuine or solid brass will be brass all the way through. A piece labeled brass plate is made of some other metal, usually steel, which is plated with a skin of brass. Brass-toned metal is simply metal that has been coated with a clear yellow lacquer for a brassy look.

When they are new, genuine brass and brass plate look very much alike. In time, however, the brass plate may pit or discolor, although better-quality plating should wear well. To check the quality of a brass-plated piece, check the surface and joints. Both should feel smooth to the touch and have little variation in texture and color.

Well-constructed genuine brass furniture will feel solid and strong. Brass parts should be attached to each other with threaded steel rods that run through the brass tubes and capped with solid brass balls. Balls, finials, castings, and other decorative parts should be made of solid brass.

Brass-plated steel parts, too, should be joined securely at each corner. The joining devices should be screwed into steel reinforcements inside the brass posts. Generally, pieces that are joined with nuts and bolts lack rigidity.

Today, virtually all brass is finished with some kind of tarnish protection, usually an epoxy or lacquer coat that needs only an occasional rub with a clean cloth.

OTHER METAL

Iron, steel, and aluminum have shed their utilitarian images to become versatile and practical for indoor use. Dressed up with a verdigris finish or a touch of brass, metal takes on neoclassic flair. Slicked up with a coat of enamel, it can add a playful touch to a bedroom. Roughly hammered and joined, it has a southwestern flavor.

As with all furniture, metal furniture is only as strong as its joints. Check for smooth, solid welds and secure bolts. Components that are screwed together (such as decorative feet or finials) should fit snugly without wobbling.

Verdigris has become a popular finish with metal furniture and accessories. In order to get the antiqued look, manufacturers brush their piece with a chemical compound that speeds the oxidation of the metal. Verdigris needs the same care as fine wood or painted furniture.

WICKER

Nothing relaxes a room like a piece of wicker furniture. Once thought of as just porch or summer furniture, wicker is now used year-round in every room of the house.

Wicker furniture can be woven of many different materials, including willow, rattan, reed, buri, raffia, and latiana. Or, it may be constructed with materials such as twisted paper or plastic. Willow and rattan are particularly prized for their strength and ability to retain natural moisture, but any well-made piece of wicker furniture should give you years of use.

Wicker can be painted, lacquered, or stained. Left untreated, it will eventually darken. If you prefer the light, natural look, choose wicker with a clear protective finish.

Wicker can last for generations, but a piece is only as good as its construction. Here's how to evaluate it.
- **Lean heavily** on a piece of wicker to test its strength. The wicker should not sag or shift. A few creaks are normal, but beware of wicker that protests loudly.
- **Go undercover.** The underside of a piece offers clues to its construction. A high-quality piece of wicker will be

woven on a frame that is at least 1 inch thick, and will have corners that are tightly and securely wrapped. Nails should be hammered all the way in.

- **Feel the finish.** Whether the wicker has been painted, lacquered, or left bare, it should be smooth to the touch, with no snags, rough edges, or hairy fibers.
- **Check the tightness of the weave.** You may have to pay extra for wicker furniture that is tightly and evenly woven, but it will repay you with years of use.

RATTAN

Rattan is a wood vine that grows in the jungles of Southeast Asia and the Philippines. Harvested and stripped to its smooth inner bark, rattan has long been prized for its versatility as a furniture material. When steamed, it can be bent into graceful curves; when dry, it is tough, flexible, and resilient.

- **Rattan furniture should be solid.** Lean on the piece to check for swaying or shifting. Make sure that nails and screws are securely sunk into the rattan poles.
- **Poles should be free** of dark blemishes that might indicate rotting. The finish should be smooth and fuzz-free.
- **Growth nodes** should be evenly spaced 12 to 18 inches apart, of uniform size, and not unduly knobby.
- **Wrappings** should be tight, smooth, and securely fastened with glue or nails. Most good rattan furniture uses bindings made from peelings of rattan bark, but some use strips of leather instead.

PLASTIC

Plastic is gaining favor, especially for shelves, occasional tables, or chairs. A vibrant, versatile material, plastic can be bent, molded, and blown into sinuous shapes. Lightweight, durable, and relatively inexpensive, it can be pigmented with any color. Most plastics in furniture are thermoplastics. Thermoplastics start out as resin pellets that are heated to a liquid state and injected under high pressure into a mold. Thermoplastics can be damaged by excessive heat, but otherwise are fairly tough and durable.

Quality influences the price of plastic furniture, but price also is influenced by the quantity in which a piece is produced. The mold is a major cost of manufacturing; if a piece is manufactured in limited quantities, it will be priced higher to cover the price of the mold.

- **Check** all the parts of the piece that will bear weight or undergo stress (shelves, chair seats, table legs). If the plastic is not thick enough to bear weight, it should be reinforced in some way.
- **Edges** and surfaces should be smooth and flawless, and all visible sides should be finished.
- **Color and glossiness** of a piece should be uniform. If the piece is assembled from several components, the tone and finish of all the components should match.

READY TO ASSEMBLE

Ready-to-assemble (RTA) furniture is a growing component of today's furniture market. Often simple and contemporary in design, RTA furniture is sold in furniture stores, hardware stores, and even through the mail.

RTA furniture is designed to be easy to assemble even for the unhandy. Some pieces don't even require a screwdriver; the parts interlock. The savings can be as much as 20 percent compared to assembled furnishings.

Popular materials include wood (finished and unfinished), composition board, and plastic laminates.

Most stores show assembled samples of the RTA furniture they sell. Put the samples through the same quality tests you would other furniture to see if they are sturdy and well made. Then, check for a few things peculiar to RTA furniture.

- **Wood corners** should be sanded smooth, and metal pieces should be free of jagged edges. Check the undersides of pieces, too.
- **Components** of the piece should fit together snugly and securely.
- **Modular units** should be uniform in color, finish, and fit, so they go together evenly and firmly.
- **Assembly directions** should be clear; examine them before you buy.

FURNITURE
SECONDHAND AND UNFINISHED

Secondhand and unfinished furniture have helped stretch many a furniture budget. When you shop for such pieces, evaluate the basic strength and quality of these pieces just as you would any other furniture. On secondhand pieces, evaluate the time and effort it will take to restore the pieces to good health and good looks, as well.

CLEANING OLD FINISHES

Renewing secondhand furniture may mean stripping away the old finish and applying a new one. But often, what looks like a hopeless finish is merely a dirty finish. So before stripping, try cleaning.

Mix a mild solution of dishwashing detergent and water and scrub an inconspicuous area. If the surface begins to cloud, it's shellac or lacquer, and you should switch to a cleaner formulated for these finishes.

If the surface doesn't cloud, continue scrubbing, rinsing and wiping dry every few minutes. Once you've washed it clean, touch up blemishes and apply paste wax.

If soap and water don't yield good results, try a furniture refinishing product. Refinishers clean and partially liquefy the finish so it melts into cracks and scratches; then it hardens again into a smooth finish. Refinishers do well on varnish, lacquer, and shellac, but aren't powerful enough to work on paint, epoxy, or polyurethane. They shouldn't be used with penetrating oil finishes.

STRIPPING

Taking furniture to a professional stripper can be a good way to get the job done, but it's also costly and risks damaging the piece. Before you have furniture stripped professionally, learn how it's going to be handled.

One common procedure is the "dip-and-strip" method. The stripping service submerges the piece in a vat of remover, then hoses it down with water to wash off the remover and old finish. This method may dissolve glue joints and should never be used on veneers or softwood pieces. Dipping usually raises the wood grain, so you'll need to do lots of sanding before applying a new finish.

Some shops remove finishes by hand, and they often sand, as well. Expect to pay more for a hands-on job.

The other option is to do it yourself. Home stripping formulas *(see box)* vary in the jobs they do best. Most formulas contain methylene chloride, which eats away the finish; because this ingredient evaporates rapidly, strippers also contain additives to slow evaporation. These end up in the goo you scrape and wash away.

The finish you apply will be only as good as what's underneath, so take your time and sand everything. As a

STRIPPING PRODUCTS

Stripping furniture takes elbow grease, but it pays off in beautiful furniture. For best results, pick the right product and follow the manufacturer's directions precisely.

Liquid removers have little or no wax. They're inexpensive and work best on large horizontal surfaces. They don't cling well to upright or rounded surfaces, so it is hard to apply the product thick enough to do the job. They are flammable and toxic.

Semipaste removers include wax to aid clinging and retard evaporation. Medium-priced, they're best for stripping paints, varnishes, lacquer, and shellac. They're unsuited for epoxies, baked enamel, and polyurethane-based enamels and varnishes.

Heavy-paste removers are the toughest and costliest removers. They work well on furniture with many layers of paint, varnish, epoxy, urethane, and marine finishes. They are toxic, are not as flammable as semipaste or liquid strippers.

Water-rinse removers can be washed away with water or a water-and-detergent solution. However, water can wreck glue joints and raise wood grain; so rinse and dry quickly. These removers work best on nonporous surfaces. Never use one on furniture with veneer. These products are toxic, but nonflammable.

rule, sand until you're satisfied with the way a surface feels, then sand some more.

If the surface is damaged, start with a coarse- to medium-grit abrasive. If you're using a straight-line or orbital sander, apply only light pressure. (Don't use a belt sander on furniture.) Remove dust and residue after each sanding by wiping with a tack rag made by dampening cheesecloth with mineral spirits. Next, sand with a medium- to fine-grit abrasive, then dampen the surface to raise the grain. Finish by hand-sanding with a very fine abrasive.

STAINING AND BLEACHING

With unfinished or newly stripped furniture, you have several color options: you can retain the natural color, modify it with stain or bleach, or paint over it.

To color and darken bare wood, use a stain. Penetrating stains soak deeply into wood fibers. Because hard and soft parts of the grain absorb them differently, these stains tend to emphasize grain patterns. Pigmented stains not only soak into the wood, but also lightly coat its surface, tending to blend and obscure the grain.

Bleach lightens wood and removes stains. To bleach with liquid laundry bleach, flood with a bleach and water solution or use bleach full strength. Neutralize any bleach left in the grain by washing it with one part ammonia or white vinegar to two parts water. Be sure to work in a well-ventilated area. To lighten wood even more, use a two-part commercial wood bleach. Brush on one chemical, wait for the specified time, then brush on another.

OIL AND WAX FINISHES

Finishes protect and enhance wood. For a bare-wood look, choose an oil or oil and wax finish. Oil soaks into the wood and offers limited protection from liquid spills. To apply an oil finish, pour some on the furniture, wipe it around with a rag, let it soak in, then wipe the surface dry. You can apply a finishing wax topcoat for a slicker look.

Varnish, polyurethane, and lacquer form a hard, gleaming surface on top of the wood. Polyurethane is impervi-

ous to water and alcohol. Varnish is impervious, too, but not quite as tough as polyurethane. Both varnish and polyurethane are applied with a brush, and both are available in gloss, satin, and flat finishes. Lacquer and lacquer-like finishes dry quickly, won't build up as thickly as other clear finishes, and can be sprayed or brushed on.

Use these techniques to brush on a clear finish:
- **Keep away dust** by putting the piece in a room where there are no drafts. Wipe the piece well with a tack rag.
- **Don't shake the can.** Stir, but avoid bubbles.
- **Use a high-quality brush,** natural- or synthetic-bristle. Load it by dipping the bristles halfway into the finish. Tap excess off the bristles; don't squeeze the bristles against the can's lip.
- **Gently pour the finish** onto the surface. When you've finished an entire panel, brush over it with long, straight, overlapping strokes, using just the tips of the bristles. Leave the room and let the piece dry thoroughly. Then, lightly sand all over with 220-grit sandpaper, wipe with a tack rag, and carefully apply another coat.

PAINTING FURNITURE

If you're going to paint a piece of furniture, you may not have to strip it first. If the finish is reasonably smooth, just wash it with turpentine or mineral spirits, then degloss the surface with 200-grit sandpaper. For chipped spots, "feather" the rough edges with 80-grit sandpaper.

Polyurethane paint is just as tough as polyurethane varnish. Alkyd enamel (oil-base) paint also covers well and provides a hard, wear-resistant finish. For best results, don't paint furniture with latex paint or wall or house paints. You can brush or spray-paint furniture. To use a brush, shake and stir the paint well. Dip the bristles about one-third of the way into the paint, and strike off against the can. Lay on the paint in long smooth strokes.

Decorative painted finishes can add a touch of the ritz to plain-vanilla furniture. The "Walls and Ceilings" chapter of this book includes instructions on stenciling, sponging, and combing painted surfaces. Do-it-yourself products are available for marbleizing and antiquing.

FURNITURE
NEW AGAIN: UPHOLSTERY UPDATES

Before you shop for new upholstered furniture, take a good look at what you have. Slipcovers or reupholstering may make that frayed, but faithful, chair new again.

Re-covering chairs and sofas can make sense for seating pieces that are well-constructed and in good condition. The wood frame should still be sound, with no dry rot or worm holes. You also should like the piece: A good reupholsterer can make cosmetic improvements in your furniture, but the shape will be unchanged. Whether you'll save money, compared to buying new, depends on what you do, the cost of labor, and the fabric you choose.

Slipcovers are fabric dressings that cover up the existing upholstery. Even if your seating pieces are in pristine condition, the slouchy, comfortable look of slipcovers is fashionable now, and they are easily removed for cleaning. Slipcovers are an option if your furniture is in good shape, with lots of bounce left in the springs and stuffing.

Reupholstery involves, at a minimum, removing and replacing the covering of a chair. If a piece has lost its comfort or shape, the upholsterer may also retie loose springs or replace worn seat cushions. Always ask for an estimate of the work needed before you decide to reupholster, keeping in mind that your upholsterer may find some surprises once the cover comes off.

GETTING IT DONE

Both slipcovering and reupholstery are jobs you may be able to do yourself. However, fitted slipcovers require careful measuring and good sewing skills, and not all home sewing machines can handle bulky projects or fabrics. They also are labor-intensive to create. It might take a professional as long as 24 working hours to make a slipcover for a three-cushion sofa. Reupholstery requires special techniques you can learn through reading or classes.

If you choose to have slipcovers or reupholstery done by professionals, use word of mouth to find competent help. Shops that carry drapery and upholstery fabrics can often supply you with names. When you talk to an upholsterer, ask to see photos—or better yet, examples—of his or her work. If you have an unusual project, such as an antique chair, or a sofa with a lot of button tufting, be sure to discuss that ahead of time.

Before you buy fabric to re-cover a piece, calculate your yardage with care. Details make a difference, and you may need extra fabric to match patterns. Skirts and loose pillows also add yards. Here are some general guidelines for reupholstery; slipcovers require slightly more fabric:

- **Three-cushion sofa:** No skirt, 10 yards; tailored skirt, 12 yards; pleated or gathered skirt, 14 yards.
- **Wing chair:** No skirt, 5 yards; loose seat cushion, 5½ yards; skirted, 6½ yards.
- **Club chair:** No skirt, 5 yards; skirted, 6½ yards.

▲

New upholstery can change the face—and character—of seating. In a fanciful play on weaves, candy-red cotton duck knocked the stuffiness right out of the formal French pieces.

NEW AGAIN: REPAIRS

Most furniture repairs are done to save money, to save the piece of furniture, or both. Knowing a few simple furniture repairs can turn a garage-sale bargain into a treasure, or spare a favorite piece from the attic. Here are some tips for putting the "sturdy" back in your furniture.

WOBBLY CHAIRS

A chair with wobbles is one small step from disaster, so take it out of circulation until you can repair it. If the symptoms are shakiness, the problem usually is chair legs and/or stretchers that need regluing. Often, the holes that legs and stretchers fit in have become enlarged.

First, disassemble the chair, using a towel-padded hammer. Label each piece so reassembly will go smoothly.

Next, remove the glue from both portions of each joint. Scrape off what you can, then sand off the rest. If, after sanding, the leg or stretcher fits too loosely in the holes, coat the rung with glue, then wrap it with a layer of strong, fine thread and let the glue dry.

Apply glue to both parts of the joint, and tap the leg or stretcher into the receiving hole. Be careful that no glue is left on the surface of the furniture. Glue will not accept stain and can ruin the final finish.

Draw the joints tight by wrapping a cord twice around the chair. Insert a small piece of wood between the two cords and turn it, tourniquet fashion, to tighten the ties.

WEAK FRAMES

When the frame of a table or upholstered chair racks or twists, turn the piece upside down and check its corner joints. They probably are reinforced with wood wedges or metal braces.

Wood wedges should be glued and screwed to rails on each side. If a wedge is loose, remove it, scrape and sand off the old glue, and apply new glue to the wedge and rails. The screws may not fit snugly. If that's the case, insert a couple of toothpicks or wooden matchsticks into the holes before reinstalling the wedges. Metal braces can be tightened with a screwdriver, a wrench, or pliers. If you find no wedges or braces at the corners, cut blocks from hardwood and glue and screw them into place.

LOOSE VENEER

When a small area of veneer is loose, follow this procedure: Lift the loose edge and squirt in a dollop of white glue. Spread the glue around with a thin knife blade. Then, put waxed paper over the glued area and a board on top; clamp it securely with a C-clamp, or weight it down with books.

When a large area of veneer is loose, or if you're replacing a section of veneer, use contact cement. Apply the cement to both the veneer and the undersurface, using a small brush. Allow cement to dry for at least a half hour.

Carefully lay the veneer in place. (Be accurate, because you won't get a second chance.) Roll the veneered area with a rubber roller or a rolling pin.

DENTS, CRACKS, AND CRAZING

• **For dents,** stick shellac may be successful in filling small areas. If not, pierce tiny holes in the dented area, using a needle. Dampen the dent with a few drops of water. After the wood swells, rub lightly with rottenstone and oil.

If furniture isn't severely dented and wood fibers aren't broken, try this on a piece that you will be refinishing:

Lay several folds of damp cloth over the damaged surface. Apply a hot iron to the cloth for several minutes. In many cases, the steam swells the wood fibers and returns them to their original state. Steam will raise the wood grain surrounding the dent as well, so you will have to do some extra sanding to smooth the surface before finishing.

• **For cracks,** fill with a good wood putty, carefully applied with a putty knife or small, thin-bladed knife. Remove excess putty with a rag or fine-grit sandpaper. Use shellac sticks to fill wide or deep scratches.

• **For crazing,** if the condition is not severe, rub the crazed area with fine steel wool, then polish with paste wax. If the crazing is extreme, you'll need to refinish the piece.

FURNITURE
CARE AND CLEANING GUIDE

Furniture is a major home investment, and with loving care, favorite pieces pay years of beautiful dividends. This care-and-cleaning guide offers practical tips for popular types of furnishings.

Wood furniture is sensitive to extremes in temperature and humidity, so consider your home's environmental factors before placing a piece. Prolonged exposure to direct sunlight or heat from a too-close heating vent can crack or discolor surfaces. Extreme dampness can cause pieces to swell or warp. To keep wood glowing:

• Follow directions on product use and on maintaining special-care surfaces. Apply products in small amounts with a clean, soft cloth, and whether waxing or simply dusting, rub with the wood's grain. Pretest new wax or polish on a small out-of-the-way spot.

• Dust frequently to remove abrasive particles from wood surfaces. To avoid scratches, lift, don't slide, objects to dust beneath them. Never dust with cheesecloth unless sizing has been laundered out. A polish-treated cloth is good for a polished finish, but may soften wax on a waxed finish. To remove everyday dust and soils, moisten a clean cloth with a spray product, because a dry cloth may leave hairline scratches on the finish.

• Protect with paste wax, applied every few months. Use two cloths—one for application, one for polishing. If streaking or a cloudy film develops, use a spray or creamy furniture cleaner to erase it.

• Use specific products on specific finishes. For high-gloss and antique finishes, use liquid polish or paste wax, and buff for sheen. For satin-gloss finishes, avoid products with silicone. For low-gloss finishes, use a liquid polish for low-luster woods or a cleaning wax that protects without shine. For oil finishes, periodically wash with a mild soap solution with a few drops of mineral spirits or lemon juice, then apply boiled linseed oil. Dust oil finishes with a cloth dampened with clean water and glycerine or mineral thinner. For painted finishes, wipe with a cloth or sponge dampened with a mild soap solution, and use products recommended for painted woods.

To keep upholstered furniture fresh, vacuum it weekly and turn the cushions to distribute wear. Before cleaning upholstery, check to see if the fabric can be shampooed or if it demands a no-water cleaning solution. Pretest the cleaner on an inconspicuous spot to make sure colors don't bleed together. Use commercial foam or home-mixed dry foam made by whipping together warm water and synthetic detergent. With a soft-bristle brush or sponge, work foam into a small area at a time with a circular motion. Remove suds with a rubber spatula, dry sponge, or clean towel. Rinse with a warm, damp cloth, and let dry.

Leather and vinyl upholstery also require special care. Dust is leather's enemy, and its abrasive action can eventually damage it. So dust often and thoroughly—especially tufted areas. Wash today's leather with warm water and mild face soap. Clean vinyl with "safe for all vinyl" products or warm water and mild detergent. For both, avoid products with ammonia, bleach, or abrasives.

To keep plastic looking good, wipe with a damp cloth and mild liquid-detergent solution. Never use abrasive cleaners or furniture polish. As a scratch deterrent, some manufacturers recommend automobile wax.

Wicker furniture is vulnerable to rain and sun damage, so keep it indoors or on a sheltered porch or patio. Dust woven areas with a vacuum cleaner brush, then wash pieces with a soapy sponge, rinse, and wipe dry. Liquid furniture wax adds a protective sheen.

When rattan snaps and crackles under pressure, it needs moisture. Being careful not to wet the frame or penetrate the weave, clean rattan with a damp sponge or mist it with a water-filled plant sprayer, then wipe, and let dry.

Use metal polish on chrome-plated furniture, but not on brass-plated pieces. Wipe brass plate with a soft cloth to keep from scratching the protective lacquer coating.

Help outdoor furniture keep elements at bay by spraying aluminum with a clear lacquer. Restore dull unpainted aluminum with fine steel wool dipped in kerosene. Wash color-coated aluminum with a mild detergent solution, rinse, and apply automobile wax. Exterior oil enamel paint or a polymer sealant, plus a top coat of automobile wax, protects wrought iron from rust, and a coat or two of preservative protects redwood from moisture. For stained-and-waxed redwood, wipe with a damp sponge.

82

FURNITURE FIRST AID

TYPE OF FINISH	PROCEDURE: SCRATCH REMOVAL
Plastic	Regular applications of automobile wax fill in minor scratches.
Dark wood	Rub nutmeats (walnut, Brazil nut, or butternut) into scratch. Or touch up with a furniture crayon, eyebrow pencil, or shoe polish in a shade to match finish.
Mahogany or cherry	Apply aged or darkened iodine.
Maple	Apply aged or darkened iodine diluted 50 percent with denatured alcohol.
Oil	Using a fine steel-wool pad, rub lightweight mineral oil, boiled linseed oil, or paraffin oil into scratch. Wipe dry.
TYPE OF STAIN	**PROCEDURE: STAIN REMOVAL**
Water marks or rings	Place a clean, thick blotter over stain and press down with a warm iron. Repeat. If that fails, try applying cleaning polish or wax. Or, apply camphorated oil with a lint-free cloth, rubbing with the wood grain. Wipe dry. Repeat.
White marks	Rub with a thin paste of wax and mineral spirits. When dry, apply a thin coat of wax or cleaning polish. Or, rub with cigar or cigarette ashes, using cloth dipped in wax, lubricating oil, vegetable shortening, lard, or salad oil. Wipe off immediately. Rewax.
Milk or alcohol	Using fingers, rub liquid or paste wax into area. If that fails, rub in paste of boiled linseed oil and rottenstone (available at most hardware stores). Use powdered pumice for dull finishes. Wipe dry. Polish. Or, apply ammonia with damp cloth. Polish immediately.
Cigarette burns	Rub area with scratch-concealing polish. If that fails, apply rottenstone paste as for alcohol stain. If burn is deep, area may have to be refinished.
Heat marks	Rub area gently with dry steel-wool soap pad a tiny area at a time, wiping up powdery residue. If that fails, rub with cloth dampened in camphorated oil or mineral spirits. Rub dry with clean cloth. Repeat. Or rub gently with fine steel wool. Wipe off. Repolish.
Sticking paper	Saturate paper with lightweight oil. Wait. Rub area lightly with fine steel wool. Wipe dry.
Nail polish	Blot spill immediately. Rub area gently with fine steel wool dipped in liquid wax. Wipe away polish. Rewax.
Paint spots	If paint is wet, treat like a nail polish stain. If dry, soak area with linseed oil. Wait until paint softens. Wipe away paint with a cloth dampened in linseed oil. If any paint remains, apply a paste of boiled linseed oil and rottenstone.
Candle wax	Harden wax with an ice cube, catching moisture as ice melts. Using fingers, crumble off wax. Scrape remaining wax gently with an old credit card. Rub with cloth dampened in mineral spirits. Or place a clean, thick blotter over stain and press down with a warm iron. Rub area with liquid polish.

COLOR

Color comes first. Whether it's in the first impression or the final analysis of what makes a room work, color is the key to successful decorating. Without it, even the loveliest furnishings go flat. Conversely, color can turn everything, even eyesores, into visual pleasures. Color works magic, too, by visually stretching or shrinking space, raising and lowering ceilings, and even altering moods. Add the fact that color is inexpensive and you'll see why it's such a decorating asset. If you've never been brave with color before, take heart. Courage comes from understanding how color works. In this chapter we'll show you how to scheme your way to success.

COLOR
COMING TO TERMS

Understanding color principles is the key to creating beautiful rooms, because color's beauty is literally in the eye of the beholder. Scientifically, color is a property of reflected light, not a fixed quality of objects we see. When light hits an object, the object selectively absorbs and reflects wavelengths. A red wall looks red because it reflects the spectrum's red wavelengths. Without light, we see blackness, but brighter light levels stimulate the eye's color receptors, and we see colors. Decorating schemes succeed if you, first, learn to speak color's language.

● **Primary colors** are red, blue, and yellow—all colors in their strongest form, spaced equidistantly around the color wheel. All other colors are derived from the Big Three. Decorating with primaries produces lively rooms, energetic and full of visual bounce.

● **Secondary colors** combine equal parts of the primaries: orange, mixed from red and yellow; green, from yellow and blue; and violet, from blue and red.

● **Tertiary colors** result when a primary color is combined with its nearest secondary color on the color wheel. Examples are blue-green, yellow-green, yellow-orange, red-orange, red-purple, and blue-purple.

● **Complementary colors** are opposite or nearly opposite each other on the color wheel. Complementary combinations, such as red and green, yellow and violet, or orange and blue, can make a lively decorating scheme, but they need deft handling to avoid overpowering a room.

● **Tints** are colors with values closest to white, such as pastels. Add white to red, and the result is pink.

● **Shades** are made by adding black to a color. Navy, maroon, midnight blue, and deep purple are shades.

● **Neutrals** are welcome in any decorating scheme because they are so easy on the eyes. Black, white, gray, brown, and beige are examples of neutral hues.

● **Monochromatic color schemes** are based on a single hue. Spice this scheme with variations of the major color for visual interest. In choosing design elements and surfaces, a textural mix is especially important.

● **Analogous color schemes** use closely related colors, those adjacent on the color wheel. Such secondary and tertiary colors harmonize well. The scheme can embrace

An essential reference in planning decorating schemes, the color wheel is a rainbow in the round, representing the brilliant bars of color that light produces as it passes through a prism. ▼

A sophisticated palette ▶ kindles color excitement in this sleek urban aerie, where varied shades of gray set the stage for furnishings in bolder blues and artworks with primary punch.

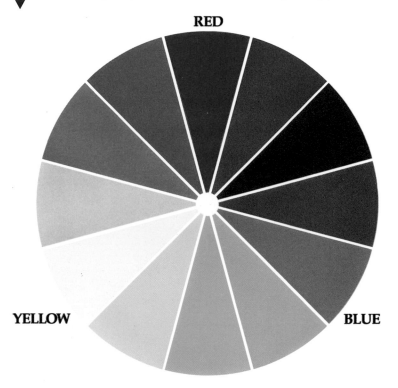

three to five hues, but only one primary color. An example is a room in blue, blue-green, and green.

● **Complementary color schemes** combine colors directly opposite each other on the color wheel. These bold-spirited rooms succeed best when one color is used more liberally than the others.

The texture or finish of a colored surface, plus the size of the area it's used on, and the size of the room all influence how a color looks. Work with large samples of paint colors and fabrics to get an accurate picture. Examine samples in the room where they will be used in both natural and artificial light.

COLOR
MOOD MAKERS

Color magically communicates with us on physical and emotional levels, influencing not only the overall look of a room—its furnishings, fabrics, and accents—but also the moods of the people within it.

We all respond to specific colors differently. To some, bold red may be energizing; to others, it's simply nerve-jangling. To some, black is sophisticated; to others, it's depressing. We may think of blue as cool and calming, but certain shades can be electrifying, too. In general, bright hues fight "blue moods," neutrals soothe the spirit, and lively reds may even stimulate the appetite. By taking advantage of color's unrivaled mood-setting talents, your room can convey a very eloquent and personalized message. But, which colors will best get that message across?

Nature sets the color thermostat, so it's important to consider the visual temperature of hues before you decide on a palette and dip into the paint. Warm colors—reds, yellows, and oranges—are fueled by sunshine. Cool hues include blues, greens, and violets. Sizing up your room's attributes will help you make appropriate color choices. What kind of natural light does the room have? If it enjoys a sunny southern exposure, temper the rich, bright light with cool or neutral colors. In north-facing rooms, let cheery warm colors compensate for the paler light. Brights can even cheer a dark, windowless room. The spectrum's cooler side fosters introspection and calm, an appealing mood for a living room or master suite. Bright warm hues, however, can buoy the spirits, producing young-looking, fun-loving rooms, no matter what your decorating style.

Because color and light are inextricably linked, check samples and swatches of your color candidates by night in the room's artificial lighting. They may look surprisingly different. Incandescent lights usually add a warm yellow cast to colors, standard fluorescents tend to cool colors down with a slightly gray cast, and halogen bulbs produce very white light with little color distortion. This relationship is especially important in night-activity rooms, or in daytime spaces short on sun. Colors that look vibrant in natural light may wash out in the low glow of table lamps.

▲
Rich chocolate-brown lacquered walls wrap the small bath in elegance and set the tone for accents, such as the window's chintz balloon shade.

The French-inspired living room derives its drama from color counterpoint, furnishings and design elements in pale hues against a deep claret backdrop.
▼

COLOR
MOOD MAKERS

In selecting colors, room function and decorating style come into play. Hues you choose for private areas—bedrooms and bathrooms—may differ from those in a home's public rooms. Here are factors to consider:

• Is the room a lively family hub, or a gathering spot for entertaining? Warm colors are good choices for action rooms, such as kitchens, family rooms, dining rooms, children's rooms, and even the nursery. Studies show infants respond happily to bright hues.

• Do you want to put your room in a formal or informal mood? The same furnishings, in different colors, can produce very different moods.

• What colors are practical for your life-style? Restful pastels may suit the bedroom, but not the family room.

• Do you want to carry the color mood beyond one room's threshold, linking spaces that flow together? Such a color link works well if one space is visible from another.

▲
Perched in a city high-rise, a heritage-rich living room counts on glossy deep green walls for drama, and light tones on floor and ceiling to keep the dark backdrop at bay.

◀ *Strong pastels, in a related-hue scheme, link an eclectic mix in this living room. Neutral elements—a pine chest and hardwood floor—temper the brights, and yellow accents add a lively counternote.*

A bold-spirited dhurrie rug ▶ inspired the vibrant colors and personality of the cozy living room. The red lacquer walls deliver intriguing texture because color was brushed over a grass-cloth wall covering.

COLOR
COLOR TRICKS

Color is the great deceiver, and by using the right hues and techniques to create illusions, you can visually remodel an awkward room inexpensively or personalize a space with special effects. Because color makes surfaces and furnishings visually advance or recede, first pinpoint your room's positives and negatives. Then decide which elements to highlight and which to hide. Here are some savvy suggestions for working design magic with color:

- In a small room, the space-expanding prescription is to unite walls and ceiling in a sweep of white or light color. Carry the light hue to the floor with neutral-toned carpet or painted or bleached wood.
- Cozy up an oversize room with a rich combination of dark or warm colors. Maximize the effect by applying the warm backdrop color over the ceiling. Use color in window treatments, and choose rough textures in carpet and upholstery, because they absorb greater amounts of light, thus appearing darker.
- Square up a long, narrow room by painting walls in advancing and receding colors. For example, use a warm, dark hue on short end walls to coax them forward visually, and use a soft white or light hue on long side walls to diminish their importance. For a long, dark hallway, keep colors light to compensate for any lack of illumination.
- Tame a too-high ceiling by painting it in an advancing color, such as brown or dark blue, that brings it down into your line of vision. Enhance the effect by extending the dark color down the wall to a picture molding or other natural demarcation line.
- Visually raise a too-low ceiling with a light receding color, such as white or a pastel hue.
- Disguise a room's flaws with color magic. If walls are broken up by doorways, windows, and various nooks and crannies, paint away such interruptions with a light or white wall color applied over frames and all. Make an unsightly feature, such as an old fireplace, seemingly disappear by painting it the same color as the walls. For uneven wall surfaces, a dark hue is the perfect cover-up.
- Play up a room's character by accenting architectural details, such as woodwork, wainscoting, or chair rail, with color or crisp white paint against warm-hued walls.

- Take an artistic approach to walls with stenciling or elegant finishes such as comb or sponge painting. With trompe l'oeil painting that literally fools the eye, you can create special effects from raised paneling and crown moldings to wall-size landscape murals.
- Furniture, too, benefits from a color boost. Painted and stained finishes and fresh-hued fabrics can revive and unify a roomful of varied-vintage pieces, but choose one color to dominate the scheme.

Elegant paneling embracing this French country living room is actually an artful impostor, achieved with trompe l'oeil painting. The realistic molding effect is done in several shades of blue and white. ▼

Plenty of sparkling white ▶ *paint and light-in-scale furnishings visually stretch the diminutive dimensions of an all-in-one living space, but it's robin's-egg blue overhead that sets the cool, refreshing mood.*

COLOR
START WITH ART

Often, favorite artwork can inspire dazzling color schemes. It's an easy starting point, because the artist has already combined hues you find inherently appealing. In translating those colors to your room, remember only one hue should dominate. Other hues should play counterpoint, in varying degrees. And, never use a color just once. For example, if you pick up a painting's brilliant red for accent pillows, add a red pottery vase somewhere in the room. Neutral backdrops can create an at-home gallery effect, always a good strategy when you're displaying dramatic art or numerous works together.

◀ *Designed around prized artwork, a living room showcases its finest in a gallerylike setting. Classic furnishings, from understated stripes on the sofas to a low-profile window treatment, don't vie with the vivid stars. Accents echo the bold primaries.*

This dining space takes its color cues from the dramatic painting by playing up the art's light/dark contrast in the backdrop and its lively hues in cushions on the wicker chairs. Midnight blue paint highlights the texture of old flocked wallpaper; woodwork is brushed in bright white, and the ceiling in aqua.
▼

COLOR
REST ASSURED WITH NEUTRALS

Unlike bold colors that instantly demand your attention, neutrals communicate in a more subtle, soothing way. Worked into a decorating scheme, these inviting "uncolors" allow the eye to set its own pace, perusing surfaces, shapes, and textures at leisure. Such highly versatile schemes are built around black, white, gray, beige, and taupe, hues that mix and match easily or solo beautifully when they're used in variations and combined with an intriguing mix of textures. Whether your style is formal or casual, traditional or contemporary, neutrals are artful mood-setters that are especially easy to work with.

One successful approach to a neutral palette is to gather a range of these easy-on-the-eye hues into a relaxing scheme. For example, you might build a room around variations of gray—a pale hue on walls, a rich charcoal in carpet, and a medium tone in upholstery—then add design elements in warm tans and accents in a soft melon hue. Another approach is to focus on one neutral, such as a refreshing white-on-white room, that may mix as many as 10 to 20 variations—from cream, bisque, and bone to ivory and white.

It's important to balance light, medium, and dark color values around the room. To heighten the drama, increase the contrast. Although neutral schemes are contemporary favorites, they work well in period rooms and showcase antique furniture and collectibles. It's essential to add pattern and texture to enliven the neutrals. Natural elements—straw, wicker, bleached and au naturel woods, nubby wools, soft suedes, crisp linens, and stone finishes—are wonderfully warm additions.

◄ *With an air of classic formality, this living room called on black, beige, and off-white to dramatically spotlight modern art. Textural interplay, from slick metals to striped silk on silver-leaf art deco armchairs, stirs excitement in this eclectic scheme.*

Picked from a warm neutral ► palette, variations of caramel, cream, and black put a den in a casually sophisticated mood and provide a perfect foil for the room's bold-hued and primitive accents. Silk fabric links a mix of sink-in seating and wraps the walls for visual softness and sound absorbency.

COLOR
WIN WITH WHITE

If picking the right palette has you in a quandary, consider an easy color equation that guarantees beautiful results. Start with white, the versatile super neutral, and add one other color. Nothing clashes with amenable white. It works in any context with even the boldest, brightest hues, and, in its myriad variations, white can be warm and cozy or crisp and cool in mood.

Proportion is the key to a successful white-plus-one scheme. One color must dominate, and white obliges in either a starring or supporting role. For example, pick white for walls and woodwork, and a secondary hue for furnishings. Or reverse roles, with a strong color in major areas, with white adding contrast and visual relief. Teamed with a bold "plus" color, white deftly keeps such assertive tones in check. You can add black to this decorating equation, but make the "plus" color bold enough to stand up to the strong contrast of black and white.

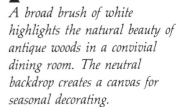

▲
A broad brush of white highlights the natural beauty of antique woods in a convivial dining room. The neutral backdrop creates a canvas for seasonal decorating.

◄ *In a restful guest realm, white provides crisp contrast to the soft gray background and carpet, and joins a mix of nostalgic furnishings in spirit.*

The living room takes on ▶ *elegant drawing-room airs with rich green spread over the walls. Refreshing lights in upholstery, carpet, and swag-and-jabot window treatments temper the deep hue's power.*

COLOR
CALL ON COORDINATES

Color-coordinated collections of design elements—fabrics, wall coverings, bed linens, and a wide range of accents from table toppers to lampshades—take the guesswork out of home decorating today. Because the harmonies, motifs, and pattern scales have been planned by a collection's design experts, it's easy to mix solid hues and a mélange of patterns, from stripes and florals to plaids and geometrics, for a successful room scheme. These elements should be linked by a common denominator color, however.

In picking coordinated patterns, remember that they should contrast in scale and fit the room's size. For exam-

ple, small prints can perk up a limited space, but they can lose their impact in a large room. Conversely, large-scale prints fare beautifully in bigger spaces. Scale is also the key to mixing like patterns. A room wrapped in countrified gingham checks avoids the busy look and becomes visually interesting if those checks contrast sharply in scale.

◄ *Here, soft peach is the major color thread and leafy green an accent hue that weave a medley of fabrics and design elements together.*

Peppermint-stick-striped fabric links the walls and chaise in the romantic retreat where accessories pick up the dominant red in various tints.
▼

COLOR
PLAY FAVORITES

Bold primary colors, in the ▶ seating, artful pillows, and favorite accents, put the sitting spot in high spirits.

Your ultimate color choices should be based on very personal criteria. Playing favorites—those colors you're comfortable with—is a good place to start. Even if a favorite hue isn't a common decorating choice, try to include it in accents. Here are some tips on color selection:

• Your closet is a clue. If your wardrobe is filled with favorite blues, consider a blue-based room scheme.

• Note your family's color preferences, a technique interior designers use to create satisfying schemes.

• Take a cue from a prized accessory, such as a pillow embroidered in bright primaries, an heirloom rug, or antique blue-and-white ware you will display.

• Consider your personal furnishings style. Are you a country buff who likes colonial blues, a traditionalist who favors rich drawing-room reds, or a collector looking for a gallery setting to showcase treasures?

◀ *A collector's passion for antique blue-and-white porcelain cued the colors in this dining room. The white backdrop provides crisp contrast to the blues in the table setting and on the chairs.*

▲ *The sunny yellow of an heirloom Grandmother's Flower Garden quilt is the color star in the romantic bower. Walls are painted in a softer buttery hue, but the exuberant chintz plays up the patchwork spectrum.*

COLOR
PATTERN AND TEXTURE

Linked by common colors, a medley of warm-up textures and artful accents adds cozy appeal to a hearthside sitting spot.
▼

Essential to any beautiful room scheme is the rich depth and visual interest only pattern and texture can provide. Each needs perfect balance to succeed.

Pattern in a quilt, rug, or fabric can inspire a color scheme, if you follow these simple rules:
- Use the pattern's dominant color for large areas—walls or ceiling—and echo it in the floor treatment.
- Use the next brightest hue as the scheme's secondary color, on large upholstered pieces and window treatments.
- Accent with the pattern's sharpest color.
- Distribute pattern evenly around the room, and factor in pattern added by art and books on open shelving.

Textures, too, require deft handling to create a well-balanced mix of smooth and rough surfaces. Smooth finishes—glass, brass, polished woods—are more formal and refined; rough textures—homespun fabrics and hand-hewn woods—are casual and informal. Capitalize on optical illusion with slick, shiny finishes to lighten a small room, and nubby, rough surfaces to cozy up a large room.

◀ *Small in size but big on charm, a romantic guest room succeeds on color-related prints and lacy textures. The precision geometry of patchwork counterpoints the soft florals.*

In this eclectic living room, a ▶ *color connection brings harmony to unlikely elements: the antique quilt over the mantel and the contemporary hand-painted fabrics on the seating.*

COLOR
AT HOME WITH HARMONY

Translated into a room scheme, colors that are close kin on the color wheel strike a harmonious chord. Such related hues are pleasingly compatible because they share family ties. For example, combine blue, green, and violet for a cool scheme; blue-green, green, and yellow-green for a spring-fresh palette; or yellow, orange, and red for a high-spirited room.

Often, the easiest starting point for a related-hue scheme is your favorite color, plus those adjacent to it. Choose only one color to dominate, and a maximum of three hues for the basic scheme. However, you can play the chosen hues like a virtuoso, varying the trio up and down the intensity scale, from warm to cool, light to dark. Then let an accent color, such as a complementary hue, add visual spark. In a living room wrapped in bright pastel pinks and lavenders, a dash of sunny yellow in, for example, art or accent pillows makes a perfect counterpoint.

▲
In a decidedly lively mood, an antiques-filled dining room plays favorites, with the backdrop's tangy lemon yellow in the starring role and related tones in the supporting cast.

◀ *Anchored by a 19th-century painted bed, this retreat relies on pinks, greens, yellows, and blues for perfect harmony against a peach backdrop.*

Capitalizing on the mood- ▶ setting magic of color, this sophisticated living room picks a vibrant red to create personality punch and a dramatic gallery for displaying prized artworks.

FABRICS

Fabrics are decorating personality you buy by the yard. With texture and pattern, they bring color schemes to life and soften the hard lines of architecture. The spirit of a fabric's design, the way it drapes and moves, the way it's used in a room—all these factors express a character you can see and feel. Choosing fabrics can be one of the most creative and satisfying parts of decorating, but it helps to be confident about practical matters as well. This chapter will help you choose fabrics that are well-suited for their job—and that function as beautifully as they look.

FABRICS
THE BASICS

For sheer decorating inspiration, spend an hour or so browsing through samples of fine fabrics. With their blend of color, texture, and pattern, fabrics suggest unlimited possibilities: They can dress a window, cover a wall, skirt a table, or surprise an old chair into freshness. If you're decorating a room from scratch, there's no better place to begin than with a piece of fabric that expresses the mood you desire.

Choosing fabrics for your home demands both artistry and practicality. When you're investing in materials you'll live with for years, you want to be sure that your selection is durable, cleanable, and well-suited to the purpose. The next few pages will help you match the fabrics to the treatment you have in mind.

SETTING A MOOD WITH FABRIC

The "Color" chapter has specific suggestions for mixing pattern and texture within a room, but selecting fabrics starts with something even more basic: a clear understanding of the ambience you're after.

Many fabrics express a distinct personality. For example, a gold-threaded brocade unmistakably connotes richness, just as a tweedy homespun implies rusticity, and a watercolor print suggests lighthearted romance. The fabrics you blend with these strong personalities should express a compatible mood. As you consider each fabric, imagine it in the room and ask yourself if it fosters the feeling you want. If it doesn't, keep looking.

Keep in mind that the style of your furniture doesn't have to dictate the fabrics you use: In fact, changing fabrics affords you a chance to give old furniture a whole new look. A vivid chintz may be just the thing to loosen up staid Victorian furniture; an elegant damask can change a countrified camelback sofa into a lady of luxury.

TIPS FOR SHOPPING

The search for the perfect fabrics may take you to decorator centers, upholstery shops, drapery shops, and fabric stores. If you're buying fabric off the bolt, be sure to look for decorative, not garment, fabrics. Decorative fabrics are constructed to be durable for home furnishings, and they usually are sold in widths of at least 48 inches.

Few people have the ability to accurately recall the nuances of color. When you shop, take along samples of carpet, other fabrics, wall coverings, and paints used in your home. And as you look through swatch books, keep in mind that small swatches can be misleading: A mini-print that looks crisp close up may blur together when you see it on a three-cushion sofa across the room.

Once you've found a fabric you like, borrow a large sample to take home with you. When you get home, hang or lay each sample where it will be used, and observe it for at least 24 hours to see how it changes in different light. For drapery material, gently pleat the sample in your hand to see how the pattern is affected. If you're buying several fabrics for a room, bring home all the samples at once: It's the only way you can be sure they'll live happily together.

PURCHASING POINTERS

When you buy or order fabric, it's important to get all you need at once, so you won't have to supplement it later with fabric from a different dye lot. Most design centers and fabric stores have salespeople who are trained to help you figure how much fabric your project will require.

If you are buying fabric to upholster a sofa or chair, come prepared with the exact dimensions of the piece and its loose cushions and, if possible, with a photo of the piece. You'll also need to supply details about your plans for the piece: Will it be skirted, and if so, in what style? Will it have tufting, buttons, or welts? Will you use the fabric vertically or turn it on its side to eliminate seams? Will you need to center a pattern on the cushion and seat backs? If the fabric features a repeating pattern, be sure to allow extra yardage for matching the repeat.

If you're buying fabric for window treatments, see the "Windows" chapter for information on measuring for various treatments. Before paying for fabric, inspect it for defects in the weave or dyeing. Remember, fabrics from natural fibers will have slight variations in the yarns.

Playful fabrics bring a breath of fresh air to this room, where the architecture is formal but the mood is not. Like the high ceilings, the patterns are oversize: an exaggerated plaid for the printed cotton draperies, a bold stripe for the petite chair. Even the tieback takes a poke at buttoned-up style.

111

FABRICS
THE RIGHT CHOICE/NATURALS

Aside from how a fabric looks, it's important to select a fabric that works well, too. Choosing an appropriate fabric boils down to three elements: fabrication (how it's made), fiber (what it's made of), and finishes (treatments after the fabric is woven). The next four pages are devoted to evaluating these three Fs.

Many of the intriguing differences in the texture, weight, and surface appearance of fabrics are due to fabri-cation. The type and weight of the yarns used and the way the yarns were woven all affect how the fabric looks and performs. The strongest fabrics, for example, are tightly woven of tightly twisted yarns. You'll find more about specific weaves on pages 116–119, but you can tell a lot about a fabric just by examining it. Fabrics with a loose weave are translucent when you hold them up to the light; these fabrics work well for window treatments or light-

THE NATURALS

	COMMENTS	ADVANTAGES	DISADVANTAGES	CARE/COST
Cotton	Creases easily; absorbent; breathes well; easily treated; highly flammable; fair resilience and elasticity.	Strong fiber; takes color well; blends well with other fibers; versatile.	Wrinkles easily; affected by mildew and sunlight; shrinks and stretches unless treated; yellows.	Machine washable; must be ironed. Inexpensive.
Wool	Very elastic and resilient; does not burn easily; absorbent.	Strong fiber; insulates; takes color well; handles and drapes easily.	Attracts moths unless treated; needs careful cleaning; weakened by sunlight; shrinks unless treated.	Must be dry-cleaned. Moderately expensive.
Linen	Low resilience and elasticity; natural luster; burns easily; absorbent.	Very strong fiber; nice texture; somewhat resistant to sunlight and mildew.	Wrinkles easily; inconsistent in quality; somewhat stiff; shrinks unless treated.	Needs special cleaning to preserve appearance; colors may run; must be ironed. Expensive.
Silk	Lustrous; elastic, resilient, absorbent; does not burn easily.	Colors have jewellike tone; strong fiber; drapes beautifully; resists mildew.	Colors may run or change with age; weakened by sunlight; water spots unless treated.	Most are dry-cleanable unless label indicates hand washable. Very expensive.

duty decorative treatments. For upholstery, you want a tightly woven fabric that regains its shape after you stretch it. Many heavy-duty upholstery fabrics also are heavy in weight, but closely woven medium-weight and lightweight fabrics in a strong fiber may be suitable for seating pieces.

Texture also plays a role in deciding what goes where, from a practical standpoint as well as a decorative one. Though highly textured weaves may seem a dirt-defying choice for upholstery, keep in mind that uneven surfaces can trap dirt, feel scratchy to bare legs, and wear unevenly.

FIBERS: THE NATURALS

All fabrics start with fiber—tiny wisps of plant or animal matter or laboratory-made chemical substances. Fiber content is more than a beauty contest: The inherent properties of these fibers help decide how strong a fabric is, how it drapes and feels, and how it stands up to wear. The primary natural fibers used in fabrics are cotton, wool, flax, and silk.

Cotton is plucked from the fluffy pod of the cotton plant. Long considered the premier natural fiber because of its low cost and versatility, it is used extensively in both draperies and upholstery. Cotton fibers handle abrasion; they also accept dye beautifully, so they are available in many colors and prints. Cotton is capable of accepting finishes and treatments that render it shrink-resistant, stain-repellent, flameproof, and water-repellent.

Linen fibers come from the woody stem of the flax plant; they are very strong, and accept dyes and finishes well. The unevenness of linen yarns gives linen fabrics a textural richness, and the waxy finish of the fibers wards off dirt and adds luster. Linen makes a good drapery fabric because it holds its shape well. Linen wrinkles easily, however, and it needs careful cleaning. It sometimes is blended with cotton to make a stronger fabric that better resists wrinkling.

Wool is clipped from the backs of sheep, goats, and alpacas. It has a natural spiral that, when woven into fabric, creates air pockets that insulate against winter cold and summer heat. That, and its smooth drape, make wool well-suited for draperies. Wool springs back to its original shape when stretched, a plus for upholstery. Wool is more resistant to sunlight than plant-based naturals.

Silk is seized from the silkworm, which extrudes the filament to form a cocoon. It also is a very strong fiber, though it is very susceptible to sun damage. Silk is as elastic and resilient as wool. It dyes so well that it picks up the most subtle shades of color. In addition to these practical properties, silk's fineness, high luster, and superb drape enable it to be made into the finest fabrics, from plush velvets to delicate chiffons. A luxury material, silk often is blended with other fibers.

FACTS ABOUT FINISHES

Special finishes can make fabrics shed wrinkles, fight flames, and even ward off mildew and insects. But perhaps the most popular finishes for home fabrics are those that repel soils and stains.

Stain-resistant finishes seal fabrics so you have a chance to blot up stains before they sink in. Silicone-based finishes resist water-borne stains only. Fluoro-chemical finishes, such as DuPont's Teflon and 3M's Scotchgard, resist water- and oil-based stains. Fluor-ochemical finishes will last many launderings and at least three dry cleanings.

The fabric label should tell you if a stain-repellent finish has been applied. Unfortunately, some dishonest merchants remove the fabric labels from treated upholstery pieces so they can sell you an unnecessary treatment. You can check with the manufacturer of the furniture or fabric to see if a treatment has been mill-applied.

FABRICS
THE RIGHT CHOICE/SYNTHETICS

Synthetic fibers, like natural ones, each have their own advantages and disadvantages. They may be used alone or blended to produce a fabric with the best qualities of several fibers.

Some synthetics actually are based on natural substances: They start out as cellulose and protein materials. These materials are then processed with chemicals to produce fibers. Rayon, the original artificial silk, is one such fiber. Made from wood pulp, rayon takes dye well and has a fine drape; it often is used for upholstery fabrics and draperies. It also is blended with other fibers to decrease static electricity, improve softness, and enhance dyeing.

Acetate also has wood pulp as its basic raw material, but it is produced by a different process, resulting in a better drape and more lustrous look than rayon. Acetate is often blended with other fibers to improve crease retention and resistance to sunlight.

PURE SYNTHETICS

Other synthetics are purely man-made; nylon was the first such fiber. Its strength, resiliency, and elasticity continue to make it useful as a blend in drapery and upholstery fabrics. However, its glassy, synthetic appearance makes nylon less attractive as an unblended fabric. Nylon also deteriorates when exposed to sunlight.

Polyester's primary strength lies in its ability to blend with other fibers, imparting qualities such as wrinkle resistance, resiliency, and cleanability, and an ability to retain pressed-in pleats. Used behind glass, polyester resists degradation to sunlight; polyester fabrics often are sold for draperies and sheer window treatments.

Acrylic's most significant trait is that it can be spun to resemble natural fibers, but with the added strength and lower cost characteristic of synthetic fibers. Acrylic's bulkiness gives it a texture similar to wool. It also shares wool's colorfastness and resiliency.

Fabrics made of glass fibers are used for draperies. Glass fabrics are durable, stable, and easy to maintain. Avoid glass fabric on often-opened windows, though; the glass filaments can break if the fabric is whipped by the wind.

Olefin is primarily used in carpet, but also is found blended into drapery and upholstery fabric. It's a lightweight fiber but is bulky enough to insulate well. Olefin also is resistant to sun and mildew. Due to heat sensitivity, olefin needs special care in cleaning.

THE FABRIC THAT FITS

The array of synthetic, natural, and fiber blends makes it possible for you to truly match fabrics to your own individual needs. These questions will help you evaluate what fabrics will work for you:

• **What is your climate?** This is particularly important in choosing drapery fabrics, because draperies can be an important insulator for your home. Natural fibers tend to be particularly good at trapping heat, but they may not stand up to harsh sunlight as well as some synthetics. If you're in a warm climate, keep in mind that if drapery fabric is tightly woven, light in color, and opaque, most of the sun's rays will be reflected rather than admitted.

• **Is humidity a factor?** If you keep a humid house or live in a humid climate, seek fabrics that resist shrinking or sagging. Look for fibers with less absorbency, like glass, polyester, or acrylic. Look at the weave as well; the looser the weave and the heavier the fabric, the greater the chance for instability. Check the fabric's label for statements about shrinking.

• **Do you prefer fabrics that don't require special care?** The most commonly used easy-care fabrics include polyester, polyester/cotton blends, and (for draperies only) glass.

• **Is the possibility of soiling great?** If so, choose fabrics that can be cleaned easily and consider colors that do not show dirt as readily. Look for fabrics that have been treated for soil and stain resistance.

• **Is flame resistance a necessity?** If the fabric will be used near a wood stove or fireplace, or if someone in your family smokes, flame resistance should be a priority. The charts here and on page 112 list flammability characteristics for each fiber. You also may want to look for a fabric with a flame-resistant finish.

THE SYNTHETICS

	COMMENTS	ADVANTAGES	DISADVANTAGES	CARE/COST
Rayon	Creases easily; versatile; high absorbency and moderate elasticity; not flammable.	Drapes well; blends well with other fibers; takes color well; can be made to look like natural fibers.	Weak fiber; shrinks and stretches unless treated; weakened by sunlight; needs special care.	Dry-clean unless label indicates hand washable; must be ironed. Inexpensive.
Acetate	Moderately good resilience and elasticity. Fair absorbency. Burns readily and melts.	Appears lustrous and silklike; drapes well; resistant to mildew; somewhat wrinkle free.	Weak fiber; weakened by sunlight; colors fade from atmospheric fumes.	Dry-clean unless label indicates hand washable; cool iron. Moderately inexpensive.
Glass Fiber	Does not absorb moisture; little stretch; poor resilience and elasticity; flameproof.	Very strong fiber; resistant to sunlight and stains; can be wiped with damp cloth; insulates.	Fibers may break along folds; may need special hardware due to weight.	Wash by hand, being cautious of glass slivers; hang to dry. Moderately expensive.
Acrylic	Low absorbency; good resilience and elasticity; does not burn easily.	Woollike in texture; resists mildew, moths, and sunlight; holds color well; fairly strong fiber.	Tends to pill; stretches somewhat; not as durable as some fibers, especially when wet.	Hand-wash unless labeled otherwise; hang to dry. Moderately expensive.
Polyester	Very good resiliency and elasticity; not absorbent; melts under high heat.	Strong fiber; resists wrinkles, moths, and mildew; blends well; doesn't stretch or shrink.	Has a slithery texture; difficult to dye; gradual loss of strength from sun exposure.	Most items can be machine-washed and -dried. Moderate cost.
Nylon	Very good resiliency and elasticity; low absorbency; melts under high heat.	Very strong; can be sponge-cleaned; blends well; lustrous; resists abrasion.	Tends to look glassy; fades and weakens from sun exposure.	Most items can be machine-washed and -dried. Moderate cost.
Olefin	Low absorbency; lightweight with good bulk; somewhat resilient and elastic; not flammable.	Strong fiber; good insulator; resistant to stains, sunlight, and mildew; resists abrasion.	Best as blend or lining due to appearance; easily damaged by heat.	Machine-wash; dry at low heat. Moderate cost.

FABRICS
A PHOTO GLOSSARY

The fabric world is filled with beautiful pattern and sumptuous color, but its terminology can be intimidating. There are literally hundreds of fabric types, some named for their weave or yarns and some by pattern, usage, or tradition. When you also consider the variety of colors and printed patterns available, your choices expand even more. Our photo glossary introduces you to some of the most popular and enduring fabric types. Many are woven in a variety of fibers and weights.

▲
Cotton Print
A favorite of designers and do-it-yourself decorators, cotton prints offer an endless variety of colors and patterns. They wear well as curtains, draperies, bedspreads, and—in heavier, closer-woven versions—slipcovers and light upholstery.

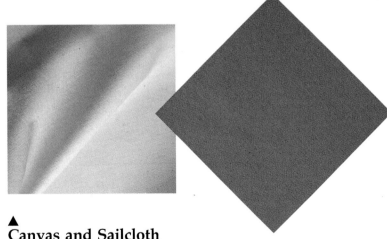

▲
Brocade
Rich and usually ornate, a brocade displays a raised pattern that resembles embroidery. Used primarily for fine upholstery, brocades traditionally were silk. Today, brocades are woven in many fibers.

▲
Chintz
This plain-woven cotton fabric is defined by its high-luster glaze. Although some chintz is solid color, the fabric often features colorful floral designs. Chintz is used for light upholstery, slipcovers, and other decorative treatments.

▲
Canvas and Sailcloth
Closely related, these fabrics feature the fundamental plain weave: one thread over, one thread under, much like a child weaves a pot holder. Canvas is the heavyweight version; and sailcloth, the lightweight. A similar fabric, duck, is medium-weight. All are woven of serviceable cotton or linen, come in a wide range of colors, and are appropriate for slipcovers, upholstery, and window shades. They are sometimes treated for outdoor use, and may be woven with wide stripes.

◄ Corduroy

Corduroy's distinctive ribs are formed by cut pile that rises above the ground of the fabric. A durable fabric, corduroy is used for upholstery, slipcovers, draperies, bedspreads, and wall coverings.

Damask ►

Damask combines two basic weaves to produce a flat pattern. A damask might show, for example, a plain-woven leaf against a lustrous satin-weave ground. Fully reversible, it is woven in many weights.

Faille ►

Faille is a delicate member of the ribbed weave (also called "repp") family of fabrics. With 36 delicate ribs woven per inch, a faille has good body and a slight luster. Consider failles for draperies and table skirts.

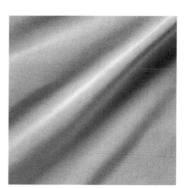

▲ Chenille

With its soft, fuzzy surface, chenille is making a comeback as a comfort fabric for upholstery and trims. Chenille is woven with a special twisted yarn, then clipped to produce the fuzz.

Flame Stitch ►

Flame stitch is a type of tapestry, distinguished by its flamelike design. It may be woven in solid colors, but more often is multicolored. Flame stitch is a time-honored pattern often used in traditional settings.

▲ Dobby

Dobby is a family of fabrics with a small raised geometric motif woven into the fabric, typically cotton or linen. Dobbies are used for slipcovers, curtains, and draperies.

◄ Dotted Swiss

A very sheer cotton fabric, dotted swiss is patterned with embroidered or chemically applied dots. It is one of several sheer fabrics often used for summery, light-filtering window treatments.

FABRICS
A PHOTO GLOSSARY

Flannel ▶

Soft and slightly napped, flannel brings home furnishings the same cozy feeling it lends to clothing. The nap is raised by bristled rollers run over a fabric of wool, cotton, or fiber blend. Flannels are used for bedding, upholstery, and draperies.

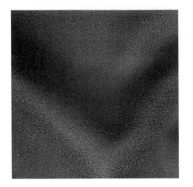

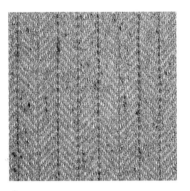

Herringbone

A twilled fabric, herringbone has a diagonal ridge that periodically reverses direction. The resulting pattern looks like the skeleton of a fish. This example is tweeded, woven with yarns that yield a nubby surface.

▲
Moiré

Moiré has a shimmering finish that resembles watermarks or wood grain. Usually, the finish is pressed into a taffeta by engraved rollers, but moire may be imitated by printing or weaving techniques.

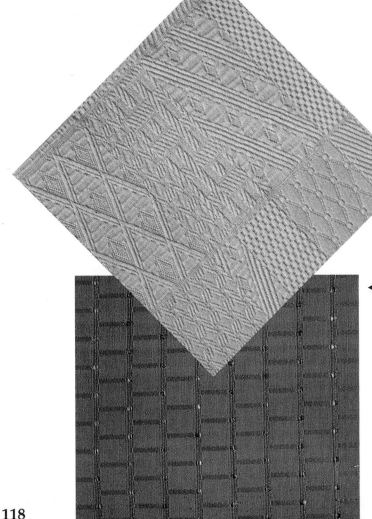

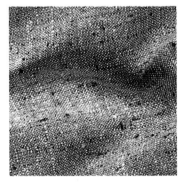

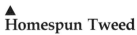
Homespun Tweed

The coarse yarns of this fabric are meant to look as though they were spun by hand; they are sometimes tweeded, like the one above. Plain-woven homespuns are appropriate for curtains, slipcovers, and draperies.

◀**Jacquard**

Jacquard is a family of fabrics that shows an intricate woven design. Named for the sophisticated loom that produces it, jacquard may be geometric, curved, or swirled; it may be solid or multicolored. Prized for its three-dimensional quality, it is suitable for upholstery in heavier weights.

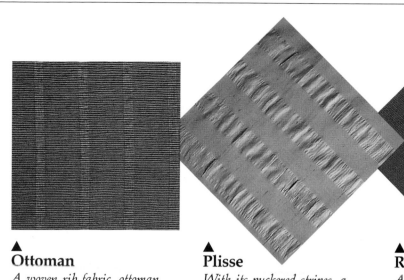

Ottoman

A woven rib fabric, ottoman has large, flat ribs that give it substantial weight and a bumpy surface texture. Its hefty weight makes it well-suited for heavily used upholstery, and the distinct texture usually suggests a casual mood.

Plisse

With its puckered stripes, a plisse resembles an overscaled seersucker. The crinkle may be formed by varying the tension in weaving or by finishing techniques. Medium-weight plisses work for curtains, bedspreads, and accents.

Repp

At first glance, repp resembles a small-wale corduroy, but the repp's rib is woven rather than cut pile. The tightly woven ribs wear well, so repps are suitable for upholstery or draperies. Failles and ottomans are variations of repp.

Sateen

Sateen is a soft, lustrous, medium-weight fabric used for draperies, linings, and table coverings. The sheen comes from threads that "float" across the surface, reflecting light. Close kin are the satin weaves.

Tapestry

Modeled after handcrafted needlepoint, tapestry is an even-textured heavy fabric. It is used primarily for long-lasting upholstery. Although tapestries traditionally featured scenes, they are equally striking in contemporary patterns.

Taffeta

A close-woven taffeta often rustles when you handle it; it has a somewhat stiff body due to a fine cross rib. Originally silk, taffetas now come in many fibers. Taffeta drapes well, making it an elegant choice for draperies and tablecloths.

Ticking

Originally used to cover mattresses and pillows, this woven striped fabric is now at home in upholstery, slipcovers, and other decorative treatments. A blue-and-white stripe is authentic, but today's tickings come in many combinations.

Twill

A fundamental weave, twill shows a distinct diagonal ridge as the weaving yarn moves up and over on each line. Tightly woven, twills are usually very strong and serviceable—ideal for upholstery. Denim, serge, and herringbone are twills.

119

ROOM ARRANGING

When it comes to arranging a room, it's not the amount of space you have that counts; it's the imaginative way you use it. Although there's no single "right" way to plan a room scheme, certain principles always apply: Proper scale, balance, and proportion are three of the most essential ingredients in successful arranging. But you also can call on other decorating tricks to make a room look and function the way you want it to. Here we show you assorted ways to shape—or reshape—the space at your place.

ROOM ARRANGING
THE BASICS

Room arrangements determine not only how rooms look, but, more importantly, how they live. Without a thoughtfully designed floor plan, a hardworking room can lapse into laziness and disorganization, a comfort zone may be plagued by irritating interruptions, and a small space can become even more claustrophobic.

The well-arranged room's success doesn't depend on the style or the status of your furnishings. The key is how the pieces work together, and how they relate to each other within the overall space.

By following basic floor-planning techniques and other guidelines in this chapter, you'll find that room arranging need not be an enigma. With an imaginative approach, even awkwardly proportioned rooms can be shaped into pleasing and practical spaces. After all, *you're* the expert. You must decide how each room will be furnished, and how it can best function to suit your life-style.

In making your own arrangements, the priorities are comfort, convenience, and composition. For livability, comfort and convenience come first, and they are the easiest elements to address. To be truly pleasing, a room must serve your purposes and fulfill your personal definition of comfort. Do you envision an easy-care, casual space for relaxing and conversation, or something formal and dramatic, strictly for guests? Convenience means that the arrangement promotes easy traffic flow and encourages the activities that you've put in the room's script. If pedestrians are a conversation stopper, constantly traipsing through the middle of the seating area, it's time to revise the arrangement in order to reroute traffic. Once comfort and convenience prerequisites are met, focus on the room's composition, the aesthetic aspects—including balance, scale, and color—that contribute to the eye appeal of the space.

Decide exactly what you want the redesigned room to do. Take the living room, for example. Is it strictly an easygoing family activity center, a space for entertaining a crowd, or both? How much seating is needed? Do you want to design-in dining potential? How much open floor space is required? In the family room, do you want work space for hobbies or a special space for child's play? In the bedroom, could you squeeze in a computer center or sitting spot?

After you've settled on the varied roles you want the space to play, size up your furnishings needs and the room's physical space—its architectural features; dimensions, including ceiling height; and immovables, such as a fireplace and built-in shelves. It's best to anchor an arrangement with one large-scale furniture piece or a wall storage system. A time-tested rule of room arranging is: Subtract to add, and divide to multiply. Eliminating nonessential furnishings frees up space. Using furniture to divide a space into various activity centers can deliver surprising new functions.

Choosing the all-important focal point around which the furniture will revolve is the initial step to an actual arrangement. When this decision is made, elements seem to fall into place according to function and size. Some rooms are quite cooperative about focal points, offering natural focus—architecturally—with a grand fireplace, a wall of built-ins, or a spectacular view through a bay window. Often, however, the focal point depends entirely upon your creativity. When a room lacks obvious focus, gather seating around a dramatic painting or an artful wall-hung grouping of collectibles, or underscore the conversation area with a colorful area rug. Cast an armoire or tall cupboard as the focal point, and pull seating around the star piece, facing it. In the bedroom, the bed usually takes the focal-point spotlight. In large rooms with secondary seating areas, plan a secondary focal point for each grouping.

In this hearthside spot, a ▶
traditional sofa steps aside, and
a quartet of rosy silk-clad
armchairs and a leggy brass
table take the spotlight.

ROOM ARRANGING
PLANNING ON PAPER

With space at a premium in today's homes, how you arrange furniture within that space ultimately determines the comfort and convenience of your home-front environment. There's no single right way to plan a room, but just as there are formulas for successful color schemes, there are guidelines for mapping out flexible, functional floor plans. All you need is a tape measure, graph paper, and cut-to-scale templates of your room's furnishings. You can put together everything you'll need or purchase one of the many kits on the market today.

Whether you're starting from scratch with a new home and new furniture, or simply revising a room, planning on paper is essential. Creating a room arrangement from your easy chair is preferable to backbreaking hours lugging furniture around a room. But, more importantly, it's a thoughtful way to explore your room's options.

To get started, here are some floor-planning tips:
• Measure the room's dimensions carefully, and transfer measurements to graph paper. As your to-scale guide, make one square, or ¼ inch, equal 1 foot.
• On your floor-plan sketch, note placement of all architectural and fixed features, such as closets, fireplaces, built-ins, windows, doors, electrical outlets, light switches, wall sconces, chandeliers, radiators, and heating ducts. Also note the direction each door, storage cupboard, and window swings open.
• Note the room's natural traffic patterns.
• Measure the height, depth, and width of each piece of furniture, using the same scale. Draw and cut simple templates on sturdy paper for each piece.
• Because a room's color balance is important, shade the templates with colored markers.
• In the living room, for example, settle large priority seating pieces first on your floor plan.

To allow space for people to live comfortably and move about the room easily, consider these guidelines:
• Traffic lanes should be a minimum of 3 feet wide. Allow 3-foot clearance at interior doorways for door swing, and 4-foot clearance at entrance doors.
• To encourage conversation, sofas and chairs should face each other and be a maximum of 8 feet apart. Each seating

piece should have adequate illumination, and a table comfortably within reach for books, beverage glasses, and lamps. End and side tables should be about as tall as the chairs or sofas they serve.
• For adequate legroom, a coffee table should be set about 14 to 18 inches out from the sofa.
• In dining spaces, leave at least 3 feet for pullout and serving room behind each chair.

▲
By sizing up your space and using cut-to-scale templates on graph paper, you can create practical and pleasing furniture arrangements to conquer even the most awkward rooms.

Facing off across a rich-hued ▶ rug, white sofas anchor this seating mix in an expansive living room. Art adds focus to the center-stage grouping and the wall-hugging desk.

ROOM ARRANGING
SUCCESS STRATEGIES

As essential to the home decorator as it is to the photographer and the artist, composition means striking a balance in scale, visual weight, and color. In room arrangements, composition translates into an appealing distribution of large- and small-scale furniture pieces, accessories, accent colors, and patterns throughout a space. It also means coaxing the eye off a single plane with intrigue high and low—from wall art and soaring bookshelves to collectibles clustered on a coffee table and area rugs for drama underfoot.

Simply speaking, balance is like a teeter-totter. If a large seating group at one end of a living room lacks a counterweight, such as a wall of built-ins, the room seems lopsided at the other end. For a well-balanced room, consider the visual weight of furnishings more than the actual size. A chunky sofa need not be matched pound for pound with another large piece. Instead, combine several pieces, such as a pair of lounge chairs with a table in between, for a grouping that "weighs" as much as the sofa. Area rugs add visual weight to any furniture grouping.

The scale of individual pieces contributes to overall balance. A lightly scaled antique tea table or open-arm French chair doesn't compete in the same visual weight class with a heavy marble-topped coffee table or an English-style wing chair. A small lamp looks lost on a massive table, and a too-large painting can overwhelm small pieces beneath it. Playing to the light scale are open-arm and slipper chairs, see-through or reflective surfaces, and unskirted upholstered pieces.

Count on color for good composition. Dark upholstery grants importance to pieces, but covering an oversize sofa to match a wall hue blends it into the background. Anchor part of a room with strong, dark colors that add visual weight, and use colorful accessories—art, pillows, collectibles—for overall balance.

Plump love seats face off over ▶
a glass-topped table, granted
visual clout with a capital base
and an area rug.

ROOM ARRANGING
SUCCESS STRATEGIES

Backed up to a narrow room's doorways, armless chairs direct traffic around a sitting spot anchored by a wall-hugging sofa.
▼

With clever furniture arrangements, you can reshape space, add function, and cope with any room's eccentricities. Simply lining the walls with furniture, soldier-style, doesn't work in many of today's homes, with their wide open spaces and windowed walls. Here are some suggestions for creating new looks and solving old problems:

• For rooms with little solid wall space and those cut up by windows and doorways, consider on-the-diagonal or floating island arrangements. Pulled-together seating is more conducive to easy conversation, and it frees up perimeter space for other duties, such as work centers or storage. Flexible modular furniture works well in such free-form groupings.

• Direct traffic and redefine space with furniture placement. If the front door opens directly into the living room, create an "entry" by walling off one side with a seating piece backed up to form an imaginary boundary.

Sumptuous seating, ▶
unexpectedly set on the bias,
banished the bowling-alley look
of a long, narrow family room
created by merging two tiny
bedrooms. Light backgrounds
visually enlarge the space and
draw attention to the artwork.

◀ *Taking geometric inspiration from*
a granite-and-metal coffee
table, this living room
gathers contemporary seating
in a triangle arrangement at
hearthside. The angled sofa
guides dining room traffic
around the conversation hub.

ROOM ARRANGING
SUCCESS STRATEGIES

The quick prescription for a room set in its ways is change. Simply rearranging the components guarantees a fresh outlook for interiors, plus the bonus of added livability. But, for rooms that satisfy today's needs yet simultaneously look forward to a comfortable, convenient future, factor in flexibility from the start.

On the furniture front, modulars are the versatile problem-solvers for rooms on the move and hard-to-arrange spaces. From upholstered seating to stackable chests and wall storage units, modular furniture is sized and shaped to fit together, so regrouping the components into a new, customized configuration is easy. But the versatility doesn't stop there. Modular styles range from the popular clean-lined contemporary pieces to traditional groupings with softly curved frames and wood trims. Some are even scaled down to fit snugly into compact spaces.

Double-duty furniture is a wise choice for today's multipurpose spaces, such as a living room with dining potential, or a bedroom that by day serves as a sitting room, home office, or entertainment center. Talented drop-leaf tables can be everyday sofa tables as well as company dining tables. Living room occasional chairs also can serve as dining chairs, and sleek sleep sofas and Murphy-style beds, hidden in hardworking wall storage, can quickly turn any living space into a cozy sleep space.

Take a thoughtful look at your furniture, because it may offer more flexibility than you realize. Capitalize on a piece's inherent function and recast it in a new, unexpected role in your room arrangement. Armoires, cupboards, dry sinks, even pie safes, can stow entertainment gear. Dressed up, daybeds make inviting settees. Chests, trunks, and benches make unique coffee tables, and an old refectory table offers luxurious work space.

◀ *It's comfort first in a living room packed with easygoing amenities. Lounge chairs and an antique blanket chest balance off the ample sofa. Expanding the focus of the fireplace wall, shelves store volumes and showcase collectibles.*

Tempting the family to ▶ gather round for television viewing and conversation, this friendly spot puts everyone at ease with its relaxed mix of seating and handy tables for books, snacks, and board games, plus plenty of built-in storage.

ROOM ARRANGING
SUCCESS STRATEGIES

With creative arrangements and light-touch design elements, small spaces become beautifully livable places. Whether you want to turn an alcove into a den, or get the most out of all-in-one-room living, here are tactics for stretching your space:

• Lighten up color schemes and keep backgrounds simple. Lots of white paint or sparkling mirrored walls can visually expand a small room's boundaries.

• Pare furnishings and clutter, and choose light-in-scale, dual-purpose pieces. Let upholstered seating hug the wall, and draft occasional chairs for dining-area duty.

• Think vertically to free up floor space. Opt for built-in storage, and lighting discreetly hidden or mounted on the walls or ceiling.

• Counterbalance floor-bound furniture groups with art or collectibles in a dramatic wall display.

▲
This cozy raspberry-hued library corrected its tunnel vision with a stepped-up floor, nifty built-ins, a wicker sofa backed into a sunny bay, and contrasting crisp-white accents.

◄ *Once an idle passage between bedrooms, this niche is now sitting pretty for reading and relaxing. A sectional sofa tucks along the walls, out of traffic, and soft neutral colors visually expand the space.*

Here, a handsome French ▶ pine bed is angled to add focus and minimize the room's spare dimensions. Treetop-view windows draw the eye upward and welcome the sun.

ROOM ARRANGING
SUCCESS STRATEGIES

For spaces with intimidating proportions, such as large cavernous rooms or long, narrow ones, the high-performance decorating solution is to subdivide and conquer with well-planned furniture groupings and design elements.

In such problem rooms, you can instantly establish new visual boundaries for activity centers by setting open, freestanding shelves or seating pieces at a right angle to the wall. Further define a room's separate conversation, entertainment, work, or dining spots with, for example, area rugs. In oversize rooms, pull the main conversation-area seating away from walls into a floating island or diagonal arrangement to grant it more importance.

For unity in such multifunctional spaces, consider backgrounds in one color or variations of a single hue. In small tunnellike rooms, light-hued palettes and airy furnishings seem to expand the space. In large rooms, consider oversize pieces, and generously repeat color and pattern throughout activity areas for a harmonious visual link.

▲
In reality quite narrow, this snug family hub squares up with crosswise seating and book-filled shelves that visually advance to shorten the space.

◀ *Making the most of its grand dimensions, a sun-washed living room floats a right-angled chaise to create the visual border between a dining spot and the relaxed conversation area.*

This gracious living room ▶ boasts a pair of separate, but equally comfy, seating groupings, composed of elegant antique pieces upholstered in toasty colors, and set off by prized Oriental rugs.

WINDOWS

It pays to explore the window treatment options available today. The possibilities are greater than ever, and good results are assured if you give your windows careful thought. Always consider first the window itself. If it's a beautiful architectural asset—or, if it affords a fabulous view—then perhaps the best treatment is no treatment at all. If privacy or energy factors take first priority, you still can select from a number of coverings that won't detract from the window's appeal. Even if your windows are nothing to rave about, there are a variety of creative ways to make them special. This chapter takes you on a window shopping expedition.

WINDOWS
POINTS OF VIEW

Windows are your home's link to the light and beauty of the outside world. Their size and location make them prominent figures in your interior landscape, as well. So, when you cast characters in a room's decorating drama, offer window treatments leading roles.

Really, window dressings play many important parts. Practically speaking, a covering can filter harsh sunlight, boost your panes' energy efficiency, and provide important privacy. Because windows frame your own special view of the world, a treatment can improve your outlook by surrounding it with the right colors or a touch of softness. On the other hand, if that view leaves something to be desired, you can choose a clever covering that will mask an uninteresting scene—and even turn the hole in the wall into a decorating asset.

WHEN LOOKS COUNT

If all that weren't enough, nothing underscores a room's style like a well-dressed window. If a room is in the mood for French-country romance, for instance, a window draped in a veil of lace makes the perfect accent. A space marked by formality and tradition will be made even more elegant if the windows are appointed with flowing fabric tiebacks crowned with a sweeping swag or a sculptured cornice. Or, a crisp curtain cut from a charming gingham pattern can lend the finishing touch to a friendly country-flavored setting.

No matter what your style, though, all windows offer an exciting opportunity to express your individuality. From sleek miniblinds to voluminous draperies, the large and varied wardrobe of window dressings available means you are limited only by your imagination when it comes to outfitting your panes.

WINDOW-SHOPPING

So, where do you begin? Consider first the window itself. If it's an architectural bonus, then the best treatment may be no treatment at all. Of course, privacy could be a factor, in which case you can select from a number of barely-there treatments that won't detract from a window's shape. Or, you may be stuck with a window that isn't so wonderful. Wrapped in a colorful fabric, for example, even a wallflower of a window can become the life of the room.

A bank of windows or a large expanse of glass (such as sliding doors) can be mixed blessings. A wall of glass invites warm sunlight to enter a room and blurs the distinction between indoors and the great outdoors. But sometimes the amount of sun is too hot to handle and you need to block the outside world. Window coverings can solve the problems presented by these tough-to-treat windows—and they can do it simply, without overpowering a room.

Sometimes windows will deal you an even tougher hand. Poorly placed panes, windows that are out of scale with the room, or those that are plainly dull stack up against a homeowner. You can use your window coverings to help even the score by planning a treatment that masks their flaws.

When you consider all the roles a window covering can perform, then factor in the many types of windows and the treatment options available, it's easy to see that picking the proper dressing is far from an open-and-shut case. So do some window-shopping on the following pages. You'll find ways with windows that will add style and personality, disguise liabilities, and accent assets. Then, you'll be better able to decide how to put your windows in their best light.

WINDOWS
FABRIC TREATMENTS

Treated as one, problem windows become decorative arches of triumph. Custom rods and floral fabric do the trick.
▼

Knot it, swag it, pleat it, stretch and staple it, shirr it, tie it back, or just let it hang—fabric's versatility makes it the ever-popular choice for covering windows. Think about what fabric can do for your windows.

A fabric's fluidity is among its strongest traits. A fabric treatment throws a room some curve, to soften the sharp angularity of walls, floors, and ceilings. This flowing nature also comes in handy for treating problematic arched windows, or for softly linking multiple windows into a cohesive design.

Fabric can be called on to perform other decorating duties, as well. Give wimpy windows more muscle in a room's design with oversize drapery treatments. With the right style and placement, fabric treatments can make windows look taller, wider, or more dramatic than they really are. Similarly, mismatched windows are no match for fabric. If your room holds windows of varied dimensions and placements, treat the panes to draperies identical in size and style. This decorating sleight of hand will create comforting visual uniformity in your room.

Pattern and color enliven any setting. Fabric coverings offer you the chance to inject these decorating elements into a room in measured proportions. There's seemingly no end to the variety of fabric designs. You can wake up a window with a bold geometric print, or keep things calm with a subtle tone-on-tone pattern. For a custom-finished look, consider the coordinating collections of fabrics and wall coverings available. The choice is yours. Remember, however, that draperies represent a sizable investment. It's wise to pick a pattern that can adapt to changes in your room's design and your taste.

Treated as one, problem windows become decorative arches of triumph. Custom rods and floral fabric do the trick.
▼

◀ *The intriguing ebb and flow of this swag treatment has a soothing effect. To create the look, gather and staple fabric to the backs of four mounting boards.*

Dressed with custom-curved ▶ cornices, slender draperies, and sheer curtains, these panes complement—rather than compete with—artful architecture.

WINDOWS
FABRIC TREATMENTS

When selecting a fabric to suit your taste, consider, too, how well it stands up to the test of time. At the window, fabrics are exposed to damaging sun and soil. Although no fabric treatment lasts forever, you can extend its life span with the proper selection and care.

Generally, heavy, tightly woven fabrics are more durable than sheer ones. What's more, some textile fibers succumb to sun damage more quickly than others. Vulnerable fibers include silk, acetate, cotton, nylon, and linen. Fibers better able to battle the sun's rays include polyester and acrylic. (The "Fabrics" chapter contains detailed information on choosing fabrics.) Lining draperies with a durable fabric is one way to fight back against the sun.

Closely follow a fabric's care instructions. It's best to wash or dry-clean draperies once a year, and vacuum regularly between cleaning. Regular cleaning won't weaken fibers nearly as much as a buildup of atmospheric soil. In addition, many fabrics are now treated for soil resistance at the manufacturing stage. When you shop, ask what special treatments the fabric has been given.

◄ *Floor-to-ceiling draperies draw the eye to this room's great height. Sewn from heavy, light-blocking fabric, the traditional draw draperies get a lighthearted kick from a petticoat of eyelet.*

▲
Laced with fringe, lush folds of cotton damask give an everyday window ballroom elegance. The mix of fabrics adds style: A pleated floral valance falls over subtly striped draperies.

◀ *More than just a pretty look, these sweeping swags solve a decorating dilemma. The problem? Low windows and high ceilings. To give the windows greater scale, fabric flows from floor to ceiling. The gap between the tops of the windows and the ceiling hides behind a lace mask.*

Hand sewn to tiny café rings, panels of lined silk make a simple yet sophisticated comment. Gathered onto a rod, the fabric between the rings falls forward for a casual twist on standard pleated draperies.
▼

▲
This swag-and-jabot treatment softly frames a garden view. A pale green lining quiets the abundant floral patterns.

WINDOWS
LIGHT TOUCHES

▲ Tacked to the window molding, lacy cloth adds a touch of frill to plain panes. A privacy-giving blind hides underneath.

▲ For a simple swag, a fabric panel is angle-cut and fringed, then looped over a rod. Tasseled rope adds a special touch.

◄ For easygoing schemes, simple treatments are best. A valance whipped up from stock window hardware and a three-seam fabric casing makes an easy-sew topper for lace curtains.

Floral fabric and lace make a pretty pair. A shirred, scalloped valance crowns lace Priscilla curtains. Reversing the curtains so the ruffle falls along the outside perks up the look.

▲ So as not to spoil the view or a relaxed family-room mood, this bay demanded a trim, informal dressing. Pleated jabots and a

tailored valance lend crispness; denim and plaid fabric keep it casual. The fabric was stapled to a board fastened to the wall.

WINDOWS
SHADES, SHUTTERS, AND BLINDS

Flowing folds of fabric make the appropriate window attire for many decorating occasions, but don't forget the many other windows of opportunity that open up for you when you consider shades, shutters, and blinds.

Some room schemes benefit from a no-frills window dressing. If you're composing a contemporary setting, the crisp geometry of a shade or shutter steps right in line with the look. Or, you many want to play up a mix of treasured furnishings in a room. Shades and blinds can be subtle supporting players that won't upstage a setting's real stars.

FABRIC SHADES

Elegant in a slimmed-down way, fabric shades treat windows with minimal yardage and maximum style. The shades can be the ideal compromise when you want color, pattern, and softness at your windows, but you don't want the heaviness of an elaborate drapery treatment.

The two most popular types of fabric shades are balloon shades and Roman shades. In each case, cording that runs through vertical lengths of ring tape raises and lowers the shade. Trim and tailored Roman shades feature flat panels that raise in a series of soft, horizontal pleats. Full and graceful, balloon shades are characterized by billowy folds of fabric that raise in scalloped poufs.

Besides a limited amount of fabric, you need only minimal sewing skills to create your own, customized fabric shades. Shop for fabric shade instructions among the home furnishings patterns at your fabric store. Depending on the fabric and shade style you choose, these window dressings can lead you in different design directions. For example, stitch a balloon shade from lace for a look that's as romantic and nostalgic as a petticoat. Or, whip up a Roman shade from a vivid cabana-striped fabric, mount it inside a brightly painted window molding, and you've got an eye-riveting, work-of-art window.

Want a no-sew option? Look for ready-made shades—many of which coordinate with bedroom linens—at department stores or home specialty shops, or in catalogs.

▲
For a soft variation on the Roman shade, run cords only along the outer edges of the fabric panel. The shade will lift in a gentle arc of fabric.

A linen Roman shade and a shirred, cotton café curtain pair up for a look as crisp and casual as a cotton sundress.

An organza shade softens the sun's rays—and the contemporary setting—without competing with special architecture.

For a different perspective, try a "down-up" Roman shade. The shade rises from the windowsill on cords so you can let the sun shine but retain privacy or block an uninspiring view.

Shirred onto a wide rod and drawn to half-mast, this ruffled balloon shade adds a delicate canopy to a tree-lined view. Sewn from fabric that coordinates with wall coverings and furnishings, the shade adds a finishing touch to the interior landscape, as well.

147

WINDOWS
SHADES, SHUTTERS, AND BLINDS

Although a room scheme often dictates the type of window dressing you choose, windows themselves can be demanding things. Certain types will call for trim, tailored treatments. Where an expanse of glass or a bank of windows might be cumbersome swathed in yards and yards of fabric, a shade, shutter, or blind covers panes in a neat and simple way. These treatments can also be the right answer if you don't want a window covering that masks fine woodwork or artful architecture—or that competes for attention with a something-special view.

Though shades, shutters, and blinds come in different styles and materials, they have similar, hardworking traits. Privacy and light control top the treatments' list of strong points. Often tightly fitted to the window frame, they offer the fringe benefit of increased energy efficiency. These long-lasting covers are also easy to maintain.

Often, shades, blinds, and shutters are used as a can't-go-wrong starting point for a window's decoration. Install them now for their practical qualities and streamlined good looks. Then, when you want to change your outlook, you have the option of topping the coverings with a colorful valance or pairing them with a drapery treatment.

▲
Palladian windows are delightful to live with but difficult to treat. Plantation-style shutters not only provide privacy in this street-level bedroom, but play an integral role in the room's stripped-down decorating scheme.

◀ *Roman and pleated shades team up to provide privacy and light control—without cluttering a contemporary setting. Pleated half-shades pull up to mask a ho-hum view without blocking sunlight. At night, Roman shades lower to cover the entire window.*

◄ Greenhouse windows bring the great outdoors into a living space. For times when you want to block the outside world, however, these panes need the assistance of a custom covering. To control light and privacy, shop for shades and blinds at window specialty stores.

◄ Without stealing the show from dramatic windows, subtle blue Roman shades lower to filter a strong midday sun. When raised, the shades disappear behind barely-there fabric valances.

▲ Pleated shades assure nighttime privacy yet unify an awkward lineup of small windows. Fully raised, the pleats stack to 2¼ inches to keep from spoiling the daytime view.

WINDOWS
SHADES, SHUTTERS, AND BLINDS

When you start window-shopping for a shade, shutter, or blind, you're likely to be amazed at the endless selection before you. Horizontal blinds not only come in a spring meadow of colors, they're now offered in a variety of slat sizes. You can pick from slick ½-inch microblinds, standard 1-inch miniblinds, blinds with sturdy 2-inch louvers—and sizes in between. Besides standard metal types, you'll choose from fabric, wood, or less costly vinyl blinds. Or, go in a different direction and shop for vertical blinds. Drawn aside like draperies, these clean-lined coverings also present a grab bag of colors and materials.

Once a shade at the window meant a plain white roller—the kind that snaps up with a quick tug. Now, the outlook has changed. Not only are roller shades offered in a wide range of textures and colors, you have the relatively new option of pleated shades. These coverings draw into neat, accordion folds. Made of synthetic, dust-repelling fabric, pleated shades filter sunlight to a soft glow.

Picking a wood shutter presents options, too. You can buy standard-size shutters through department store catalogs and home centers, or have them custom made to suit your taste—and window.

◀ *Sleek miniblinds are an interesting visual contrast to traditional architecture, yet fit right into the light and airy scheme of things.*

▲
A series of different-sized windows becomes a single design element with plantation shutters. Custom-cut shutters are available.

Because they block light, plus ▶ provide privacy and energy savings, horizontal blinds are a good match for sliding glass doors. When raised, the wood blinds hide under a soft swag.

WINDOWS
JUST BROWSING

SINGLE WINDOWS

Let this sketchbook inspire you with ideas for covering all types of panes. If you're dressing a single window, consider first its size. Does the window look small compared to the size of your furnishings or the room itself? Give it fullness with ruffled tiebacks or flowing curtains. If its scale matches other elements, treat it simply with a shade or a top treatment. For the drama of height, mount the rod higher than the top of the window.

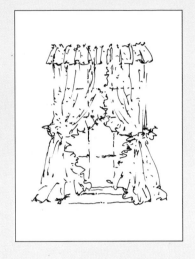
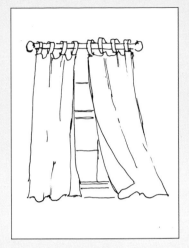

MATCHED SERIES

A series of windows not only offers a room an eye-grabbing focal point, it invites the light and beauty of the outdoors inside. Even more, this type of window offers you a host of decorating options.

Multiple windows, however, do demand that you make a decorating decision: Do you treat each window as a separate unit or unify the series into a single design element? To reach a conclusion, think about your room's style. In a clean-lined contemporary setting, the geometric look of a bank of windows can be an asset. To get the full architectural impact, try a top treatment only. A valance or cornice adds a punch of interest and color to the blank expanses of glass, without masking the window's design. Need more privacy, light control, or energy efficiency? Shades and blinds mounted inside each window's molding perform those tasks, and still offer a tailored look.

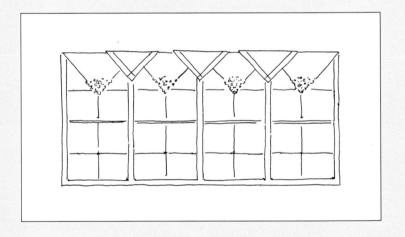

If your tastes dictate a softening solution for multiples, fabric options abound. Flowing, to-the-floor draperies lend grace and elegance to traditional schemes. Crown the draperies with a sculpted cornice for added height and formality. In a casual or pared-down setting, simple side curtains flank windows with color and pattern without "overdressing" them. For an even lighter look, half-curtains add French-café charm and coziness, while providing privacy and allowing sunshine to stream in.

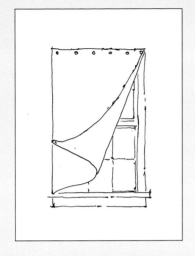

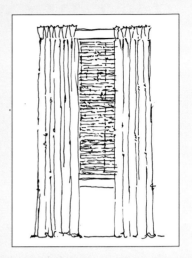

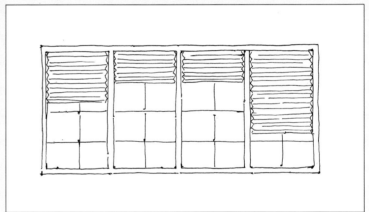

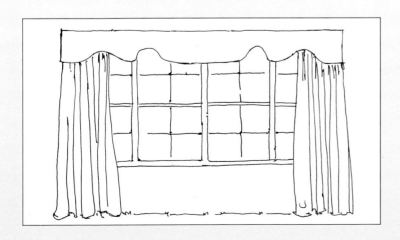

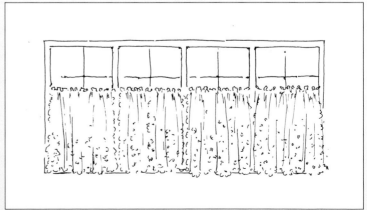

WINDOWS
JUST BROWSING

CORNER WINDOWS

Mirror-image dressings allow you to treat corner windows separately, but achieve the effect of a single design. Be sure that draperies or vertical blinds draw to the outside, and that blinds raise and lower without clashing.

BAY WINDOWS

Like its cousin the corner window, a bay window demands separate but equal treatment. Like its other cousin, the matched series, there are many ways to treat bays, depending on the look you're after. To keep things clean, stick with trim shades or blinds. Or, outline those tailored treatments with fabric—such as a sweeping swag or a scalloped balloon valance—for eye-pleasing softness and color. Want to fabricate a formal look? Install draperies to stretch across the front of the window alcove.

SLIDING DOORS

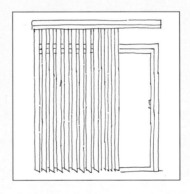

Sliding glass doors present a unique decorating situation. Because they are doors, a covering must allow them to open and close freely. Yet, as windows, they still require a dressing that enhances their appearance and provides privacy and light control. Finally, because glass is a poor insulator, you should also choose a treatment with energy savings in mind. Blinds of all kinds, fabric shades, draperies, and sliding panels are options to consider.

HIGH WINDOWS

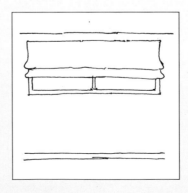
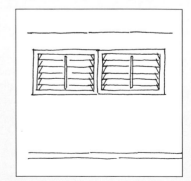

Many bedrooms and most basement rooms present high windows, or a narrow strip of windows. To best dress these panes, think about the other elements in the room. For instance, if you place a piece of furniture under the window, a fitted covering—such as shutters, shades, or blinds—will stay out of the way of the furnishings. If your room is full of horizontal elements (beds, bureaus, chests), add visual interest with a vertical, to-the-floor treatment.

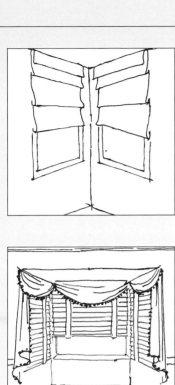

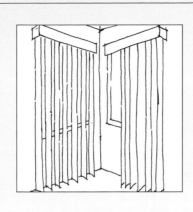

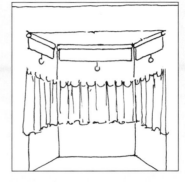
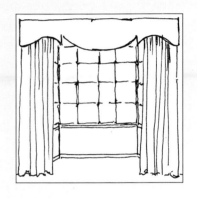

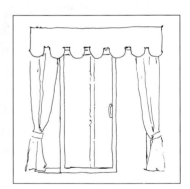

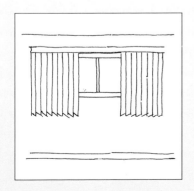

155

WINDOWS
JUST BROWSING

CASEMENT WINDOWS

Standard casement windows swing out, and can be treated similarly to a single window. There is one special consideration in a casement's case, however: The covering you choose should mount on the outside so that it falls over the window's cranking mechanism. For in-swinging casements, you'll need a treatment that doesn't interfere with the window's operation. Inset curtains or blinds on each window section, or mount shades or blinds far enough above the window's molding so that they can be raised to let the windows open freely.

FRENCH DOORS

Although an architectural asset, French doors can be tough to treat. They combine the problems of outfitting in-swinging casement windows with those of covering sliding glass doors. The solutions? For a look that won't interfere with the architecture, mount blinds or shades on each door. If your decor calls for a softer touch, consider shirred lace panels or door-mounted tiebacks. Traditional drapery treatments are options, too. Simply make certain the rod extends well beyond the frame so the draperies can be drawn out of the way of the doors.

 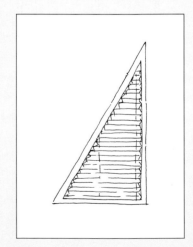

PALLADIAN/ODDLY SHAPED WINDOWS

Shapely windows have long been used to add drama to a home's design, in traditional architecture as well as in the most up-to-the-minute construction. The trick to treating these special panes is to flow with the curve—or bend with the angle—of the opening. Where privacy and light control are needed, custom-fitted shades, blinds, or even shirred fabric will do the job without altering the window's shape. To call more attention to the artful architecture, outline the window with the texture, color, and pattern of fabric.

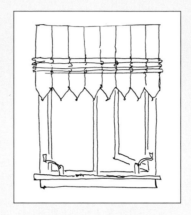 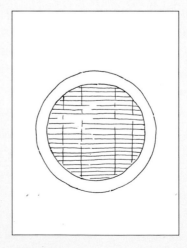

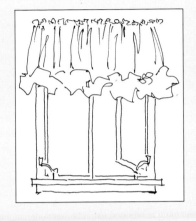

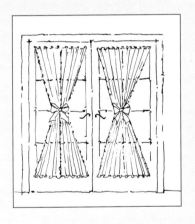

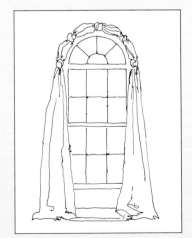

WINDOWS
DRAPERY SHOPPING AND HARDWARE

Draperies can be a major purchase, so arm yourself with as much information as possible before you begin shopping. Whether you plan to buy ready-mades or invest in custom draperies, you'll want to make informed choices about color, fabrics, and hardware. Taking paint and fabric swatches to the store can help with preliminary selections, but make your final decision in the room the draperies will be used in. Your room's light (both natural and artificial) will greatly affect color.

For most windows, you'll want a fabric with good drapability. Wool and silk drape well, as do rayon and acetate. Climate should also play a role in fabric selection. If you're in a cold-weather area, remember that natural fibers tend to prevent heat loss at windows. Synthetic fibers (except nylon) are less resistant to disintegration from sunlight, an important consideration in a warm climate. The "Fabrics" chapter contains more information on drapery materials.

Today's draperies include ready-mades; special-order ready-mades; made-to-measure draperies; workroom customs; and draperies selected through a department store's in-home shopping service.

READY-MADES

Ready-mades offer many advantages to the drapery shopper with limited time or money. A large selection of fabrics, colors, and patterns is available in ready-mades. You can walk into a store and walk out with draperies. The least expensive type of drapery, ready-mades cost about half the price of workroom customs and 40 to 60 percent less than factory-made customs. They only come in standard sizes, however.

FROM THE FACTORY

Factory-made customs also are called special-order ready-mades or made-to-measure draperies. You choose your fabric from store samples, provide the window measurements, and the draperies are made to your size specifications (up to 108 inches in length). Prices vary greatly, with differences often due to the fullness of the drapery and the quality of the workmanship. Factory-made customs are usually ready in four to eight weeks.

CURTAIN RODS

1
2
3
4
5

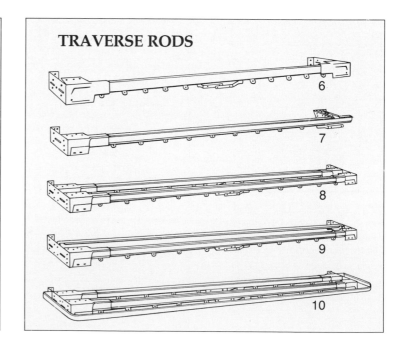

TRAVERSE RODS

6
7
8
9
10

CUSTOM-MADES

Custom draperies made in a retail store or a decorator shop are called workroom customs. They're at the high end of the drapery spectrum but offer an unlimited selection of fabrics, styles, and sizes. These draperies are delivered to your home and, for an extra fee, can also be installed.

Charges for workroom customs depend on the price of the fabric, the labor charge, the price of the hooks, and whether the draperies are lined or not. This type of drapery will cost you about twice what ready-mades of a similar fabric would cost. Workroom customs generally take from four to eight weeks for delivery.

HOME SHOPPING

Some department stores offer the convenience of shopping for draperies in your home. And at the same time, you can get design advice from knowledgeable personnel. Your draperies also will be installed for you, all without leaving home. Costs of these draperies are nearly as high

as workroom customs, with only a slight savings in the labor charge. The waiting time for these draperies is usually six to eight weeks.

THE RIGHT RODS

Finding the right hardware is essential to the success of your window treatment.

Functional rods include *single curtain rods (1), sash rods (2),* and *swivel end sash rods (3).* Often used for shirred curtains or simple cafés, these rods all have adjustable lengths.

Sash and swivel end rods allow you to hang lightweight curtains over windows where the rods must be close to the glass. *Spring tension rods (4),* for example, fit snugly between the two sides of a window casing, making them ideal for shirred curtains hung inside the window frame.

Drapery cranes (5) are the appropriate hardware where installations have to be flexible. On French doors or in-swinging casement windows, this drapery rod, with its hinged bracket, allows the free end to swing out away from the door or window.

Traverse rods come in many types. The *conventional traverse rod (6)* is used with classic pleated draperies that pull from the center to either side. A *one-way-draw traverse (7)* lets you pull your drapery back to one side of the window or the other. Ideal for corner windows, one-way traverse rods are available in a right- or left-hand draw. *Double traverse rods (8)* let you hang two pairs of draw draperies and open and close each drapery independent of the other.

Combinations of traverse and curtain rods, such as the *traverse-and-plain rod (9),* allow you to layer draw draperies over a shirred curtain. For two pairs of draw draperies topped with a valance, choose a *triple rod (10).*

Decorative traverse and café rods transform the hardware of your window treatment into a decorative accent. *Decorative traverse rods (11 and 12)* look just like café curtain rods, but let you attach pleated draperies with hooks inserted into the slides of the rods just as you would into the slide of a conventional traverse rod.

Café curtain rods (13) are used with café rings, and curtains are opened and closed manually.

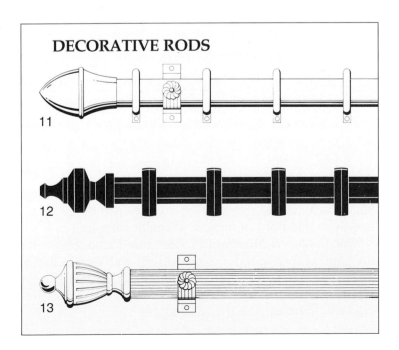

DECORATIVE RODS

11

12

13

WINDOWS
MEASURING AND INSTALLATION

Your draperies and the rods you hang them from are inseparable. You need to know the length of the rod to accurately determine the drapery width, but you also need to know how large an area you want your draperies to cover to accurately determine rod length.

For ready-made draperies, buy the width that best covers the area you want treated, then buy and install an appropriate-length rod, taking into account that drapery panels should overlap 2 inches at the center and cover the "returns" on each end. For custom-made or home-sewn draperies, determine the exact area you want covered, buy and install the rod, then use the rod to establish the measurements of your finished draperies.

MEASURING TIPS

When measuring for draperies and drapery hardware, always use a steel tape. A cloth measuring tape may stretch somewhat, giving you inaccurate measurements. To avoid costly errors, always write down all the measurements as you make them. Measure every window you intend to treat, even though several windows in a room may appear to be the same size. Size is deceptive, and certain windows, particularly those in older homes, can vary slightly.

POSITION THE ROD

Hardware may be mounted in four ways: on the wall, on the casing, inside the casing, and on the ceiling.

Rods to be mounted on or inside the casing are simply sized to fit the casing. To size a rod that will be mounted on the casing, measure the distance from outside edge to outside edge of the casing. For interior mounts, measure the distance inside the window casing.

Rods mounted on the wall or the ceiling can be any length you want; window size doesn't have to determine the size of the treatment. Rods that are longer than the width of the window visually expand the window's size and give the window more importance. You can place a wall-mounted rod at the ceiling line, giving you a floor-to-ceiling drapery effect. If not installed at ceiling height,

wall-mounted rods are usually placed 4 inches above the window glass to mask the heading and hardware when the window is viewed from the outside.

The length of the rod establishes how much of the window will be exposed. If you're not using an extra-wide drapery for a special decorating effect, you will want to calculate just how wide your draperies have to be to pull open and yet reveal the entire glass area of the window. This means allowing extra space at either side of the window for the draperies to "stack" when opened.

To help figure the stackback for each window, divide the window's glass width by three, then add 12 inches. This will give you the total stacking area required for a pair of draperies. To determine the position of your rod, divide the stackback figure in half, measure that distance from either outside edge of the glass, and make a mark. The distance between these marks represents the length rod you will need.

When planning for decorative traverse or café curtain rods, take into consideration that the measurement of the rod doesn't include the finials. If space is tight or you're working on a corner installation, be sure to figure the size of the finial into your window treatment.

MEASURE FOR DRAPERIES

Once the rods are installed, you're ready to measure for custom draperies.

To figure the length for draperies hung by hooks from conventional traverse rods or curtain rods, measure from the top of the rod to the sill (A), the apron (B), or the floor (C). If you are planning to use decorative traverse rods or café rods with rings, measure from the bottom of the rings. For rooms with baseboard heating, remember that the length should not interfere with the heating unit.

The drapery width should be measured according to the diagram at *right*. Start by measuring the length of the installed rod (D). Then, measure the side returns (E). For treatments with an overlap at the center, add 4 inches. Add the figures to get the total width.

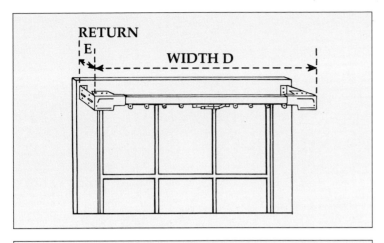

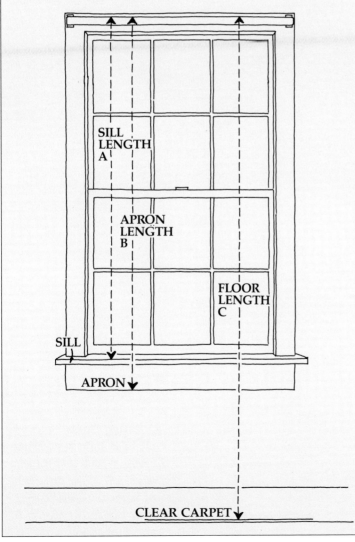

KNOW THE BASICS

Follow these guidelines in measuring standard draperies and other popular window treatments.

Draw draperies: Measure the length of the rod, plus the returns and overlap at the center. Remember that one-way-draw traverse rods have no overlap.

Café curtains: Measure the width of the rods between the finials. To determine the length of each tier, measure from the lower part of the clip or ring on the upper rod to 3 inches below the clip or ring on the lower rod. This is the finished length (including overlap). If you're using decorative café rods and want the bottom rods and rings exposed rather than hidden, measure from the bottom of the ring on the top rod to the top of the lower rod. For the lower tier, measure from the bottom of the ring on the lower rod to the desired finished length.

Window curtains mounted inside the casing: Measure the length from the top of the rod to the sill.

Shirred curtains: Finished length is from 1 inch above the top of the rod to the desired length.

Casement curtains and French doors: Measure the length from the top of the upper rod to the bottom of the lower rod. Measure the rod width inside the brackets.

INSTALLATION

Measuring accurately, installing the right rod, and selecting high-quality draperies all contribute to the beauty of your windows. But all those quality-conscious preliminaries are a waste of time if you do a haphazard job of installation.

The hooks you select play a big part in how a drapery panel hangs. Several types are available, and there is one that's right for each drapery-and-rod combination.

Hook placement determines the placement of the drapery or curtain heading in relationship to the rod. For a conventional traverse rod, the heading should be level with the rod top. With decorative traverse rods, you'll want the rod and rings to show. The top of the heading should come to the bottom of the rings.

WINDOWS
SIMPLE YET STYLISH

▲
Delicate details and layers of lace recall Victorian grace. Raise it to the top, and a striped balloon shade edged in lace becomes a frilly valance. Gauzy cotton curtains and a wispy lace panel make a pretty petticoat. Below, a fringed shade is as dutiful as it is beautiful.

▲
For a slightly different slant on standard tiebacks, this sheer fabric panel is raked to one side only, as if to invite a glimpse of the view beyond. Shirred onto a tension rod, a half curtain screens the sun—and the outside world. The tasseled trim gives visual weight to the fabric.

A slight twist of the thinking cap yields this one-of-a-kind window dressing. Flipped on its side, pleated shade material makes a crisp valance that cleverly contrasts with the horizontal lines of the blinds. Then, ordinary draw draperies get a kick from a petticoat of crinoline—the stiff, open-weave fabric that put the pouf in '50s skirts.

As light and fluffy as a summer cloud, this dreamy organza window outfit adds a touch of romance to a guest room. It's a dream to make, too. Simply knot a hemmed fabric panel at the corners, secure it with a loop of string, and nail it to the molding. Voile-ah!

163

WINDOWS
CREATING WINDOW TREATMENTS

ROLL-UPS

Window treatments you sew yourself are a wonderful way to personalize your home—and save yourself some money. Simply follow the instructions on these two pages to create two popular custom window treatments quickly and easily: fold-back curtains and roll-up shades.

FOLD-BACKS

Fold-back curtains require four panels of fabric, a double curtain rod, and tiebacks. Each panel is cut the length and width of the area of the window. You'll need to decide beforehand whether you want to inset the curtain into the window casing or cover the casing, as shown at *left.* For the most accurate width determination, measure the rod from bracket to bracket. Include ⅝-inch seam allowances on all four edges.

Cut two panels of curtain fabric and two panels of contrasting lining fabric of approximately the same weight. It's important that these four panels be cut exactly the same size. When folded back, the underpanels become an interesting design element. With right sides together, stitch the top and side seams of each panel, leaving an opening at the top of each side (approximately 1 to 1½ inches) so the curtain can be slipped onto the rod.

Turn each panel inside out and press the top and side seams. Press up the seam allowance along the bottom edge of each panel; finish each with a blind-stitch hem.

Hang the finished curtain panels on a double rod, then fold back each to expose the contrasting lining. Secure each panel with a tieback.

ROLL-UPS

For roll-up shades, choose a sturdy fabric, such as chintz or cotton duck. Cut the shade fabric and a contrasting lining to the measurements of the inside of the window frame; add ⅝-inch seam allowances on all four sides. With right sides facing, sew the panels together on three sides, leaving the upper edge open. Trim seams and clip corners diagonally, then turn the finished shade right side out and press.

FOLD-BACKS

The shade attaches to a mounting board of equal width, about ½ inch thick, and 1½ inches deep. Staple the shade's unfinished edge to the ½-inch side of the board. (See the illustration *above.*)

To make the fabric sash, cut a strip of fabric about 3½ inches wide and twice the length of the window. Fold the strip in half lengthwise, bringing right sides together; sew along the bottom and side edge, forming a long tube. Turn right side out, slip-stitch the unfinished edge, and press. Drape the sash over the board, center, and staple in place.

With the stapled end next to the window frame, attach the board with nails or screws. To operate, roll or unroll the shade to the desired position and tie it in place with the sash.

▲

"Campy" but fun describes these muslin fold-backs. Cut to fit the attic roofline, the fold-backs are held together with rings and rope.

165

WINDOWS
CROWNING TOUCHES

▲ *A blooming valance grazes the ceiling to give this window the illusion of height and to add visual punch to sheers.*

Looped around both fabric and rod, floppy floral bows throw a creamy fabric panel some curve—and verve!
▼

◄ *It's no coincidence that the snappy striped valances match the bed linens—the toppers were made from pillowcases. Opened at the side seam, the cases were cut and hemmed to the desired width.*

▲ *A wallpaper border that mimics swagged fabric customizes shutters in a clever and colorful way. The border was applied to wood that was custom-cut to the contoured shape.*

WALLS AND CEILINGS

Walls and ceilings are more than the packaging your furniture and accessories are wrapped in. They are decorative elements in their own right, and account for the largest portion of color, pattern, and texture in a room. Walls can set the mood of your room, can warm it or cool it, can visually expand or contract it. They can showcase your design imagination or reflect your skill as a do-it-yourselfer. And with the wide variety of materials available on the market today, neither your walls nor your ceilings need look like anyone else's.

WALLS AND CEILINGS
BEAUTIFUL BACKGROUNDS

Furnishings may represent the cast of characters in your decorating drama, but walls and ceilings—as the all-important backdrop—set the scene. By virtue of their vastness alone, walls and ceilings call for some thoughtful stage management.

It can be intimidating to pick out paper, paint, or some other covering, knowing what a dominant role the colors and patterns will play in your room scheme. On the other hand, your rooms' backgrounds can also represent a wonderful blank canvas on which you can express your style, personality, or creativity. And you have so many clever and colorful covering options from which to choose. So why not relax and explore the decorating opportunities your walls and ceilings offer you.

ESTABLISHING DOMINANCE

How dominant a role you want the walls and ceilings to play in your home is entirely up to you.

If you prefer a spare setting, brushing your walls with a strong color can fill in empty spaces and warm up a sometimes cold minimalist scheme. Or you may want the walls and ceilings to fade into the background so your furnishings hold onto the spotlight. Neutral colors or subtle prints can soften a setting without stealing the show.

You also can use walls and ceilings to establish a mood. Dress walls in traditional coverings to set a formal tone. Splash on paint in lively, Caribbean-inspired shades and you'll give your rooms an ever-sunny disposition. Want to cozy up a den or library? Rich red tones or mellow golden browns will embrace a space with warmth.

PUTTING WALLS TO WORK

Even more than a mood-maker, though, a wall and ceiling treatment can be a handy decorating tool you wield to accomplish many tasks. In today's open floor plans, for example, rely on a wall treatment to define separately functioning areas within a large space and help the space to appear more cozy than cavernous.

▲
The owner of this city apartment wanted a formal feeling in her living room, but didn't like the heaviness of the original dark paneling and ceiling beams. Her solution? Raise the roof with a coat of creamy enamel, then lighten up the walls with a sophisticated, faux-marble paint finish.

This bedroom's residents ▶ sought the elegance of an English manor, but didn't have the traditional raised wall panels to complete the look. Once again, paint performs its decorative magic. Brushed-on borders and garlands fool the eye into seeing an architecturally embellished room.

WALLS AND CEILINGS

BEAUTIFUL BACKGROUNDS

Walls and ceilings can do much more than simply add color to a room; they can add pattern, texture, and special interest, as well.

Faced with a place that lacks architectural sparkle? Use paint, paper, and a bit of creativity to build character into your backgrounds. Want to call attention to a room's architectural features? The same suggestions apply.

Add a spark of individuality and style to ho-hum walls with a painted or papered border. Give a room definition and dimension with any one of a dozen decorative painting treatments—comb painting, for example, is one of the easiest. (See pages 190 and 191 for instructions.)

When you cast the role you want walls and ceilings to play in your own home, let the rooms in this chapter inspire you.

▲
To beat the high cost of papering her huge dining room in the floral wallpaper she loved, this imaginative home-owner made a stencil of the wallpaper pattern and painted on the blooms.

◄ *The aged-parchment look here is achieved by dappling plaster on the walls until it peaks like meringue. Sand off the peaks and you have a crack-led finish. A stenciled-on border of blocks highlights the rough texture.*

Blushing pink paint and a ▶ decorative graining technique highlight this room's architec-ture. Dare to be bold with color for dramatic results.

WALLS AND CEILINGS
WALL-COVERING BUYMANSHIP

◀ *Reach out and touch these walls and you might expect to experience the soft texture of aged leather. But looks can deceive. In reality, the walls are covered with a block-printed wallpaper.*

▲
Recognize the marbled finish on this wall? The covering used here is actually squares of bookbinding paper that are applied with wallpaper paste. The mirrored far wall doubles the decorative impact.

Apart from the grab bag of colors and patterns available in wall coverings today, you'll also be faced with a vast array of materials, textures, and specialized finishes when you shop. Before you buy, think about how the room is used and the condition of your walls.

There are two types of wall coverings: prepasted and unpasted. Prepasted coverings already have paste on the back. All you need to do is wet the backing to activate the adhesive. These types save you the trouble of deciding which type of paste to buy, and the expense and inconvenience of mixing a sticky concoction. Add to that their low-cost, easy installation and their availability, and it's no wonder prepasteds are so popular.

Under those two headings fall a variety of wall-covering materials. For a covering that's tough enough to stand up to grease, scuffs, and fingerprints, scrubbable vinyl coverings can't be beat. Look for cloth-backed, strippable vinyl coverings if you want a wall covering that will eventually strip clean from a well-prepared wall.

Wallpapers remain another popular covering category. These machine-printed or more costly hand-printed papers come in a wide range of widths, with or without pretrimmed edges. Many of today's papers are treated for stain resistance or have vinyl-coated surfaces. Although not as durable as vinyls, papers offer clearer patterns and richer colors.

The remaining wall-covering types are more specialized in their application, but each offers fine qualities. Grass cloth adds intriguing texture to a room and discreetly hides wall damage. A close cousin, string cloth offers many of the same advantages—and then some. Made from strings applied to paper in vertical rows, string cloth comes in a variety of colors and patterns. A bonus? This textural covering goes on virtually seamless.

The list goes on. Metallic coverings (or foils) offer dramatic good looks, but generally require professional installation. Embossed papers hide a host of wall flaws and have textural appeal. Flocked coverings, cork, wood veneer, and fabric are all available as wall dressings. Be sure to consult a professional paperhanger before you attempt to install an exotic covering.

WALLS AND CEILINGS
WAYS WITH WALLPAPER

Wall coverings can be the right answer to a number of decorating questions. Need to camouflage damaged walls? Looking for a decorative focal point to add interest to a boring room? Want to smooth out rough or irregular architectural features? Wondering how to make a strong decorative statement out of a plain box of a room? Have a dark room that demands a brighter outlook? Wall coverings solve these decorating dilemmas—and more!

From delicate florals to bold geometrics and from tailored stripes to artistic faux-finished looks, the wide variety of wall coverings means that your biggest problem is not so much finding the look you want as it is narrowing your choice to a final selection. While you shop, think about what colors and patterns appeal to you, as well as any decorative goals you want to accomplish. As a starting point, consider what wall coverings did for these rooms.

▲

◀ *Papering walls and ceilings unifies awkward angles in this room. Using a tiny print on a white background visually expands the area.*

Team wallpaper with companion fabrics for custom-finished looks. Here, coordinating fabric, wallpaper, and border tie elements together.
▼

Focal-point wallpaper in a fool-the-eye tile pattern is used to counterbalance appliances and cabinets that weigh down the other end of this room.

Richly hued wallpaper embraces visitors with a cozy feeling. Light touches—a mirror, lamps, and white fixtures—keep the dark walls from closing in.
▼

WALLS AND CEILINGS
APPLYING WALL COVERINGS

Attention to detail makes all the difference in the quality of wallpapering, so take your time with each step.

Most single rolls of wallpaper contain 36 square feet of paper. But allowing for waste and matching pattern, a roll covers only about 30 square feet. To figure how many rolls you'll need:

• **Measure** the distance around the room. Multiply this figure by the height of the wall.

• **Subtract** from this total the square footage of all windows, doors, and other openings.

• **Divide** by 30.

If your wall covering is not a standard 36-square-foot roll, you'll need to adjust your calculations accordingly.

A dealer can help you fine-tune your estimate. It's wise to order an extra roll as a margin of error and for future patches. When your paper arrives, check to see that the rolls are color matched.

PREPARING WALLS

For paper to adhere properly, start by washing your walls to remove grease and soot. Rinse them with clear water.

• **Remove old wall coverings,** if they are vinyl or the new paper is vinyl. If your new covering is paper, nonvinyl

wallpaper can stay, providing it still adheres well with no overlapping edges. Apply sizing before you paper.

• **Prepare walls.** For old gloss or semigloss oil-base paint, roughen with coarse sandpaper. Seal water-base paint with a fast-drying glue sizing.

Wait a month before papering newly painted walls or new plaster. A coat of glue sizing should be applied. Unpainted wallboard needs sealing with an oil-base primer; dry for 24 hours.

• **Repair blemishes** as you would for painting.

• **Paint the woodwork** and moldings and let them dry.

GETTING STARTED

The first step is to plan the match—or more accurately, the mismatch. A mismatch is inevitable, because the last strip you put up will have to be trimmed lengthwise to meet the first strip. To minimize the problem, begin at a spot where the flaw won't be noticed—in a corner, or by a door or window, where you'll have only a few inches of discord.

Now you're ready to hang the first strip—all-important because it "locks in" all the strips that follow. Unless the first one is absolutely vertical, all the other strips will be out of alignment, and the error will compound itself.

▲
A wide wall scraper and a steamer do a fast job of removing old, loose wall coverings. Strippable papers pull right off.

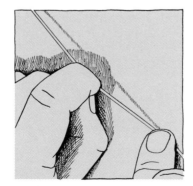

▲
Snap a chalk line for a true vertical where you plan to line up your first strip. If you don't have a plumb line, use a level.

▲
Smooth each strip of wall covering onto the wall by wiping it with a clean sponge or a paperhanger's brush.

▲
Extend the covering ½ inch around the corner. Plumb the next strip (it should overlap the corner strip). Trim both pieces.

To establish a truly vertical (plumb) line, use a plumb bob or level. Measure the width of the wall covering from your starting point. Then, subtract ½ inch and mark your plumb line. The first strip of wall covering goes to the left of this line. If you started by a corner, press the paper into and around the corner. Cut the first two strips so their patterns match. They should be cut several inches longer than the height of the wall.

PREPASTED STRIPS

Today, most wall coverings except heavy vinyl come prepasted. For prepasted paper, reroll strips, patterned side in, starting from the bottom. Then place the roll in a water box so the top of the strip comes out of the box. When you're ready to hang the strip, place the box on the floor below where the strip will be hung. Draw the roll up onto the wall and smooth into position along the plumb line.

Go over the paper with a wall brush or clean sponge to eliminate air pockets. Double-check the position, then use a utility knife and straightedge to trim the excess.

Line up the second strip with the first, butting it up to the edge of the first strip carefully. After 15 minutes, smooth the butted edges with the seam roller. Remove

squeezed-out paste with a sponge and clean water (except on raised-pattern coverings).

PASTING STRIPS

To apply heavy vinyl or any unpasted wall covering without getting paste everywhere, "book" each strip. Use the adhesive recommended by the wall-covering manufacturer. Place the first strip on a pasting table, facedown; spread paste on it from the center to the top edge. Fold the top half of the strip back to the center, pasted surfaces together. Do not crease. Repeat with the bottom half.

While this strip is resting, paste the second strip. If you cut all of the strips for a wall at once, mark one end "up" and number the strips. Hang the first booked strip by opening the top half and lining up the motif at the top. Smooth this to the wall, then unfold and smooth the bottom half.

OPENINGS AND CORNERS

Do doorways and windows as you come to them. Let the strip adjoining the opening overlap the casings. Crease the covering at the molding's vertical edge and cut it with a razor blade or very sharp knife. Then crease and cut at the top of the casing and—for windows—underneath.

To keep corners in kilter, as you near the corner, measure from the edge of your last strip to the corner. Cut a piece ½ inch wider. Hang it, bending the ½-inch margin around the corner. Snap a plumb line on the second wall. Using the new line as a guide, hang the next strip so it overlaps the ½-inch margin and extends ½ inch back around the corner. In the corner, cut through both thicknesses. Peel off the top strip, then lift the edge and peel off the inner layer. Roll the newly exposed seam.

▲
Work out any small wrinkles and bubbles that remain, using a pin to release trapped air, if necessary.

▲
For fixtures you can't remove, cut an X in the wall covering and slip it over the fixture. Cut the power off, then trim.

WALLS AND CEILINGS
CREATING FABRIC TREATMENTS

Fabric-covered walls not only can give a room a luxurious look, they also can quickly and economically cover up a wall in poor condition. Two popular fabric treatments used on walls and ceilings are stapling fabric directly onto walls or shirring fabric panels onto rods. The method you choose will depend on the look you want to achieve, the type of fabric you use, and the condition of your walls. Here's how to fashion your own custom treatments.

STAPLING

Stapling is the simplest and fastest way to attach fabric to a wall. You can staple directly to most wall materials.

Use a heavy-duty stapler and ½-inch staples. The staples will barely show if you use a nubby or textured material. Spray-painting the staples to match the fabric before loading the stapler to help help to hide them.

Plan your fabric yardage in terms of panels around the room. Start by cutting panels the height of the wall from ceiling to baseboard, allowing enough extra length to

match any patterns, plus a few inches for handling ease. After you've calculated the amount of yardage you'll need, cut the panels.

Staple the first panel in place along a true vertical line, established by using a weighted string. Chalk the string and snap it against the wall for a reference, or simply leave the weighted line hanging on the wall while you work.

Pushpins and double-faced tape can secure panels temporarily while you work. To finish the top and bottom edges of each panel, turn under 1 inch on each edge and staple it down, or trim excess fabric after stapling. If staples along the side seams aren't noticeable, simply staple the second panel snugly along the first. If staples are noticeable, back-tack to produce a concealed seam.

To back-tack, when the first panel is stapled in position, place the second panel facedown on the first with the pattern matched at right-hand seams. Staple the seam in place every 6 or 8 inches. Press a panel-length strip of upholsterer's tape along the seam (to help it keep its shape) and staple in place. Open the second panel so the

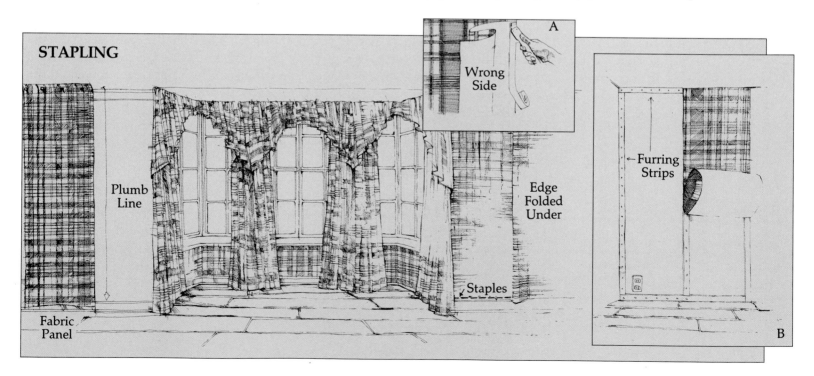

STAPLING

Plumb Line

Fabric Panel

Wrong Side

A

Edge Folded Under

Staples

← Furring Strips

B

Here, printed sheets are ▶ shirred and stapled to a wall. Cording and swags made of plain sheets conceal staples.

pattern faces you, and staple the fabric to the ceiling and baseboard edges.

If your walls are highly textured, are in poor condition, or are too hard for staples to penetrate, attach ¼-inch-thick furring strips to the wall with nails or paneling adhesive, then staple the fabric to the strips.

SHIRRING

Gathering or shirring fabric to cover walls takes two to three times as much material as that needed for a flat application, but it will create the most elegant look. Shirring also will conceal more than stapling: structural faults, fading color, and unwanted texture can disappear beneath the folds of the fabric. Lightweight materials, which have good drapability, work better than most types of heavy fabric for this method.

Depending on the degree of fullness you want to achieve, you'll need between two and three times the amount of fabric required for a flat application. When you cut the fabric panels, allow an extra 6 inches in height to allow for the fabric taken up by the hems, top and bottom. Turn the top hem over 3 inches and press. Turn the raw edge under ½ inch and machine-stitch the hem in place as close to the inner fold as possible. Run another row of stitching approximately 1 inch from first, depending upon the size of the rod you're using for the installation. Repeat this procedure at the bottom of each panel.

Use extendable rods and extension brackets to hang the fabric, or shirr the fabric on cable cords and staple it to the wall. A third option is to use dowels and cup hooks. Let the fabric hang for a day before finishing the bottom hem. Then, insert the rod through the casing and ease the fabric evenly along the rod. Don't worry about side seams; the selvages will disappear in the folds of the fabric.

SHIRRING

1½" Top Heading

1" Rod Casing

½" Folded Under and Stitched Down

A

WALLS AND CEILINGS
OTHER COVERINGS

Wrap a space with wood, glass, brick, or tile and you've not only given a scheme decorating distinction, you've also chosen an easy-care and durable option for covering walls. Before you roll out the wallpaper or pop open a paint can, consider other ways to work wonders on walls.

WOOD LOOKS GOOD

Want to give your room natural warmth or nostalgic appeal? Wood is the answer. Although there are endless types of wood coverings, you have two basic installation options: put it up in sheets or pound it on plank by plank.

Usually sold in 4x8-foot sheets, manufactured paneling is less expensive and easier to install than single slats of solid wood. What's more, today's manufactured sheet goods come in a virtual forest of styles and finishes.

Hardwood plywood paneling consists of wood layers joined by an adhesive and topped with a face veneer. Offered in many woods, colors, and patterns, plywood paneling dominates the market. You'll choose from a long list of wood veneers—from whitewashed pine to rich cherry—or choose a painted finish. You'll also choose from a rustic and a polished surface, random and uniform planks, a full wall of paneling and a wainscot effect.

Hardboard panels are rigid sheets pressed out of heat-bonded wood fibers. Less expensive than plywood, hardboards get their finish from a photoengraving process that simulates all types of wood-grain and painted looks, as well as brick, wood, marble, and tile surfaces. This paneling boasts cleanability and moisture resistance.

Although manufactured sheet materials are the easiest and most popular way to panel a wall, they aren't the only way. Boards or strips of solid wood offer versatility and unbeatable beauty. Thicker than plywood or pressed fiber panels, solid wood is a natural insulator. Let your imagination be your guide when deciding what kind of "board-room" you want. You can nail on wood planks vertically, or give your room a twist with a horizontal or diagonal pattern. Choose from rustic, unfinished wood types, or treat elegant woods with a clear sealer. Don't forget recycled woods—reborn oak flooring or barn boards.

MIRROR, MIRROR ON THE WALL

Loved for its fool-the-eye effect, mirror is a decorative magician that has been called on to perform in many a home. Mirrored walls brighten and visually enlarge small areas, plus add dimension to dull, boxy spaces. This covering is durable and easy to keep clean—unless you install the glass in a close-traffic area that attracts daily smudges.

Order plate mirrors cut to size and install them with mirror adhesive and special steel clips found at glass outlets. Or try mirror tiles, 1- or 2-foot squares of reflective glass that go up like ceramic tile.

EARTHBOUND BEAUTY

Brick and ceramic tile are wall-covering options with a lot in common: both begin life as an earthy material, clay; both are hardened with heat into durable, low-maintenance, fire-resistant building materials; and both offer the charm and warmth that only earth-born objects can give.

If you live in an older home, you may be lucky enough to have a treasure trove of well-aged brick hiding behind cracking plaster walls. If not, there's an easy route to the beauty of brick: brick veneer. Brick and stone veneers look like the real thing because they *are* the real thing—cut into thin slices. Choose from many colors and textures, and apply them like ceramic tile.

Tiles are as varied as pebbles on the beach. From hand-painted beauties to natural terra-cotta looks, tiles come in all types of textures, patterns, colors, shapes, and sizes. Although prices range from moderate to expensive, ceramic tile guarantees a good-looking, long-lasting return on your investment.

Cloaked in mirrored glass, a ▶ partition wall lends function times two. The partial wall conceals a dressing area; reflective covering adds depth to the small bedroom.

With its nubby textures and earthy colors, brick is a natural beauty. Like prospectors discovering a vein of gold, these homeowners delighted at uncovering brick walls during a renovation. Polished wood counters and smooth, laminate cabinets offer intriguing textural contrast.

Knotty pine gets a fresh face with a whitewashing technique. The paneling was stripped, then brushed with thinned-down white paint that was quickly wiped off to allow the wood grain to shine through.

WALLS AND CEILINGS
THE POWER OF PAINT

Paint is not only one of the least expensive decorating materials available, it's also the most versatile and dramatic tool in your decorating kit. Never underestimate the power of paint to perk up a dull room, bring an aging room up to date, add architectural impact, or even visually alter a room's dimensions.

Paint's list of fine qualities doesn't end there. This decorative element goes on in a hurry and without requiring a skilled applicator. So why not experiment with bold color or a fancy, decorative finish? If you don't like the end result, you can simply erase your error with a new coat.

▲
Rich taupe paint warms up this long, narrow dining hall. The deep color helps battle the glare from south-facing windows.

Here, painted moldings frame ▶ a room with interest. Pink paint weaves colors found in the furnishings around the room.

▲
Courageous colors brand this room with a new breed of frontier spirit. White walls give the eye a rest and visually separate the vibrant hues.

Bright white and pewter ▶ gray make a striking couple in this foyer. Use contrasting paint on trim and walls to point out architectural pluses.

WALLS AND CEILINGS
PERFECT PAINT JOBS

Even novice painters can get professional-looking results with the right materials, good wall preparation, and the right techniques.

Ask your dealer to help you select the right type of paint, primer, brushes, and rollers for your job, because different paints and surfaces require different products. For example, a natural-bristle brush is best for use with alkyds, but a latex paint requires a synthetic brush.

To calculate the amount of paint you'll need:
- **Measure** the perimeter of the room and multiply the result by the ceiling height to get the number of square feet. Round off wall measurements to the next full foot. (Don't deduct for windows or other openings unless they total more than 100 square feet.)
- **Divide** the result into the number of square feet a gallon of paint promises to cover (check the label). Round off to the next gallon to get the number of gallons you'll need for the room. Double that number if you plan two coats.

A dealer also can help you estimate the amount of paint you'll need. As a rule of thumb, one gallon of latex or alkyd paint covers about 400 square feet.

Even the best paint job can't hide blemishes such as cracks or chips in the underlying surface. Before you open a can of paint, take time to prepare your walls and ceilings:
- **Scrape or sand away** rough spots in the old paint and woodwork.
- **Mend blemishes** with spackling or joint compound, let dry, and sand smooth. Repair cracks and patch plaster.
- **Strip off wallpaper.** If you must paint over it, test a small area, and wait for a few days to see if the pattern bleeds through or the paper peels.
- **Dull glossy surfaces** with sandpaper or a liquid (chemical) sandpaper.
- **Wash or dust** the surface to be painted carefully and allow it to dry.
- **Prime bare spots** or places you've repaired with an appropriate primer. Treat stained spots with a special primer that prevents bleed-through.

STEP-BY-STEP PAINTING GUIDE

◀ *After walls are prepared, assemble painting supplies: brushes, rollers or paint pads, masking tape, a sloping paint tray, drop cloths, and an extra roller "sleeve" for each color or type of paint you use.*

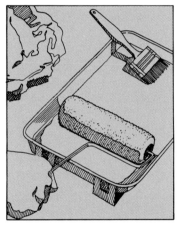

◀ *Load the roller by rolling it into the lower end of the tray, then smoothing it on the sloping surface until the paint is distributed evenly. Fill the roller with as much paint as it will take without dripping. (Roller covers have naps of ¼ to ½ inch. Use long naps for rough surfaces; short, for smooth.)*

◀ *Paint the ceiling first, using a roller attached to an extension rod. Or, erect a scaffold. Paint in 2- or 3-foot strips across the shorter dimension of the ceiling. Use a small brush or trim roller for corners.*

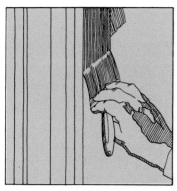

◀ Paint a narrow strip at the ceiling line, around openings, and along the baseboard using a brush, edging roller, or paint pad. For flat paint, do all the edging around a room before painting the walls. With glossy or semi-gloss paint, do one edge at a time and fill in immediately.

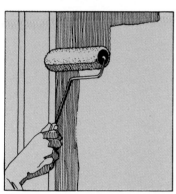

◀ Switch to a roller or paint pad for the rest of the walls. If you used a brush for edging, run the roller close to the trim, over the brushwork, because a roller leaves a different texture than a brush. Paint the open area first, so the roller is drier when you get near the trim.

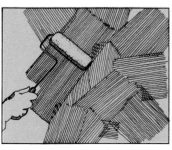

◀ To paint large surfaces, roll a big M on the wall and fill in. Strokes should not be parallel, up and down, or across; roll on paint every which way. If you're using gloss paint, finish up with vertical strokes.

◀ Take your time painting woodwork and features such as raised door panels. If you are using the same paint for walls and woodwork, paint woodwork as you come to it. If it will be another color or a higher gloss, do it after painting the walls.

◀ Paint a door in this sequence: door frame first, then the top, back, and front edges. If the door is paneled, paint the panels and molding, then the rest of the door, starting at the top. If you can't remove hardware, paint around it with a trim brush, then fill in with a roller or brush.

◀ For windows, paint the lower part of the upper sash first. Then raise the upper sash to finish painting it. Do the lower sash, then the recessed part of the window frame, the frame, and the sill.

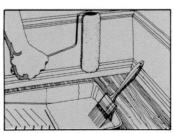

◀ Paint the baseboard last. Do the top molding and base shoe, then fill in the space between the two. Protect flooring or carpet with masking tape or with a cardboard or plastic guard.

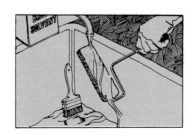

◀ To clean up, remove masking tape; wipe or chip off with a razor blade scraper any paint you may have missed. Clean brushes, pads, and rollers according to directions on the paint can label.

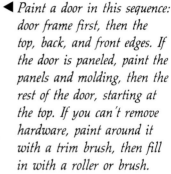
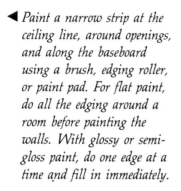

WALLS AND CEILINGS
SPECIAL TECHNIQUES

Not only does paint provide coats of many colors to dress your walls, it offers coats of many kinds as well. The special effects you can create with an applicator and a can of paint are limited only by your imagination. More common decorative paint techniques, such as sponging, combing, and spattering, are easy ways to spark a space with color, pattern, and texture. Or try your hand at fancier finishes—marbleizing, rag rolling, and trompe l'oeil, for instance—to give your backgrounds personality.

You don't necessarily need the brush strokes of van Gogh to dabble in many of these decorative paint techniques. (Turn the page for how-to instructions.) For finishes that require more skill, contact a local art center, gallery, or school. It may be easier and more affordable than you think to find an expert in your community that will help you transform your ordinary walls into masterpieces of one-of-a-kind style.

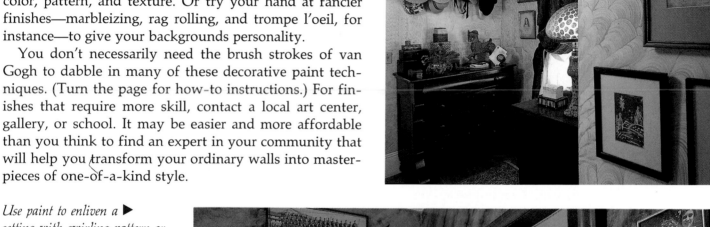

Use paint to enliven a ▶ setting with swirling pattern or intriguing texture. The fancy finishes shown on this page mimic the creative designs found in nature: malachite (top right) and tortoiseshell (bottom right).

◀ *Paint fools the eye into believing this room's old plaster trim is elaborately carved, knotty pine moldings. The technique is called "faux bois" (literally make-believe wood), and is one of the many tricks paint can do.*

WALLS AND CEILINGS
SPECIAL TECHNIQUES

SPONGING

 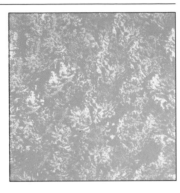

COMBING

 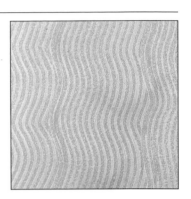

Sponging allows you to produce a fanciful wall finish with basic painting skills. Created by dabbing paint onto a surface with a sponge, this easy technique can be used throughout a room, on an accent wall, or as a crowning touch for trim and woodwork.

Sponging can create many different effects. A wall with close, overlapping sponge marks adds subtle richness to a room. Widely spaced sponging with little or no overlap will produce a heavily textured, casual appearance. Natural sea sponges with large pores are best for a finish with coarse texture.

Sponging is done on top of a dry, painted surface; you can use latex or oil-base semigloss paint for the sponge coat. To begin, dampen the sponge to soften it. Place about a cup of paint in a paint tray and dab the sponge into the paint, but don't overload it.

Practice your technique on a newspaper. Blot excess paint from the edge of the sponge and dab sponge prints on the paper. Space the patches of color randomly yet evenly. Change the position of the sponge often for an irregular, mottled effect.

Begin at the top of the wall and sponge quickly until the paint fades from the sponge. Reload the sponge and repeat. (Keep newspaper handy to check the effect each time you reload.) Replenish the paint tray as needed.

Combing, as the name suggests, is achieved by raking a toothed instrument through a wet topcoat of latex or oil-base paint or pretinted decorator's glaze. Combs for this purpose are available in most well-stocked paint or hardware stores. You also can make a comb by notching the edge of a stiff piece of plastic, such as a dustpan.

Prepare the walls by applying a base coat. Although any type of paint can be used for the base, semigloss or high-gloss paint is preferred because it creates a slicker surface for combing.

When the base coat is dry, apply glaze or a contrasting color of paint over it. Keep in mind that glaze will darken the color of the undercoat.

You must comb the surface while the paint or glaze is still wet. It's best to have two people on the job—one to brush on the coating and the other to comb it. Comb over the wall with long, smooth strokes; wipe the paint off the comb after each stroke. Try to continue these strokes until you reach a corner, which is a natural breaking point. Comb the wall twice, beginning the second layer centered between adjacent comb strokes.

Don't worry if you can't keep the pressure or design precisely consistent. Irregularities help create an appealing textural finish.

RAG ROLLING

STENCILING

Rag rolling is a fairly precise technique carried out on a wall of pretinted decorator's glaze. Rag twists are rolled through the glaze to produce the effect of moiré or watered silk. You also can rag roll on semigloss or gloss paint; for best results, stick with neutral or pastel shades. You must complete a whole wall or room at a time, using the same batch of glaze or paint. So, it's best to work in pairs: One person applies the coating; the other follows with rag rolling.

Prepare the walls and a wide practice board with a coat of semigloss oil-base paint. Lightly mark vertical plumb lines in several places on the wall.

Before you begin, practice on the board. Twist a piece of fabric into a tight 6-inch-wide sausagelike roll; the weave of the fabric will determine the texture of the finish. Paint or glaze the board. Hold the rag twist at each end. Working from the bottom up, roll the rag through the glaze. The fabric will pick up excess glaze or paint and create a pattern.

After practicing, prepare enough rolls to do the entire wall or room; you'll need to change twists when they become saturated. Brush a 1-yard-wide glaze strip evenly onto the wall. Roll through the glaze along the plumb line. Roll the next row parallel to the first, using a slight overlap and merging edges. Continue until you've covered the entire area.

Stenciling adds hand-painted detail to a room. Used as a border on walls and ceilings, stenciling highlights a room's contours. Stencil motifs also can be applied overall to mimic wall covering. Most craft and decorating centers carry precut stencils. Or, cut your own design from commercial stencil sheets.

Plan the placement of your stencil design carefully. Measure the stencil motif and the area on which you will apply it. Divide the length of the area by the stencil size to figure the number of times the design can be repeated. Plan for even spacing, and a neat arrangement at corners. Lightly mark where the stencil will appear, using a level to keep the design straight.

The secret to successful stenciling is to use a nearly dry brush; a short-bristled stenciling brush will make the job easier. Put a small amount of paint on a palette. Dip the tip of the brush into the paint and remove the excess by twisting the brush bristles onto a paper towel. When you apply the paint, it should be almost powdery.

Anchor the stencil to the wall with masking tape. Holding the brush perpendicular to the stencil, use a firm up-and-down motion to apply the paint. Do not stroke or drag the paint across the stencil. For the best results, work from the edges of the stencil toward the center.

191

WALLS AND CEILINGS
EYE-APPEALING CEILINGS

The ceiling stars in this ▶ bedroom production. Neon lights are installed like ceiling fixtures in the second-floor room.

Given the right treatment, a ceiling can be your room's crowning jewel. Just as you would the floor underfoot or the walls that surround you, think about how you want the ceiling to fit into the decorating scheme of things.

If your ceiling is low, a coat of white or light paint will make it a less imposing element. Pale shades also keep the ceiling subtle, so that it doesn't battle for the attention that more interesting elements deserve. Try stronger hues on a high ceiling to make the space feel more intimate.

Wall coverings can give your ceiling character that the builder may have left out. Almost any wall covering will do; simply smooth out the ceiling's surface before you apply it. Check a local building supply store for other application options. Easy-to-install beams, plaster moldings, or ceiling tiles are other decorative details available.

The ceiling stars in this ▶ bedroom production. Neon lights are installed like ceiling fixtures in the second-floor room.

◀ *Elements borrowed from the great outdoors give this sun-room natural warmth. Beams are coated the color of an ivy-draped trellis, and sky-blue ceiling insets are tinged with cloud-white wisps of paint.*

▲
Like a custom-wrapped gift, this boxy room gets something-special status with cleverly applied wrapping. Applied from floor to ceiling, coordinating wall coverings and borders give the space architectural appeal.

WALLS AND CEILINGS
FAUX ARCHITECTURE

Create architectural details with paint. This brushed-on design echoes original moldings in a colorful way.
▼

Architectural detailing does a lot for a space. Besides defining interior areas, architecture builds strong and dramatic character into a home's design. Is your house short on architectural assets? Simply deposit a little creativity.

Before remodeling your spaces, decide what you want to accomplish. Do you want to increase visual interest? Replicate the mood of a bygone era? Make a dramatic statement? Keep in mind that you don't have to limit yourself to typical materials, such as wood trim or reproduction moldings. Out-of-the-ordinary ideas—ribbon, fabric, or paint, for example—create similar effects with a smaller investment in time and money.

These ideas may inspire you: Painted- or papered-on murals offer an endless variety of outlooks, from primitive to panoramic. To put a room in an Early American mood, add a plate rail a foot below the ceiling, or a chair rail 30 inches from the floor. Use ready-made moldings or wood, or even paint and wall coverings to do the trick. For a garden-fresh feeling, install white-painted lattice as a wall covering or room divider.

◀ *Rectangular frames fashioned from strip molding work like a mantel to give a marble hearth more height and prominence. Given its dynamic dimensions, the artwork over the sofa also works as architecture.*

They look as if they've been ▶ carved from stone, but the columns that appoint this raised dining area are really plastic tubing pipes from a plumbing supplier. Paint supplies the grainy marble finish.

WALLS AND CEILINGS
CLEVER EFFECTS

When deciding how to decorate, people today follow their hearts rather than chase after fleeting design trends. That means homeowners everywhere are getting more personal with their decorating schemes—and having fun doing it!

Like a blank canvas, your home's backgrounds invite personal expression. Just as you needn't limit yourself to standard building materials to create a bit of architectural oomph—you can dare to be different with paint as well.

Trompe l'oeil (French for "fool the eye") is a witty paint technique that also packs a decorative punch. You can use it to add architectural dimension that isn't really there— even add decorative accessories that aren't really there—or to make walls and ceilings disappear into a painted-on landscape. Why not grab a paintbrush and try your hand at your own custom wall design? Start small, by sponging white clouds on a sky-blue ceiling, for example, and build your confidence. And, remember, if you don't like it, all you have to do is brush over your mistake.

▲
This painted tree is fun and functional. It draws the eye to the back of the room, and away from the space's tunnellike dimensions.

◀ *Electronic entertainment hides behind this "bookshelf." The trompe l'oeil design lends color, whimsy, and library coziness to the room.*

When she couldn't afford the ▶ wall covering she wanted, this clever homeowner made a stencil of the pattern and painted it on. She brought unadorned cabinets to life with painted-on pulls and shelves of collectibles.

197

FLOORS

In more ways than the obvious one, the floor is the foundation of every room. It is the "fifth wall," so to speak, a large surface that demands both practical and decorative consideration. The floor covering you select will have a major influence on the way a room looks and functions, so be sure to explore the options—carpet and rugs, resilient vinyls, ceramic and vinyl tiles, wood, and numerous other materials—before making a choice. You'll find flooring to fit every budget and style preference, with a wide selection of colors and patterns. This chapter is filled with plenty of ideas—and lots of information—to help put your floors in focus.

FLOORS
SURFACE MATTERS

Selecting the right kind of floor covering to beautifully underscore your rooms means more than picking a pretty pattern or luscious color. How a floor covering functions is equally important. Will it stand up in a high-traffic area? Are easy-care and stain-resistant features important? Do you want sleek hard-surface flooring or the plush comfort of carpet?

Today's wide-ranging floor covering options make it easy to match decorative appeal with durability. Here are some popular choices you'll want to consider:

● Installed wall-to-wall carpet can add a splash of color, texture, and pattern to any space. It warms up a cold room, deadens sound, and provides a quick fix-up for a less-than-attractive floor.

● Room-size or area rugs share some of the same carpet advantages, but they are portable and can be shifted around to distribute wear evenly. Rugs may require a finished resilient or hard-surface floor surrounding them, depending on their size.

● In sheet goods or tile, resilient floor coverings offer easy maintenance and a range of colors, patterns, and textures. Location may influence your choice, and you may save money with do-it-yourself installation.

● Wood floors are natural beauties. Vary the look with bleaching, staining, painting, or decorative techniques, such as stenciling or spatter painting.

● Ceramic tile, quarry tile, brick, and other hard-surface materials lend a natural look and rugged texture.

By profiling your home's traffic and use zones, you can make wiser floor covering selections. For example, high-use areas demand top-quality resilient coverings, hard-surface materials, or heavy-duty carpet, but low-use areas welcome delicate colors and plush surfaces. Heavy traffic and use areas include entryways, hallways, stairways, kitchens, family rooms, and baths. Entryway floor coverings must make a good first impression, be easy to clean, and be resistant to water and abrasives, such as sand. Stairways should be carpeted for safety reasons. In the kitchen, hard-surface or resilient floor coverings are practically impervious to traffic and spills. Active family rooms welcome rugged carpet and spillproof resilients.

Consider easy-clean vinyls or ceramic tile in the bath. Formal dining and living areas see light to moderate use, but dining room floor coverings need to survive occasional spills. A formal living room is a good spot for plush carpet, hardwood, or area rugs. Bedrooms see the lightest traffic, so aesthetics can outweigh durability in the floor covering.

Floor coverings can be hardworking design elements, so it's important to decide their role in your overall decorating scheme. Consider these strategies:

● To make a small room appear larger, avoid pattern and use a solid color, preferably a light tone. Try a solid or slightly textured resilient covering, flat-pile carpet, or bleached or painted wood.

● Add pattern to a room with any type of floor covering or let a patterned area rug accent a neutral setting.

● To unify space within a room, try one great sweep of floor covering, and avoid area and room-size rugs that tend to chop up space visually.

● Warm up a large room with area rugs that define activity centers, such as dining and conversation spots.

● Make your floor a focal point with an interesting treatment or material, such as an exquisite Oriental or other area rug with a spectacular design.

In shopping for floor coverings, buy the best quality you can afford and choose a reputable dealer who offers a wide selection and is well-versed in the advantages and disadvantages of specific materials. Measure your room accurately and factor in installation, plus cushioning for carpet, to set a general cost figure. Bring floor covering samples home, so you can view them in natural light and with the room's other design elements, such as drapery and upholstery fabrics.

Durable, natural-fiber coir ▶ floor covering adds texture and the mellow color of wood to this living room. For contrast, an area rug defines and warms the conversation area.

FLOORS
CARPET

From sumptuous pastel plushes to rugged tweeds, carpet is a universally popular floor covering. Wall-to-wall carpet has long been synonymous with comfort and luxury, but in today's eclectic room schemes, it's just one of numerous soft options for a high-fashion floor.

Whether you choose a room-size loose-laid rug, area rug, or wall-to-wall carpet permanently installed over a cushion, this soft floor covering offers many practical advantages. Its sweep of color and underfoot comfort gives any room—even sparely set ones—a more "furnished" feeling. Carpet colors can work magic, too. For example, a light hue visually expands a small space, and a dark one cozies up a large room. Carpet in a sunny color can visually warm a room short on natural light. Cool colors will temper an overly bright space. Before you buy, study carpet samples at home, and remember that the color of a room-size carpet will be more intense than the samples.

Materials and construction give carpet inherent virtues that may suit your decorating needs.

• Carpet absorbs sound, an appealing feature for condominiums, town houses, and homes with high ceilings.

• Its yarn construction and surface texture add soft contrast to a room's angular architecture.

• Carpet provides psychological and real warmth to a room, and helps eliminate cold radiating from a chilly hard-surface floor, all energy-conscious advantages.

• As versatile camouflage, carpet goes over any existing floor, with no need for a new subfloor, and it hides uneven surfaces and existing floor damage.

• Technology has enhanced carpet's low-maintenance appeal. Today, carpet is available with soil-, stain-, odor-, and static-resistant features, and manufacturing techniques have increased its durability and cleanability.

Wrapped in buttery yellows, ▶
a traditional living room works
color magic at floor level. The
carpet's pale hue and diagonal
pattern team up to make this
small space appear larger.

FLOORS
CARPET

Whether you're rolling out new carpet in a single room, or giving every floor the magic carpet treatment, learn the basics about fibers and construction before you buy. Carpet is a major decorating expense, so you'll want to make your carpet decisions well-informed ones for the best return on your investment.

First, consider carpet construction. A carpet made of good fiber, but of poor-quality construction, can soon prove to be a costly mistake. Most carpets are produced by one of four basic construction methods:

- **Tufted carpets** are made on tufting machines, similar to sewing machines. Yarn is punched through a preformed backing material. A coating of latex adhesive locks yarns in place, and a second backing, or cushion of high-density foam rubber, sponge, or vinyl, is added. Many domestically made carpets come from tufting machines, and can vary widely in quality and style.
- **Woven carpets** are made on power-driven, high-speed looms, operating on the same weaving principle but producing different surface finishes. Famous carpets have taken their names from loom types, such as velvet, Wilton, or Axminster. Pile, weft, and warp yarns are interlocked into a solid fabric.
- **Needle-punched carpets** are made by using hundreds of barbed needles to interlock a mat of fibers on a woven fabric core. These sturdy carpets resist damage by water, insects, mold, and sun, making them good candidates for indoor/outdoor use and for high-use areas such as baths and kitchens.
- **Hand-knotted and hand-tufted carpets,** such as Oriental rugs, generally hail from the Middle East, where makers follow centuries-old traditions and patterns. These inherently expensive, handmade carpets are highly durable and often unique works of art.

From chemist's laboratory to your living room, that's the route many of today's carpet fibers take. The result is a wide array of carpet options and special features, from richer colors to stain resistance. The rule is to match good fibers with good construction for longer wear and better value. Each natural and man-made carpet fiber has specific advantages. For example, nylon holds color well and stands up to heavy cleaning. Wool is warm and durable, but not the best medium for bright colors.

Density is a reliable key to carpet quality. To determine density, give carpet the "grin test" by rolling back a corner to see how much of the backing shows through the pile. The more backing you see, the less dense the carpet and the less fiber you have to walk on, making the carpet less durable. Two factors that affect density are denier, which refers to fiber size and weight, and ply, the number of strands twisted together to form a single strand of yarn. For example, three-ply carpet has three yarns twisted together in each tuft. Generally, higher denier and ply figures indicate higher quality carpet.

Carpet texture, or surface finish, is also an important consideration. In general, the tighter the yarn twist, the longer the carpet's beauty will last. Look for tight, even ends and ask if yarns have been heat-set to lock in the twist. Here are some common textures:

- **Plush carpet** has a luxurious look, features velvety even-cut pile, and shows footprint shading easily.
- **Saxony carpet** has soft, dense cut pile with well-defined individual tuft tips. It is the most widely used type of residential carpet. Many dealers call their smoother finished saxonies "plushes."
- **One-level looped carpet** has tufted, uncut loops on the same level, a pebbly look, and good durability.
- **Two-level looped carpet** is formed of a high-and low-looped pile, left uncut.
- **Cut-and-looped carpet** is similar to the two-level looped style, except that the lower level of loops remains uncut and the top level is sheared. This produces a sculptured effect, as though a pattern has been carved into the carpet.
- **Embossed carpet** is of the multilevel-loop variety and has a lush, sculptured look.
- **Random-shear carpet** combines single-level loops and sheared yarns.
- **Frieze or twisted-pile carpet** has a plush look, but yarns are uncut. Tight twists are locked in by a heat-set process.

Saxony ▼

An underfoot favorite, saxony is noted for its elegance and array of solid hues. This versatile, tufted carpet features yarn loops, clipped for a soft, dense pile. New-generation saxonies resist stains and are less susceptible to traffic wear.

Cut and Loop ▶

Subtly multicolored and less formal, cut-and-loop carpet achieves its sculptured-pattern effect with varied-level pile of uncut low loops and sheared top loops. This shift in texture and the variegated color help disguise soil and traffic wear.

◀ Berber Carpet

Usually made of tweedy, heathered yarns, berber carpets have a distinctive, large multilevel-loop construction with no uncut pile to crush or mat. Berbers are popular in contemporary interiors, and they wear well.

▲ Textured Carpet

Made with tight-twist construction and two-toned yarn that produces a salt-and-pepper finish, textured carpet has a casual look, but resists soil, traffic laning, and footprints. It's a durable choice for kitchens and other active-use rooms.

FLOORS
CARPET

Beneath every beautiful, long-wearing carpet and area rug, there's a good cushion. Not only is this foundation padding important to a carpet's longevity, it also provides underfoot comfort, helps absorb noise, and prevents slippage of small rugs.

For walking support and comfort, a cushion for wall-to-wall carpet and large area rugs should be about ⅜ inch thick. It should be resilient and soft, but of high enough density to give firm support for the carpet's backing, so the carpet won't stretch and wear out as quickly. A thin, resilient cushion is better for small area rugs, and a common rule of thumb is that the rug should be no more than ⅛ inch to ¼ inch from the floor. To lie flat over a rough-surface floor, such as brick, increase the cushion thickness. Even if an area rug will be placed atop broadloom carpet, it still needs a cushion, such as stiff-finished cotton or linen, or sturdy felt, to keep it from shifting and rippling.

Selecting the right cushion type depends on the quality of the carpet, its location in the home, and how much wear it will get. Most cushions are priced according to weight per square yard, and may not be included in the carpet's purchase price. For most rooms, 40-ounce padding is adequate, but a 48-ounce cushion may be wiser for stairs and heavy-traffic areas. Padding is available in several types and prices, and it's always a good idea to purchase the appropriate padding along with the carpet to ensure proper fit. Here are some common cushion types:

- Urethane foam padding, made in a continuous, flat sheet, has excellent durability and strength. It's the most popular padding for residential use because it offers comfort and support. It resists moisture, but may lose its bounce and wear thin over time.
- Sponge or foam rubber padding comes in sheets with waffled or flat surfaces, and the top surface usually is bonded to a facing material to facilitate even carpet wear. Use the flat padding under area rugs to reduce slippage. These cushions tend to wear out more quickly if exposed to floor polishes and cleaners.

Foam rubber padding is nonallergenic and mildew resistant. Sponge rubber padding is not recommended for outdoor use.

- Felted padding, made of animal hair, jute, or a felt-and-fiber mixture, wears well and provides firm support, but tends to shed. For the most part, felted padding has been replaced by more cushiony synthetics and foam rubbers for residential use. It mildews in high-humidity areas and may aggravate allergies.
- Self-cushioned carpet has a layer of latex cushion bonded to the underside. It is usually thinner and less dense than a separate cushion, and may be less resilient. This carpet can be installed directly over concrete or other subfloors, however.

When shopping for carpet, check one of your best and most important information sources, the label and the warranty, on the carpet back. Such labeling is required by law. The label should list manufacturer's name, location, and fibers used in the carpet. With carpet technology ever changing, it's wise to buy from a reputable manufacturer and dealer. If the carpet is a blend, the label will list fiber percentages with the majority fiber first. For example, a carpet that is 80 percent wool and 20 percent acrylic will look, feel, and perform like wool, with acrylic added for cleanability. The label may also list the pattern name, number, and color, and special features such as mothproofing or antistain treatments.

Read the carpet's warranty to learn what to expect from your carpet, and ask the dealer to explain the warranty's specifics. Warranties differ in scope and length, but commonly cover: fiber wear; manufacturer's defects; carpet performance, which protects against crushing, unraveling, and twist loss; and special features, such as antistain treatments. A strong warranty is a good indication that the manufacturer has confidence in the product. Beware of warranties that are watered down by disclaimers and limitations. For example, a warranty may not cover certain types of installation or certain locations, such as stairs. Most performance warranties require "proper maintenance," so know what you need to do to keep the warranty in effect.

CARPET/RUG CONSTRUCTION FACTS

	CHARACTERISTICS	ADVANTAGES	DISADVANTAGES	CLEANABILITY
WOOL	Deep, warm, rich look. Excellent resiliency, abrasion resistance. Warm, natural feel.	Excellent durability; flame resistant; crush resistant.	Can be damaged by alkaline detergents; needs mothproofing. Not best medium for bright colors.	Greatly resists soil. Not cleaned as easily as many synthetic fibers.
ACRYLIC	Closest to wool of man-made fibers. Non-allergenic, resists mildew, moths, insects. Wide choice of colors.	Crush resistant; springy; resists fading. Generates minimal static.	May form pills, or beadlike balls of fiber on face of the carpet.	Cleans very well. Smooth fibers resist soiling.
MOD-ACRYLIC	Modified acrylic; blended with acrylics in carpet; used alone in bath, scatter rugs.	Abrasion, mildew, moth resistant; non-allergenic. Enhances flame resistance of acrylics. Easily dyed.	May form pills.	In blends, easy to clean and maintain. Some rugs washable.
NYLON	Wide choice of colors; excellent color retention. Soft and resilient.	Strongest synthetic fiber; resists abrasion, mildew, moths. Non-allergenic. Continuous filament fibers minimize pilling, shedding.	Static-prone, unless treated. Cut-filament loop carpet may pill.	Good cleanability, enhanced by new anti-stain treatments.
POLYESTER	Similar to wool in look, touch. Good color and texture selection, color retention. Resists moths, mildew; non-allergenic.	Very durable, resilient; abrasion resistant. Sheds moisture. Less expensive than nylon or wool carpet.	Some pilling and shedding; susceptible to oil-based stains.	Good cleanability, enhanced by new anti-stain treatments. Sheds moisture; static resistant.
POLY-PROPYLENE OLEFIN	Primarily in loop and random-sheared textures; nonabsorbent; resists abrasion, pilling, and shedding.	Fibers can withstand moisture; use indoors or outdoors. Very durable in level-loop styles.	May fade in direct sun. Lower grades may crush and flatten.	Excellent cleanability, especially with new antistain treatments. Resists static, most acids, chemicals.

FLOORS
RUGS

For spreading personality around a room, the area rug has few rivals. What could be more elegant than an heirloom-quality Oriental atop a gleaming hardwood floor, or more charming than a handcrafted braided rug on timeworn pine planks. In myriad styles and prices, versatile area rugs set the mood—and more.

Beyond beauty, these stage-setters are hardworking design elements. They bring softness and warmth to any hard-surface floor, instantly infuse color and pattern into a space, and make comely cover-ups for soiled or damaged carpet. They are great unifiers, sparking entire color schemes. One of the best decorating strategies is to use area rugs to define specific activity centers within a room, especially important in large rooms and in today's flow-

◀ *In this redesigned solarium, a dramatic area rug, in soft greens and blues on a black background, unifies elements from the 1930s checkerboard tile floor to blue-gray seating.*

▲

Imbuing the living room with formal flair, a distinctive Heriz Oriental rug defines the seating area, warms the hardwood floor, and inspires rust hues of coffee table and wing chair.

ing, open-plan homes. For example, let one rug set boundaries for a conversation area and another outline a dining spot. Area rugs can be used alone or in conjunction with carpet.

Rich in history and hue, jewel-toned Oriental rugs are the aristocrats of area rugs and are prized in traditional, formal, and eclectic schemes. Authentic hand-knotted Orientals may take years to create, but can wear well for more than a century. Equally elegant and formal are French classics, such as Aubusson and Savonnerie rugs, and hand-stitched needlepoint rugs.

Popular in contemporary and eclectic room schemes are wool dhurrie rugs, produced in India for centuries. Sumptuous colors, stylized motifs, and vivid geometry characterize these flat-woven rugs that are durable and reversible. Other picks include Scandinavian ryas, shaggy Greek flokatis, and modern rugs in bold, graphic designs.

Colorful braided, hooked, and rag rugs bring homey, handcrafted appeal to country-spirited rooms, and antique examples are increasingly prized by collectors. Many reproductions are made by traditional methods and reprise historic motifs, and there are contemporary interpretations in fresh pastels. Another option is the floorcloth, a favorite of colonial America, with designs from primitive to formal painted on canvas, jute, or other fabric backing.

If you're shopping for an authentic or antique rug, research the techniques, materials, and designs of the period and the region of origin, as well as the rug's identifying characteristics. For example, high-quality Oriental rugs are made of sheep or lamb's wool yarns, hand-knotted through linen or cotton backing. The more knots per square inch, the better the quality. A superb Persian carpet may have more than 500 to 1,000 knots per square inch. There are handsome reproductions made on power looms, and less-costly facsimiles with designs printed on the pile surface. Antique rugs, especially Orientals, are always expensive and often difficult to find. Although good examples turn up at estate sales and auctions, your best shopping bet is a reputable, established rug dealer.

FLOORS
RUGS

From the sophisticated beauty of dhurries and Orientals to the homespun charm of rag and braided rugs, there's an area rug to suit every taste, budget, furnishings style, and palette. Although antique examples rest at the expensive end of the spectrum, there are many reproductions and adaptations of timeless designs available today, and some styles are still handcrafted using age-old techniques. Here is an international sampler of classic area rug designs.

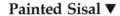

Painted Sisal ▼
A contemporary creation inspired by 18th-century floor-cloths, this sisal carpet has the design painted on the surface. The paint permanently stains the sisal, or vegetable fiber, pile.

◄ Bessarabian
Geometrics and florals char-acterize these flat-weave wool carpets, made by nomads in Russia, Romania, and Tur-key. Vertical looms dictate the long, narrow shapes.

Rag ▼
Hand-loomed around the world, cotton rag rugs have been a decorative staple for centuries. These sturdy, flat-weave rugs range from traditional stripes and multicolor designs to contemporary pastels.

Aubusson ▼
Prized for classical French styling and fine craftsmanship, Aubusson rugs have a hand-stitched tapestry weave and an elegant, formal air. They usually come in soft pastels with a center medallion design.

Dhurrie ▼

Handwoven in India and noted for soft colors and varied designs, wool dhurries are descended from ancient cotton coverings for floors and beds. Dhurrie is from "dari," meaning threads of cotton.

Oriental Turkish ▶

A treasured art form from about 3000 B.C., hand-knotted Oriental rugs, especially rare antique ones, are highly valued. This new oushak is hand-knotted in a timeless geometric design.

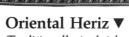

Hooked ▼

Hooked rugs, such as this early American example, derive their pattern from yarns or fabric strips pulled through mesh backing.

Braided ▼

Although the graphic design is decidedly contemporary, this rug follows the age-old method of braiding cloth strips, then stitching them together.

Needlepoint ▲

Developed in 18th-century Europe, needlepoint rugs are stitched in wool on canvas and distinguished by floral or geometric motifs.

Oriental Heriz ▼

Traditionally in brick reds and blues, these Oriental rugs hail from Heriz, Iran, and are noted for large-scale patterns, medallions, and corner designs.

FLOORS
WOOD

The rich, natural beauty of wood floors has long been an elegant hallmark of gracious homes. A gleaming expanse of mellow-grained wood underfoot not only sets an appealing stage, but also can enhance your home's value because, today, well-cared-for wood enjoys the luxury status once reserved for wall-to-wall carpet.

Beyond simple beauty, wood has numerous advantages. Unlike many synthetic materials, a wood floor has an inherently warm look, and, practically speaking, wood is one of the best insulating materials around. Its durability is excellent, and, if properly cared for, a wood floor ages well to a fine patina. Because graining, colors, and textures vary widely, wood flooring is a versatile option for any decor, from contemporary to country to more traditional settings.

The type of wood flooring you choose is strictly a matter of personal style. Hardwoods, from leaf-bearing trees such as red or white oak and walnut, produce some of the finest flooring material. Softwoods, such as pine, are from cone-bearing trees and are equally beautiful and functional. Oak is the most popular wood for flooring because it is so durable and because it beautifully accepts so many stains. Maple is the runner-up favorite in residential flooring. Also available are birch, beech, pecan, and pine. For a special project, it's worth searching lumberyards for relatively rare woods, such as heart pine, a much harder cousin of common pine used in cabinetry.

Consider your room's furnishings style in selecting wood flooring. In a casual, country-style setting, for example, a random-width, pine-plank floor is a fitting choice, reminiscent of the early American flooring that colonists hewed by hand and fitted with pegs. Wood floors make a delightful visual warm-up in contemporary rooms, playing off the cool palettes and sleek-lined furnishings. And in traditional and eclectic schemes, a treasured Oriental rug atop a burnished hardwood floor is an enduring, classic look.

Wood is graded—and priced—on appearance rather than on strength or durability, so match the flooring to the desired mood. More expensive, high-grade wood has a straight, clear grain and is free of knots and other blemishes. In public rooms, such as living and dining rooms, for example, you may want to set a luxury mood with top-grade wood flooring. In private family areas, you may opt for a rustic, informal feeling, achieved with lesser-grade woods with character-filled imperfections. Both grades will deliver similar long wear. After top-grade woods come select, No. 1 common, No. 2 common, and finally 1½-foot shorts, which are remnants from the other grades. You can purchase all grades and types of wood flooring, finished or unfinished. High-grade finished flooring costs more and usually requires professional installation to avoid damaging the wood. Unfinished flooring requires less precision, but may need touch-up sanding to smooth out surface irregularities.

▲
In this refreshingly casual living room, an old oak parquet floor was darkened to heighten the contrast with cool blues and the white backdrop. Topped with an Oriental rug, the flooring warms up the stage.

Taking a cue from the angles ▶ in this contemporary kitchen, rich-hued hardwood flooring runs on the diagonal to visually expand the space. Wood offers a natural counterpoint to chrome, tile, and other slick surfaces.

FLOORS
WOOD

Wood floors have come a long way since the days when the only option of early settlers was humble, hand-hewn planks. Two centuries later, those ancestral floors are treasures in historic homes and remain a testament to wood's durability and long-lasting aesthetic appeal. Inevitably, things have changed, and technology has improved upon a good thing. Today, wood flooring is available with stain-, wear-, and scratch-resistant features that make it an easy-care choice and a fitting floor for almost any room in the home. Wood is impregnated with an acrylic filler and finished with polyurethane and wax to make a tough surface, and wood that has not been treated can be stained, bleached, or painted after installation, then sealed.

Before buying, be certain of the kind of wood floor you're looking for because the styles, sizes, grades, and finishes vary. Here's a summary guide to some of the most popular types you'll encounter:

- Strip flooring is the most popular wood flooring. It is made of long, narrow boards that are tongue-and-groove-matched and end-matched, and such flooring comes in a variety of widths and thicknesses. Usually preferred is flooring 2¼ inches wide and ¾ inch thick. Although not as intricate in design as parquet flooring, it turns any floor into a warm, rich-grained expanse of wood. Strip flooring is usually nailed to a subfloor, and professional installation is recommended.
- Parquet floors are composed of small pieces of wood fitted together, in puzzlelike fashion, in a variety of designs, including herringbone, basket weave, and checkerboard. Parquet flooring, made of 12x12-inch squares, is a favorite with do-it-yourselfers because it's easy to install, especially with adhesive backing on the squares. With a parquet floor, you can have a wood floor practically anywhere in your home, although wood is not recommended for areas where there is likely to be standing water. For underfoot comfort and sound absorption, some types of parquet flooring come with a built-in foam cushion.
- Block flooring is another hardwood option, and is produced as a block or as a laminated block, cross-banded much like plywood. It comes in parquetlike designs, appropriately called parquetry.

- Plank flooring is wider than ordinary strip flooring, with planks available up to a foot wide. This flooring is especially effective laid in random widths and can be accented with wood or brass plugs. Like strip flooring, most plank flooring is nailed to a subfloor, although some adhesive-backed varieties are available.

The polished, planked or parqueted floor you're looking for just may require no shopping at all because your home may have one hidden beneath decades of old resilient flooring or yards of carpet. It pays to see what's underfoot. If you live in a home that was built in the 1930s or before, there's probably a hardwood floor that can be refinished to recapture its beauty. Newer homes often have softwood floors that lend themselves to painted finishes.

To refinish a natural-wood floor, you can hire a professional or do it yourself with rental equipment—an upright drum sander for open floor areas and a disc-type edger for working close to the baseboards. You'll need to sand off the old finish, fill in cracks and gouges with paste wood filler, and apply a protective finish such as a polyurethane sealer. If you want to change the floor's color, apply a stain before finishing. Good-quality enamel paint, plus a protective finish, can rescue a worn wood floor. Embellish old wood with any one of a variety of painting techniques from marbleizing to stenciling and spatter painting. A bleached wood floor is a dramatic option, but should be done professionally because of the caustic compounds used and the multistage process.

Vacuum regularly to eliminate dirt and grit, the major source of surface destruction. Even small soil particles, ground in by foot traffic, wear away at the protective coating and eventually damage the grain. Use a slightly damp mop for cleaning; standing water can cause swelling and staining. For small surface scratches, use steel wool dampened with a solvent, such as cleaning fluid, rubbing with the grain; rinse and refinish the spot. Gouges need to be filled, sanded, and refinished.

Herringbone ▶

For traditional elegance underfoot, wood flooring has an intriguing herringbone pattern that's a favorite parquet design. Its color and grain can carry a decorating scheme alone or in tandem with an area rug.

Parquet

A parquet floor, such as this mellow-hued example, is a design element that guarantees visual interest in schemes from traditional to contemporary. It's made of small pieces of wood fitted together into geometric patterns, and look-alike block flooring is called parquetry.

▼

◀ Tiles

Easy-to-install, adhesive-backed parquet tiles sometimes have a built-in foam cushion that adds resilience. Basket-weave, checkerboard, and more intricate patterns are available.

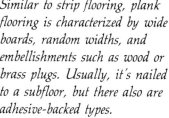

▲

Planks

Similar to strip flooring, plank flooring is characterized by wide boards, random widths, and embellishments such as wood or brass plugs. Usually, it's nailed to a subfloor, but there also are adhesive-backed types.

◀ Strips

The most common wood option is strip flooring, narrow boards fitted together, side by side, to give the appearance of a smooth expanse of wood. The flooring grants timeless appeal to any setting, is easy to customize with stains and bleaching techniques, and is easy to maintain.

FLOORS
RESILIENTS

Durable, care-free, and beautifully designed, the new generation of resilient floor coverings is the answer to numerous decorating problems and works as hard as today's homes. Resilient floor coverings are softer than clay tile or wood, and more stain resistant than carpet. They're an especially good choice in heavy-traffic areas and rooms prone to spills, although, aesthetically, they complement any floor in the home.

Technology has enhanced the many talents of resilients. With modern printing, embossing, and finishing processes, these floor coverings not only wear longer, but also are more appealing in color and pattern. Many of the new vinyls are great impostors, realistically mimicking patterns and textures of natural materials such as brick, stone, clay tile, intricate wood parquet, and even hand-painted tile. This design versatility allows you to customize the flooring to the mood you want to create. For example, you could revive the dining room floor with an elegant sweep of creamy white vinyl that looks like aged stone or marble. Upstairs, where flagstone flooring would be too heavy, you could use its resilient counterpart.

Vinyl flooring comes on wide rolls or in tile form. Although sheet vinyl is more expensive than tiles and can cost up to twice as much for a comparable grade, it offers the advantage of few seams. In many cases, sheet vinyl can be installed without any seams to catch dirt or to come unglued, an especially desirable feature in rooms that see splashes and spills. Adhesive-backed resilient tiles, in 9- and 12-inch squares, are easy for a do-it-yourselfer to install and provide decorative flexibility.

Like carpet, sheet vinyl comes in many grades and price ranges and is made in several ways. Inlaid vinyl designs are created by layers of colored vinyl granules fused under heat and pressure. Inlaid vinyl is the top of the line in durability and price. Because the design goes all the way through to the backing, the pattern is not as likely to suffer from chips or gouges and will last as long as the flooring does.

Rotovinyl has the pattern imprinted on the surface, protected by a layer of vinyl or polyurethane. One advantage is that it comes in sheets up to 15 feet wide; inlaid vinyl is available in only 6-foot widths.

Vinyl tiles are available in 9- and 12-inch squares that are individually glued to the subfloor. The most durable tiles are of solid vinyl. The other common type is vinyl composition floor tile, a mixture of vinyl and other less-expensive materials.

◀ *Easy-care vinyl tiles underscore a no-fuss, high-function kitchen redesigned to make the most of minimal space. The checkerboard flooring mixes light and dark shades for a wide-open feeling.*

Old meets new in a kitchen's charming dining spot, where a sweep of bright blue, rubber-base resilient tile sets a handsome, yet durable, stage for antique pieces, a 17th-century refectory table and chairs. ▶

FLOORS
RESILIENTS

A high-quality resilient floor is usually a sizable investment, but with careful installation and minimal upkeep, you can expect a high return—in good looks and long wear—on that investment.

Most tiles and sheet goods can be installed right over old resilient floors, except cushioned ones. The old floor must be in sound shape, firmly bonded to the subfloor, and the surface must be smooth. If this is not the case, consider covering the old flooring with an underlayment of ¼-inch sheets of plywood or hardboard. Cushioned vinyl flooring, however, can be installed over floors in relatively poor condition, often without the underlayment. You will still have to patch large holes and gouges to make the old surface smooth before the new flooring is laid. In working with sheet goods, any seams must be tight and patterns must match precisely. Inlaid vinyls are heavy and may require professional installation to avoid damage and achieve perfect fit. Some vinyl flooring, however, is specially designed for loose-lay installation, secured only around the perimeter with adhesive. Although the problems of weight and precise measurement remain, loose-laying sheet flooring is a task the skilled do-it-yourself homeowner may want to tackle.

In maintenance, resilient floors demand little, just damp-mopping with mild detergent to keep their no-wax finishes looking great. If constant wear dulls the sheen, use an acrylic-based dressing from your flooring dealer. An even newer twist is never-wax flooring that needs only a water-ammonia rinse and occasional buffing with a lamb's wool pad to stay bright. Because resilient flooring gives a little, it's susceptible to nicks and dents. Heavy furniture should be fitted with glides or casters to distribute weight. If your floor does get a dent, you may be able to plump it up by warming the area with a hand-held hair dryer. Vinyl floors are prey to discoloration from certain dyes and chemicals, such as those found in shoe polish, wax crayons, furniture oils, and tar, so wipe up any spills immediately. Chlorine bleach will remove some stains; leave a bleach-soaked cloth on the stain overnight.

◄ Solid Vinyl Tiles
Solid vinyl tiles make a top-of-the-line choice for almost any room because they are durable, easy to install, impervious to many stains, and easy to maintain. The tiles' wear layers go through to the back, so patterns wear longer. Designs often simulate natural materials, such as brick, ceramic tile, or even parquet-style wood. The tiles also come in solid colors.

Vinyl Composition ►
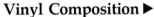
A combination of vinyl resins and filler materials, vinyl composition tiles offer moderate pricing, durability, easy installation, and assorted colors and patterns. They resist scuffs, burns, dents, and grease, but may require heavy-duty cleaning because the embossing can trap dirt.

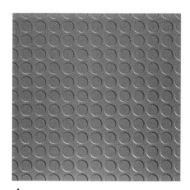

▲ Rubber

Once used primarily in commercial settings, rubber tiles are hard-wearing, colorful, and resilient, but costly. Because rubber can become slippery when wet, ribbed or studded rubber tiles are recommended for good traction, and work well in kitchens and active-use rooms.

▲ Sheet Vinyl

A good choice for kitchens, bathrooms, and surfaces likely to get wet, sheet vinyl is more watertight than tiles. Easy to install, sheeting comes in inlaid and rotovinyl types, with special features such as no-wax finishes. For basements, get below-grade sheeting with a backing that withstands dampness.

Solid/Inlaid Vinyl ▼

Made of solid vinyl and considered top-of-the-line flooring, inlaid vinyls come in sheets. The surface design is built up, in layers, with colored vinyl or polyurethane granules fused under heat and pressure. Heavy inlaid vinyls are less likely to chip or gouge, but may require professional installation.

▲ Inlaid Vinyl

Although more expensive than other types, inlaid vinyls offer long-wearing beauty. Inherently thick and soft, some have extra layers of foam to provide added underfoot comfort and to muffle sound. Because the colors and patterns go all the way through the material to the backing, they don't wear off.

▲ Printed Vinyl

Also called rotovinyl, this flooring is made by a photography-and-printing process, allowing realistic simulation of stone, wood, and other natural materials. Price and durability increase in ratio to the thickness of a clear vinyl or polyurethane layer over the printed image.

FLOORS
OTHER OPTIONS

Beyond the conventional carpet, vinyl, and wood, there's an exciting array of classic hard-surface, or nonresilient, materials that you can choose from to create the ultimate fashionable floor. Options, such as clay tile, slate, marble, terrazzo, and brick, offer unrivaled beauty, durability, decorative versatility—virtues appreciated throughout the home. Many of these options are easy care, as well.

Technology has buoyed the popularity of nonresilient materials by producing tile and glazes that tolerate heavy floor traffic, quarry tile with rich wood graining, stain-resistant finishes, and other special features. Tile is no longer strictly bath-and-kitchen flooring. From sun-rooms to foyers, living rooms to family rooms, these non-resilients are being used to create stunning underfoot effects, define separate activity areas, and set a mood. Brick adds rugged rusticity to casual and country schemes, terrazzo or clay tile makes a sleek stage for contemporary living spaces, and marble is inherently elegant anywhere.

Clay tile comes in ceramic and quarry forms, with glazed or unglazed finishes and a rainbow of colors and designs. Unglazed quarry tile that often has an irregular, handmade-looking surface is well suited to high-traffic areas and informal interiors. Glazed floor tiles are available in matte surfaces that make them less slippery than un-treated glazed tiles. Stone offers almost as many styles as clay tile, with polished marble, granite, or travertine hall-marks of formal interiors. In choosing any tile or other nonresilient material, it's important to make sure that it is recommended for floors. Although professional installa-tion is more expensive than a do-it-yourself flooring proj-ect, nonresilients may call for professional expertise for the best results.

▲
A painted border, echoing the chair cushions' paisley motif, embellishes handsome terra-cotta tile in the dining room of a seaside retreat. A practical choice, the tile is impervious to wet feet and tracked-in sand.

High-polish, high-style ▶ travertine was used to create the two-toned floor treatment in this elegant sitting room. The custom design outlines the seating area with a dramatic black travertine inset.

In this Southwest-flavored ▶ hallway, rugged antique bricks are set in sand to create old-world-style flooring that complements stucco walls and rough-hewn ceiling beams.

FLOORS
OTHER OPTIONS

Ceramic tile has been a popular decorating material for 7,000 years, plenty of time for it to build an·impressive record of durability and versatility. And it takes to customized designs, unique glazes, and special effects with ease.

One way to create an eye-catching floor with tile is to use subtle gradations in color across the entire floor. Or, you can frame the room's perimeter with tiles in a different hue or pattern from those used on the rest of the floor. You can create your own "tile rug" or one-of-a-kind floor by taking ordinary stock tiles and setting them in an original pattern. If you have an area rug for the room, set it off with a border of tile inset in the flooring. Today, tile grout comes in many colors, adding yet another design option. You can also design a floor that combines ceramic tile with other nonresilients, such as granite and marble, or wood.

How you install ceramic tile depends on the tile itself and the surface where it is to be applied. Each brand of tile is different, and each manufacturer usually includes specific recommendations for use and installation. Pregrouted panels or ceramic mosaics are within the realm of capability for many do-it-yourselfers who can muster the time and patience and ably wield a straightedge, tape measure, and carpenter's level. Specialty tools, such as cutters, nippers, and trowels, are often sold or loaned by ceramic tile dealers. It's wise to order tile for the entire project all at once, plus 10 percent more tiles than you'll need to cover breakage and replacement. Ceramic tiles can be installed over most structurally sound floors, but for new or uneven surfaces, or elaborate installations, consider hiring a professional for the job.

Of common nonresilients, ceramic tile demands minimal upkeep—regular vacuuming to remove gritty particles, mopping with a mild detergent and water solution, and a grout cleaner if the area's prone to mildew. However, brick, slate, quarry tile, and marble need occasional waxing to look their best.

Marble ▶

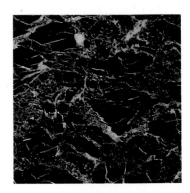

Marble floors are found in few new homes because installation is expensive. The surface is hard and colorful, stains easily, and needs regular waxing. The look is elegant and formal. Marble slabs, in sizes up to 40 square feet, come in a wide range of colors. Marble tiles offer a more limited selection.

Slate ▶

A beautiful choice in rustic settings, slate is stain resistant and relatively easy to install. It does, however, scuff in heavy-traffic areas, and it does need waxing to keep it looking good. Slate, like fieldstone and ceramic tile, holds heat well, making it a good choice for passive solar homes.

Terrazzo ▶

Smooth terrazzo flooring is made of marble or stone chips embedded in a cement binder, then highly polished for a multicolored effect. It's strong and resists moisture, stains, and abrasions, but needs a concrete base for installation. The flooring's cement is apt to show dirt and traffic patterns in time.

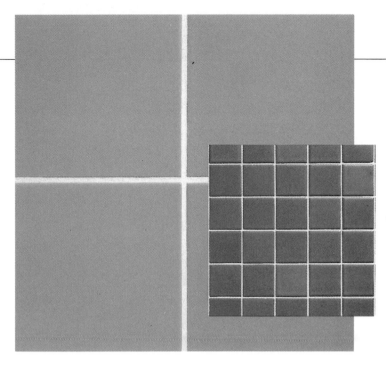

▲ Quarry Tile

Glazed or unglazed, quarry tile is made by an extrusion process from natural clay and shale, and is usually found in squares 6 inches or larger. It's durable, but may need a stain-resistant sealer. Although highly impact resistant, it will chip under severe blows. Common colors are terra-cotta, buckskin, and earthy browns.

◀ Glazed Tile

Clay tile technology has changed little over the centuries; clay is still shaped into a tile ¾ inch thick or less, then fire-hardened. Because clay is naturally porous, finishing tiles with a matte or high-gloss glaze or sealant makes them more resistant to water. With a rainbow of colors and designs from delicate florals to contemporary geometrics, this flooring is at home in a variety of settings.

Mosaic Tile ▶

Probably the most versatile of tiles, ceramic mosaics can be made of natural clay or hard porcelain, glazed or unglazed. They are small tiles, about 1 or 2 inches square, that are sold in groups, mounted on a backing. They can cover floors, walls, and any flat surface and conform to contoured shapes.

◀ Unglazed Tile

Unglazed tile is fire-hardened clay tile with color running throughout and a matte-type surface finish. Its appearance doesn't change as the tiles wear, and this flooring is not as slippery as one of glazed tile. Many shapes, colors, and designs are available, and cleaning requires only occasional mopping.

◀ Bricks

Whether bricks are old or new, they make an appealing flooring choice for rooms in a country, casual, or rustic mood. They add earthy color, rugged texture, and interesting shapes to flooring. Bricks are hard underfoot and need occasional waxing. Stain resistance may be enhanced with a sealer; overall, bricks offer long-lasting durability.

FLOORS
PAINT TECHNIQUES

A colorful and easy-to-clean painted-on-the-floor floorcloth lifts the decorative spirits of an all-beige kitchen.
▼

With artful painting techniques, you can stage delightful, and inexpensive, floor shows, whatever your room's mood—country, traditional, or contemporary. In borders, allover patterns, and painted-on rugs, stenciling adds unrivaled charm underfoot. Sources for precut stencils include art and specialty paint shops and museums and historic sites that offer vintage stencils in do-it-yourself kits. If marble is beyond the budget, try an elegant faux marble floor treatment that mimics classic "veining" with brushstrokes and sponges. Or create a tile look with an easy painted-on checkerboard pattern. For durability, seal your floor masterpiece with several coats of polyurethane.

▲
Contributing to the old-fashioned feel of this thoroughly modern kitchen is a wood floor transformed by a painted-on pattern of black and white squares and intricate veining.

A vintage paint pick-me-up ▶ called spattering rescued this timeworn wood floor. First painted in a pale color, the floor is then brush-spattered with a medley of hues.

224

RESILIENT AND HARD-SURFACE FLOORING

TYPES	CHARACTERISTICS	ADVANTAGES	DISADVANTAGES	CLEANABILITY
ASPHALT TILE	Porous; resists alkalis; low cost	OK on cement floor; can be below grade	Noisy; dents easily; needs waxing	Damaged by grease, harsh cleansers
VINYL CORK TILE	Handsome, sealed surface	Warm and quiet underfoot	Not for heavy traffic	Easy upkeep; similar to vinyl tile
RUBBER TILE	Handsome, clear colors	Excellent resilience; quiet; durable	Expensive; slippery when wet; must be above grade	Resists dents, stains; damaged by strong detergents, grease
VINYL COMPOSITION TILE	Resists alkalis; easy to install; low cost	Durable; colorful	Not very quiet; not very resilient	Embossing traps dirt; clean with heavy-duty detergents
CUSHIONED SHEET VINYL	Wide range of colors, patterns, surface finishes, and prices	Superior resilience; quiet; comfortable; stain resistant	Expensive; lower-cost grades susceptible to nicks and dents	Easy upkeep; some with no-wax or never-wax feature
SHEET VINYL	Wide range of colors, patterns, and surface finishes	Good resilience	Less-expensive grades susceptible to nicks and dents	Easily maintained; some with no-wax feature
SOLID VINYL TILE	Often simulates natural materials	Easy to install; durable	Only fair resilience	Stain resistant; easily maintained
WOOD	Natural or painted	Good resilience and durability	Only fair stain resistance	Easily maintained
BRICK, SLATE, QUARRY TILE	Natural look; variety of exciting shapes	Durability; beauty	No resilience	Needs waxing; may need sealer; good stain resistance
CERAMIC TILE	Colorful; many shapes and designs	Beauty; resistant to stains, fading	No resilience	Clean with soap and water only
MARBLE	Costly; formal	Beauty	Hard underfoot and stains easily	Needs waxing; stains difficult to remove
TERRAZZO	Smooth shiny finish; multicolored effect	Durable; resists stains, moisture	Limited design; permanent installation	Easily cleaned

LIGHTING

These days, there's no need to be in the dark about lighting. Advances in product design and technology have made it possible for us to be lighting magicians, enhancing our homes not just with lamps and light to see by, but with truly dramatic effect. With a mere flick of the switch, you can manipulate light in myriad ways. With the right light, you can make an average room look spectacular, disguise flaws, and emphasize assets. Lighting can enhance color schemes, make boxy rooms look spacious, and make overly large rooms seem more intimate. Filled with illuminating ideas, this chapter will show you how to turn on a room with light.

LIGHTING
THE BASICS

Artificial lighting, the sunshine substitute, is a vital component of successful room design. To maximize its myriad practical and decorative talents in your home's lighting plan, consider function first. Basically, general lighting must ensure safety and allow us to move about a room easily, avoiding collisions with furniture and the children's roller skates. Once that prerequisite is met, you can customize lighting to brighten work areas, enhance color, spark drama and interest, change moods, cozy-up large spaces, and make small rooms appear larger.

Interior lighting falls into three categories: general, task, and accent. The most appealing room schemes, however, mix them all from a variety of sources.

● General lighting is glare-free indirect lighting that bounces off walls and ceiling, providing comfortable background illumination. It should be evenly distributed, with no extremes of superbright or shadowy spots. General light sources, such as recessed or track fixtures, should be flexible enough to suit the room's needs. For example, an easy-to-install dimmer switch in an everyday dining room softens the mood for entertaining.

● Task lighting delivers essential illumination for specific jobs: writing, reading, cooking, computer work, grooming, or hobbies. It's localized, shadow-free, easy-on-the-eyes lighting, such as study lamps, bedside reading lamps, or countertop illumination in the kitchen.

● Accent lighting is purely decorative and creatively planned with a combination of sources, such as floor-based uplights, sconces, or spotlights. Use it to highlight a room's appealing aspects—artwork, collectibles, vignettes, or architecture. With inexpensive clamp-on lamps and bulbs of varied colors and wattages, experiment with accents before buying costly fixtures.

Short on sunny exposure, an ▶
English-style living room
brightens up with multilevel
lighting for comfort, reading,
and artful accents. Pale colors
enhance the illumination.

LIGHTING
THE RIGHT LIGHT

In creating a successful room-by-room lighting plan, it's important to match each fixture to the role you want it to play and to provide enough light sources to make each room pleasant, safe, and comfortable.

Because it hosts a range of activities, the living room requires several types of lighting. Soft, general lighting from indirect sources—wall washers, uplights, lamps, recessed fixtures, or cove, cornice, or valance lighting, for example—is appropriate for relaxing, conversation, entertaining, and television viewing. Downlights, spotlights, and table and floor lamps provide good direct light for reading. Accent lighting can be an important design element in the living room. To create a focal point for a furniture grouping, wash a wall of artwork with clear, soft light, or focus a spot on an important furniture piece, such as an armoire. Shine portable and fixed spotlights on collections, and stage an intriguing light show in a hard-to-decorate corner with an uplight behind a plant. Lighting to accent objects should be at least three times brighter than general lighting.

Flexible lighting is imperative in the dining room, where the ubiquitous chandelier may be elegant, but too bright unless it's tamed by a dimmer switch to soften the mood. Placing a chandelier off-center or over the buffet makes a room appear larger. Valance or cove lighting, recessed fixtures, and over-the-buffet spotlights supplement this general source. Use the same accent lighting strategies as in the living room to highlight glassware or art.

For family room or den, the lighting plan should be similar to the living room, with greater emphasis on direct light for games, hobbies, and desk work. If the room includes a computer center, avoid reflections and choose a fixture, such as an adjustable pendant lamp, with baffles that shade the light source.

Bedrooms need versatile general lighting, ranging from soft for relaxing to bright for cleaning, all on a dimmer control. A shared room should have separate task lights, such as bedside lamps or adjustable track lights above the headboard for reading. In a child's room, ceiling or wall fixtures are a better choice than portable lamps that can be broken in play. In baths, light for safety and eliminate shadows with fixtures on both sides of grooming mirrors.

Kitchens need multilevel lighting for efficiency. General illuminators, such as a luminous ceiling, track lighting, or pendant fixtures, should be teamed with task lights beamed on counters and cooktops.

In entries and hallways, lighting should ensure safety first, but it also can add drama. Up a stairway, three or four elegant wall sconces make more sense than a hard-to-clean hanging fixture on the landing. Or, turn a hallway into an art gallery and spotlight paintings and the passageway simultaneously.

▲ *The bedroom glows with off-the-track halogen fixtures, ceiling-mounted separately. A pair of classic Tizio lamps personalize light for reading.*

Crowning the dramatic ▶ dining room is a multilevel recessed ceiling, studded with spotlights focused on each place setting, artwork, and glassware.

230

LIGHTING
THE RIGHT LIGHT

Without proper placement and fixture accessories, a lighting scheme may miss the mark *and* the mood. Thus, finding the right spot for the right fixture is important, especially in accent lighting. Bulbs and shades also make a difference in overall effect.

Today's homes have taken some exciting, special-effects lighting cues from the theater. The most practical way to add dramatic accent lighting is with a well-placed mix of uplights and downlights, spotlights, and floodlights, used to highlight a room's pleasing aspects, from architecture to furniture to treasures.

Ceiling- or wall-mounted downlights cast pools of directed light below, on sculpture or paintings, for example. Uplights work in reverse, beaming up from the floor to accent objects and produce dramatic patterns of light and shadow. Spots and floods work on the same accent principle. Some accent lights come with adjustable reflectors or louvers to focus light where you want it. Bulbs, such as eyeball spotlights and low-voltage halogen bulbs, offer excellent light-beam control. Equip spotlights with low-voltage transformers to prevent heat damage that incandescent lights can cause to art and furniture finishes.

Here are some measurements for siting your lighting:
- Space recessed fixtures 6 to 8 feet apart for general lighting and use flood bulbs. For task lighting, install them 15 to 18 inches apart.
- Hang pendant lights and chandeliers with the bottom about 30 inches above the table. If the fixture has a bare bulb and open bottom, hang it low enough to avoid harsh light in diners' eyes. A hanging light's diameter should be at least a foot less than that of the table beneath it. When a room's ceiling height is more than 8 feet, keep the room in balance by raising the chandelier 3 inches for each additional foot of ceiling height.
- At a chair or bed, site a hanging light with its lower edge about 4 feet from the floor. Hang a fixture with its lower edge about 15 inches above a desktop.
- The bottom of a table lamp should be at eye level, about 38 to 42 inches above the floor, when you are seated. For tasks, the ideal light source is 10 to 12 inches below the user's eye level.

- Short floor lamps, 40 to 42 inches high, should line up with your shoulder when you're seated. Taller lamps should be set about 15 inches to the side and 20 inches behind the center of the hypothetical book you're reading.

In shopping for shades, special lighting needs determine the type of shade to buy. A translucent shade bathes everything in a soft glow. An opaque shade casts light upward and downward for good reading.

▲
With Hollywood-style grooming lights and a sparkling wrap of mirrored panels, this powder room earns star status.

Nostalgic, green-glass ▶ *fixtures suspended above the countertops spotlight efficiency in a cook's-choice kitchen.*

LIGHTING
A PHOTO GLOSSARY

Study Lamp ▼

Whether the task is balancing the checkbook or homework, a desktop study lamp offers easy-on-the-eyes illumination. A diffuser disk that fits above the light source eliminates glare. Choose a shade broad enough to wash the work area in light.

Torchère ▶

With its sleek sculptural base and flared torch-shape shade, the torchère bounces light off the ceiling for a soft ambient glow. Slim lines make it popular for small spaces, and it's a good choice for lighting dark corners and making ceilings appear higher.

▲
Ginger Jar

Among portable light sources, the ginger jar lamp is a favorite because its versatility suits any room. Fitted with a white, translucent shade, the lamp provides reading light and casts a wide enough glow to qualify as a general illuminator. The ginger jar is among classic lamp designs inspired by ordinary objects: tea canisters, candle-sticks, and apothecary and other jars. The ginger jar at right represents the contemporary end of the lamp's spectrum of styles.

Pharmacy Lamp ▶

Developed by pharmacists in the 1920s, the pharmacy lamp serves reading and conversation areas. You can adjust the lamp's beam and height with a telescoping shaft and movable shade, commonly in a tent, shell, or parabolic shape. Some lamps feature a flexible arm.

▲
Floor Canister

Canister uplights create special decorative effects, and can be used on the floor or a tabletop. Beam them on artwork or sculpture, or tuck one behind a plant in a dark corner for a dramatic show of light and shadows.

▲
Cylinder

High function and a stylish range of colors and finishes make the cylinder lamp a decorating staple. Its flared shade casts a wide glow for task and general lighting, and its sleek base is a tabletop space saver.

▲
Halogen Balance

A contemporary classic for task or accent lighting, the halogen lamp features counterweights and a heavy base. Often it rotates 360 degrees for vertical and horizontal adjustment. The bulb provides pure, white light without color distortion.

◀ Adjustable Arm

The highly versatile flex-arm lamp has become an inexpensive answer to many home lighting needs, serving desk, hobby center, and reading nook. An adjustable elbow and head suit it for accent lighting, too.

LIGHTING
A PHOTO GLOSSARY

Cylinder Light ▼

Mounted on the wall or ceiling, or even in outdoor living areas, downlights have multipurpose appeal. They usually feature a glare-reducing baffle. Use them to supplement general illumination. Or, use them as high-lighters, focused, for example, on artwork, collectibles, or plants.

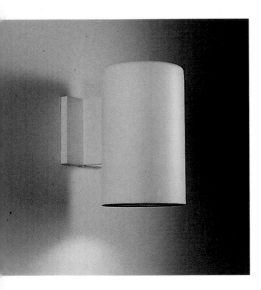

▲
Chandelier

Long ago created to hold candles and suspended from the ceiling to avoid fire risk, the graceful chandelier offers general and task light. From antique reproductions to sleek modern versions, it suits any decor and guarantees impact in dining room, foyer, or living room.

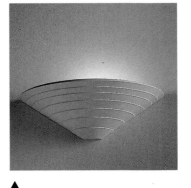

▲
Wall Sconce

No longer confined to the powder room and nightclub circuit, wall sconces direct light up, down, or both ways, and come in halogen, incandescent, and fluorescent models. Use them to enhance light in a large room, accent art and architecture, or brighten a foyer, or as task lighting in a bedroom or bath.

Ambient Wall Light ▶

Taking a design cue from a ship's bulkhead lights, this fixture is a classy, functional general illuminator. It comes in varied finishes and shade types, such as frosted glass, and adapts to any setting, from living room to outdoors. Use it in dramatic groupings or solo.

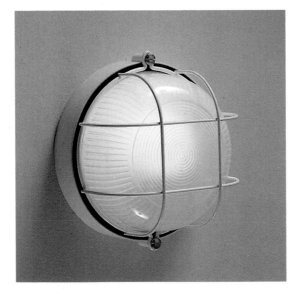

Track Lighting ▼

Suspended on wall- or ceiling-mounted tracks, track lighting is wired to hold individual fixtures. Track systems offer ambient light, or spotlighting, depending on the bulbs used.

◀ Pendant Light

The polished brass pendant light brings a touch of tradition to the living room, dining spot, or worktable. If there's no electrical box, run a ceiling track to the light, or discreetly run a cord up a corner and along the ceiling line to feed the "swag" lamp hung on a hook.

Louver Tube Light ▼

For focusing light where you want it, this sleek fluorescent tube has a louvered canopy that rotates 360 degrees for special effects, such as up- or down-lighting. It can be hung from the ceiling or wall mounted.

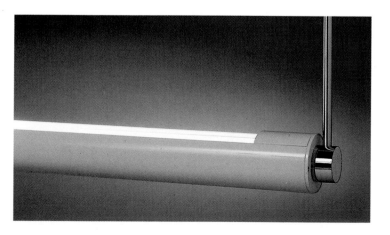

Recessed Lighting ▶

Versatile ceiling-recessed fixtures offer unobtrusive built-in lighting. Depending on the type of bulb used, they handle general illumination in living areas and task lighting in work areas. Directional versions adjust for spotlighting and washing walls in a soft glow.

237

LIGHTING
A PHOTO GLOSSARY

Undershelf ▶

Easy-to-install undershelf lighting in spotlights or sleek bar-type fixtures can be added to highlight displays of collectibles and sparkling glassware, or to illuminate the dark corners of deep storage.

◀ Reading and Study

Eye comfort comes first in this trim-lined reading-and-study lamp, with adjustable swing arm and stylish finish to fit any room's decor. Floor and wall-mounted versions meet task lighting needs.

Magnifier ▼

For artists, needlecrafters, model-makers, or other hobbyists, an adjustable magnifier lamp is the ultimate accessory, giving a detailed look at works in progress. It tucks neatly by a worktable or chair or rolls out of sight.

Pendant Light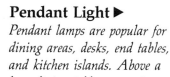

Pendant lamps are popular for dining areas, desks, end tables, and kitchen islands. Above a long dining table or counter, hang two lamps, evenly spaced. Rise-and-fall fittings make the lamps adjustable.

▲ Art or Piano Lights

These bracket-mounted lamps dramatically spotlight individual artworks. The adjustability and concentrated beam also make them a good light source for the piano's music rack.

Makeup Lights ▶

Striplights (top) that take their cue from movie stars' dressing rooms and familiar fluorescents (bottom) are bathroom naturals. The striplights' backplates come in colored and metal finishes and attach vertically or horizontally. Consider complexion-flattering deluxe warm white tubes for fluorescent lighting.

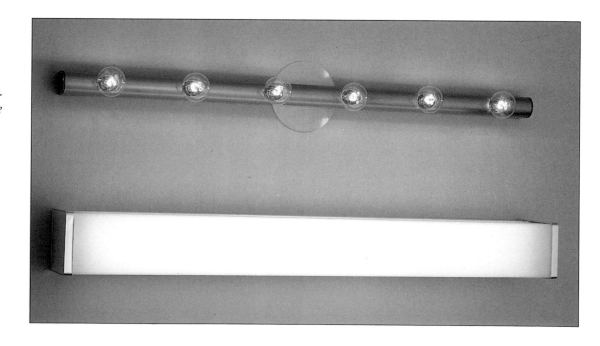

239

PERSONAL TOUCHES

Often, it's the small touches that have the greatest effect on a decorating scheme. Accessories, art, and treasures of all kinds are what give a room its unique character. Because accessories are the most personal part of decorating, they should be chosen with care and displayed to advantage. Accent items should reflect your personality and give you pleasure, too. Accessories and art needn't be equated with one-of-a-kind objects. As long as an item holds meaning for you, it's certainly worthy of attention. This chapter will show you how to give your rooms character.

PERSONAL TOUCHES
GETTING TO KNOW YOU

Never feel shy about showing off your treasures: art collections, mementos, heirlooms, photographs, or trinkets. The objects of your affection are always worthy of display, be they simple seashells or a fine collection of porcelain figurines. Indeed, when it comes to personalizing with favorite things, cost is of little or no importance. What *is* important is that your accessories say something about you—your likes, your hobbies, your history, even your eccentricities. Without exception, the most interesting interiors are those that tell a visual story about the people who live there. The dullest houses, on the other hand, are devoid of hints as to who the owners are. Stripped of special touches, a room is bland at best, barren and forbidding at worst.

Many people, especially first-time homeowners, feel stumped when it comes to personalizing their surroundings. First of all, keep in mind that personalizing is a personal matter; no one can really do the job for you. Sure, you can get ideas and help from others—interior designers, friends, magazines, books, and store salespeople—but in the long run it's your own preferences that count. The whole idea of personalizing, after all, is to create your own unique look. The point is lost if you accessorize with anonymous knickknacks that have no meaning for you.

LOOK AROUND YOU

It may well be that you have a wealth of accessories and prized possessions just waiting to be put on display. Take books, for example. Are yours hidden away in boxes? If so, bring them out; they're tops for adding warmth and interest to a room. Look, also, to things you're fond of but may not have considered as accessories before. Old family photographs, memorabilia from your travels, art created by your children (or by you, for that matter!), cherished valentines or postcards (framed)—these are all candidates for special treatment.

◀ *In this serene, sophisticated setting, personal touches are limited to contemporary art and colorful pottery, all carefully placed for aesthetic effect. The child-size rocking chair and table are old Stickley pieces that are accessories unto themselves.*

A couple who are avid ▶ travelers let their living room reflect the fact. The French porcelain fireplace screen was bought in Paris, as were the toiletry jars on the mantel and the colorful fabric draped with panache on the back of the sofa. The cornice crowning the window is a relic from Boston's first drugstore.

PERSONAL TOUCHES
FIRST IMPRESSIONS

Fresh flowers can always be ▶
counted on to provide a personal
touch. Peachy pink tulips
enhance this charming scene.

As the old saying goes, "You only get one chance to make a first impression." And because your entryway is the first thing guests see upon entering your house, you'll want to make it as pleasing and memorable as possible. Even the tiniest vestibule should bid a warm welcome and provide a decorative sneak preview of what's to come in the rest of the house. To this end, art and accessories can do a lot, especially in entries where furniture won't fit.

Embellishments can be as practical as they are decorative. Mirrors, for instance, not only make an entry seem more spacious and gracious, they're also handy for checking one's appearance upon entering or leaving the house. A lovely old trunk can make a fine accessory while serving as storage for boots, gloves, and other seasonal items. Similarly, hat racks and umbrella stands can be as eye-pleasing as they are practical.

◀ To create a grand entrance—and to announce their passion for collecting—these homeowners turned a foyer stairway into a dramatic gallery-on-the-rise. At the foot of the stairs: a Fledermaus chair and a sculptured pedestal.

▲ This entry hall is filled with an intriguing mix of special finds, among them a trio of Oriental rain jars, a Chinese wedding basket, and a contemporary oil painting. Next to the skirted table is a Thai settee upholstered in Peruvian fabrics.

PERSONAL TOUCHES
ON DISLAY

Collections of nearly any kind offer wonderful decorative potential, but only if properly displayed. Scattered willy-nilly around a room, collections aren't collections but orphaned objects in search of a home. Similarly, collections are dishonored if placed slapdash-fashion on a table or shelf.

The way you display your collections will depend somewhat, but not entirely, on their worth. Fragile items and those of great monetary (or sentimental) value obviously deserve special care. Consider glass-enclosed display cases (custom-made or store-bought) for priceless or irreplaceable objects. Enclosed display cases also make good sense if you don't like dusting, or if you have rambunctious children or pets about. Open shelves, bookcases, china cabinets, and other kinds of storage cabinets are ideal for displaying many types of collections. When arranging objects, keep scale and balance in mind, and—most importantly—don't overcrowd. To call attention to your collection, especially at night, consider using spotlights or specially designed display lights.

▲
An 1860s grain-painted cupboard makes an appropriately rustic home for a collection of Indian baskets and pottery.

A homeowner who uses china accents in every room highlights a collection of Royal Copenhagen in an Irish pine dresser.
▼

◀ *A single bell, a gift from a friend, was the beginning of this now-sizable bell collection. Amassed over a period of years, the bells are showcased in a wall-mounted, mirror-backed Lucite display case, completely enclosed so that dusting is never necessary.*

Here again, a Lucite display ▶ case was used to display—and call attention to—a cherished collection of old toys.

PERSONAL TOUCHES
CREATING VIGNETTES

Vignettes are special treats for the eyes. They are small scenes in a larger setting; islands of beauty to behold. Any surface—table, desk, mantel, or ledge—is a candidate for a vignette. Furniture, too, can play an important role. The idea is to create a composition that invites viewing and stirs interest, even if just in passing.

The ingredients of your composition can include just about anything. The only *must* is that the items relate well to one another visually. You wouldn't, for instance, place a large earthenware bowl next to a dainty demitasse cup—not, at least, without regrettable results. Shown here are a smattering of ideas, but the possibilities are infinite. More than likely, you already have the makings of a lovely vignette on hand. Consider books, framed art, candlesticks, and flower vases for starters.

◀ *It's the sum of the parts—shapely furnishings, a single framed print, and a simple spray of flowers—that makes this scene a small work of art. Even the parquet floor, with its faux marble inserts, plays a part in the picture.*

▲ *This charming vignette was created in the entry of a New England cottage. The Empire table was rescued from a dump, then painted on top to resemble granite, and shaped into an eye-pleasing scene with assorted treasures.*

A mantel is the perfect place for a still life. This one, consisting of shells, flowers, and a pastoral print, is a gem.
▼

▲
An antique tole tray table, nestled next to a sofa, displays an array of miniature trompe l'oeil delights. The fruits are made of silk and velvet, the corn cob is wooden, and the tiny watermelons in the woven basket are painted pecans.

Yet another eye-pleasing ▶ equation—law books, old boxes, a lovely painting, and an antique lamp—all beautifully balanced for exquisite effect.

PERSONAL TOUCHES
PICTURE PERFECT

This designer-homeowner ▶
practices what she preaches. Her
advice? Personalize bedrooms
with photos of people you love.

Photographs offer a wonderful way to make your presence felt. Placed in groupings on walls or tables, framed photographs grab the attention of passersby, inviting them to linger and look. There are a number of ways to personalize with photos. One approach is to create a visual history of your family, mingling pictures of long-gone ancestors with present-day pictures of yourself and other family members. Another idea is to create a gallery of baby pictures, featuring yourself, your spouse, and your children. Photographs depicting special occasions—weddings, birthday parties, graduations, and homecomings—are always of interest, and can be grouped together or placed in separate arrangements.

When putting photographs on public display, be sure to use frames worthy of—and compatible with—your decorating scheme. They come in all sizes, shapes, and price ranges, and can be store-bought or custom-made. Consider having prized photos professionally matted and framed.

▲
Framed photos should be hung
with the same care as artwork.
This striking arrangement of
black-and-white photos was
composed to complement the
window's stately proportions.

◀ This dramatic display niche was
designed for a collection of
family photographs and a
magnificent tapestry depicting
the Hungarian village where
the owner once lived. Re-
cessed lights and a halogen
track fixture focus on the
tapestry, the photos, and the
elegant, no-two-alike frames.

▲
Fond memories, in the form of photographs, top this white-painted gateleg table. Even the table itself has sentimental value: It's the same table where the owner, as a child, ate breakfast every day.

◄ *Photos don't have to be large to make a big impact. Here nine standard-size photos are given display-worthy importance by matting and framing them in identical simple pine frames, then hanging them on a background of pin-striped linen-covered walls.*

PERSONAL TOUCHES
ARTFUL ASSETS

Artwork comes in many forms: paintings, posters, prints, sculpture, even furniture. It can be original or reproduction, be quite costly or cost nothing at all. Whatever your preference in art, make it a point to incorporate the art in your surroundings. Not only will your rooms benefit by its presence, so will you. Art's purpose, after all, is to give visual pleasure.

GETTING ACQUAINTED

If you're a stranger to the world of art, there are many ways you can become acquainted. Begin by visiting museums, galleries, and art shows. Browse around to get a feel for what you like. Then, start asking questions of the curators, the art dealers, or the artists themselves. Study one art form at a time until you become familiar with its fine points and can distinguish good-quality work from bad or mediocre.

Once you've developed an appreciation for art, you can begin building a collection. Fine-art prints and posters are in the realm of most budgets. Posters, especially, offer excellent value for the money. Many are created by famous artists, usually as lithographs or silk-screen prints. Instead of being printed in limited editions, however, posters are often run off in the thousands. Unsigned ones are the least expensive. Those with signatures in the printing impression are more costly, and a limited number, pencil-signed by the artist, cost the most. Look for them in galleries, museum shops, and department stores, or order them by mail from a poster catalog company.

Don't be shy about showing off your own art creations or those of your children. Also, keep an open mind about what constitutes art. Quilts, for instance, when hung on the wall, become instant works of art. The same is true for rugs, framed silk scarves, framed postcards, unusual masks, and any number of other everyday or offbeat items.

▲

Given prominence and placed in the right context, nearly anything is fodder for art. This picture of a heart (made by a friend of the owner), an artist-designed clock, and a whimsical hand-painted cat chair (made by the French artist Rigot Gerard) are teamed together for just-for-fun effect.

In this dining area, art is a ▶ major and powerful presence. The triptych (a painting done in three parts) depicts the living room in the owner's former house. Placed on a dark lacquered wall, the contemporary painting adds a sense of daring and theatrics to the otherwise subdued, traditional setting.

PERSONAL TOUCHES
MULTIPLE CHOICES

The highlight of this elegant setting is a symmetrical grouping of identically framed 19th-century English prints.
▼

Certain types of art, particularly fine-art prints, look best when displayed in multiples. Although there's nothing wrong with showing off a single print, the strongest decorative impact is made when there are several, or more, in the arrangement. Botanical prints—detailed engravings of plants, flowers, fruits, or trees—are delightful additions to both contemporary and traditional settings. Also effective are old architectural engravings, nautical prints, and those depicting animals. Original prints and complete sets from old folios can be quite expensive. Many reasonably priced reprints are available, however.

◄ *It isn't necessary to invest in authentic fine-art prints to create an arresting display. These homeowners devised a creative alternative by individually framing 36 colorful fruit prints from an old seed catalog.*

Here's proof that slanted ► walls can be used for art. To secure an octet of black-and-white French engravings, the designer attached eye hooks to the bottom corners of the prints, ran wire through the hooks, then tied the wire to tiny nails in the wall.

PERSONAL TOUCHES
FRAMING AND HANGING

One of the keys to an effective art display is well-chosen framework. Keep in mind that a frame should never be more important than the picture it surrounds. The frame should complement the subject matter, tonal value, and size of the picture. It also should integrate well with the decor. How you frame your art affects not only how it looks, but how it lasts—protecting it from soil, fingerprints, and other damaging factors.

When you're ready to frame your artwork, you have a basic decision to make: to have it custom framed, use ready-made frames, or do the framing job yourself.

Custom framing is the easiest option, but also the costliest. Indeed, it's not uncommon to pay more for the framing than the art within. However, it takes a special blend of craftsmanship and creativity to see and bring out the best in a piece of art. It also takes time, skill, and patience. These are what you pay for when you hire a professional framer. Also, professional framers generally offer a larger selection of frames and other materials than you'd find anywhere else.

Ready-made frames are adequate for many purposes, and cost much less than other types of framing. These come complete with glass, stapled fitting devices, backing, and hanger. Ready-mades are limited in terms of size, style, and quality, however.

Make your own frame—but only if you have lots of patience, the proper tools, and knowledge of matting and backing techniques. If you don't have a home workshop, consider going to a do-it-yourself framing shop, where you can buy framing materials, use the shop's tools, and get free help and advice.

TIPS ON FRAMING

- Original watercolors and prints look best when framed simply, with shallow, narrow frames, glass, and mats. It isn't usually necessary to mat posters.
- Traditional oils usually have heavier frames, sometimes in a style that matches the period of the painting. Mats and glass are *not* used on oil paintings. Modern oils and acrylics often are unframed.

- Glass is needed on all art you want to preserve except oils. You can buy nonreflective glass that is glare-free, but it tends to distort colors and deaden black and white.
- Acrylic, like nonreflective glass, is more expensive than regular glass, but it is much lighter in weight. This can be an asset when you are framing a large picture. Acrylic dosen't break as easily as glass and you can drill holes in it. However, acrylic does scratch easily. Do not use it over pastel chalk or charcoal drawings, as it generates static electricity that will attract the chalk or charcoal dust.

HANGING TIPS

If you've ever pounded a nail in the wall and watched the plaster come crumbling down, you know that picture hanging can be nerve-racking business. To reduce the risk of damaging the wall, make a cross with masking tape over the spot where you want to drive the nail. This will greatly reduce wall damage.

An alternative to the standard nail and metal hanger is wall-mounting tape. The double-side adhesive strip or square is applied to the back of the picture, then the picture is pressed to the wall. Disadvantages of this type of hanger are that the tape won't hold heavy pictures, nor will it work on porous or textured walls.

PLAN FOR SUCCESS

The *real* secret of achieving picture-perfect art groupings is to select and arrange your pictures first before ever pounding a nail in the wall.

To plan a grouping, piece together sections of paper until you have a mock-up of the same size as the wall space you want to cover. Lay the paper on the floor and arrange the frames so the grouping is balanced in size, shape, and weight. Trace around the pictures and mark where the nails will go. Tape the paper to the wall, making sure the center is at eye level. Remember, too, that a picture should be no wider than the piece of furniture below it or narrower than half its length.

To give this sizable art grouping a sense of unity, the arrangement was first plotted on paper, like pieces of a puzzle.
▼

▲
Don't let slanted walls or lease prohibitions stand between you and your love of art. If hanging is out of the question, show off artwork on an easel, like this one, or prop your paintings on a ledge or mantel, and lean them against the wall.

◄ *It takes a keen eye and a great sense of balance to create an asymmetrical arrangement like this one. A key factor in this room is visual "weight." The four portraits of women flanking the clock, for example, are counterbalanced by the visual weight of the single painting placed squarely below.*

257

PERSONAL TOUCHES
A PRO'S APPROACH

◀ *The living room in Richard FitzGerald's carriage house is abundant with personality and a potpourri of art, oddments, and other treasures.*

▲ *Opposite the fireplace is a small vignette consisting of wedge-shaped table deftly accessorized, pair of comfy armchairs, and a collection of Chinese paintings.*

Richard FitzGerald is a highly successful interior designer with an enviable eye for details. His home, a delightful remodeled carriage house in Boston, is small in square footage, but filled with more personality than many houses twice the size. For Richard, space—or lack of it—is immaterial to successful scheming. What counts is character: the sum total of a room's furnishings, colors, art, accessories, and other items of interest.

In his sophisticated living room, *opposite,* Richard emphasized the snugness of the space by painting the walls a dark bottle green. Actually, the walls were first painted with off-white enamel, then glazed with green paint, vertically and horizontally, to create the crosshatched textured look of linen.

Another detail worthy of note is the use of mirror on the flat plane where the ceiling drops (to accommodate plumbing pipes) from 11 to eight feet. The mirrored surface, Richard explains, reflects the room's angles and creates the illusion of uniform height.

The L-shaped seating banquette looks built-in, but it's actually movable. Richard upholstered the banquette in the same color tone as the walls to make it "disappear," a good trick in a small room, or if you want to direct attention to art and accessories.

Adding spice to the soothing setting is a colorful Portuguese needlepoint rug and a red lacquered tray table topped with a bowl of pink posies and a pair of shaded candlestick lamps.

◀ *The designer's attention to detail even extends to the stairway, where he's embellished an old brass handrail with trompe l'oeil tassels— actually antique wooden carvings.*

PERSONAL TOUCHES
A PRO'S APPROACH

▲
Unique window treatments are one of the designer's many fortes. Here, what looks like a flower-bedecked cloth festoon is actually a wooden valance, cut from a template, then painted.

Chinese red is a commanding ▶ *presence in the master bedroom. All of the artwork and most of the accessories hail, beautifully, from the Orient.*

◀ *The carriage house kitchen is invested with personal style. This view focuses on a tête-à-tête table, set for nibbles and drinks. Forming a delectable backdrop is an engraving of a melon, surrounded by Italian lettuce-leaf plates.*

Helping his clients with the finishing touches is a big part of Richard's job. Indeed, it's only after the furnishings are in place that the "soul" of a room begins to take shape. Although some of his clients need little assistance in personalizing a room, many need—and ask for—direction. Often he suggests that they:

- **Try a treasure hunt.** Before rushing off to stores or galleries to buy art and accessories, Richard embarks on a treasure hunt in the owner's own house. He rummages (with permission) for interesting objects, collections gone astray, heirlooms hidden away, and other overlooked items. It's a rare hunt where he emerges empty-handed. Have you scoured your house for hidden treasures?
- **Experiment.** Stagnant, "just so" rooms are boring. Try rotating your accessories, and now and then, be bold. Don't be afraid to put a $2 "find" next to a $500 lamp, as long as they're visually compatible.
- **Learn.** Visit the best galleries and accessory shops to develop a discerning eye. Ask questions.

STYLE STRATEGIES

In developing this book, we traveled around the country, visiting hundreds of homeowners who graciously allowed us to tour their rooms. As you might imagine, we saw all kinds of homes and decorating schemes. Some were splendorous, but many were simple and small. Some were luxuriously furnished, but the lion's share were not. The schemes that impressed us most were not the showiest or the costliest. Our favorites, including the delightful homes featured in this chapter, were those rich in character, warmth, and personal style. Let us take you on a tour.

STYLE STRATEGIES
PURELY PERSONAL

Traffic-clogged expressways and city bustle seemed a world away from the quiet shady lane that greeted house-hunters Reecie and Gary Mestman and guided them toward a 1920s colonial. The serenity was instantly enchanting, but the old home begged for renovation. With loving labors, the Mestmans designed a surprise package, wrapped in tradition. Today, the home's inviting interiors reflect their free-spirited decorating philosophy and capture the essence of eclectic style.

◀ *Nestled among towering sweet gum and lush dogwood, the colonial-style home boasts Taraesque columns and classical details in southern Greek Revival tradition.*

Adobe-pink walls and old ▶ woodwork in creamy white enhance the fresh-and-formal mood of the living room, at ease with timeless seating atop a soft-hued dhurrie rug. Prized pottery delivers lively accent.

264

STYLE STRATEGIES
PURELY PERSONAL

"We wanted an old home, with lots of trees, and we wanted something we could fix up," Reecie recalls. "Once we recognized the home's potential—knocking out a wall here, adding a room there—we got excited."

With work to be done inside and out, the Mestmans wisely set renovation priorities, allowing time between major projects for the dust to settle and for the family and the house to "relax." Outside, the main problem was landscaping: there wasn't any. Now, a serpentine border encloses rampant ivy, prolific yews, and billowy Korean boxwood, edging the front of the home. In spring, the yard explodes in a vibrant patchwork of blossoms. And a new brick walk meanders up to the grand-columned porch, set, in warm weather, with white rococo-style iron chairs.

Heightening the decorating excitement were the Mestmans' evolving design tastes. Their former home was "very, very country." But, after years of collecting and honing their knowledge of good design, they were ready for a change, ready to write a new chapter in their personal style. "I was a little tired of the tried-and-true look. We wanted something appealing, something unique. I find eclectic rooms so interesting," Reecie explains. "I like a whole range of things: antiques, contemporary art, a touch of the Southwest, even French country. I used to have 15 little things together on a wall. Now I need only one smashing thing."

As comfortable for the family as it is elegant for entertaining, the formal living room (pages 264-265) shows how Reecie uses rich colors for drama. The walls' matte adobe pink was originally a warm shade of rust that has turned rosier with age. The massive dhurrie's muted hues play to the overall tranquil palette, but the rug's precise geometric pattern is a perfect counterpoint to the curvy seating and pottery accents in soft sun-baked colors.

Although the redesigned rooms are a masterful mix of old and new, the home's traditional charm has been carefully preserved. For example, creamy white accentuates the living room's original detailed woodwork and the mantel, topped with a favorite modern painting that echoes the furnishings' fresh pastels.

▲
Butterscotch woods, continental collectibles, and contemporary accents mix delightfully in the casual dining spot, once an untamed breezeway and now annexed to the family room. Country oak chairs ring the table, skirted in saucy stripes under glass. The 18th-century Welsh cupboard brims with antique porcelain.

Rough earthy textures and ▶ rich red colors kindle uncommon warmth in the cozy family room, a garage in a past life. From the subtle verdigris base of the coffee table to the Aztec-style pattern in the upholstery and the unexpected angle of the woolly rug, thoroughly modern elements play to an intriguing geometric theme.

266

STYLE STRATEGIES
PURELY PERSONAL

More traditional in mood than any other room in the home, the formal dining room gathers an antique table and Queen Anne chairs at the bay window, with a view of the manicured gardens. The window treatment is intentionally light, just a gracefully scalloped valance in a bright salmon-toned fabric coordinated with the wall covering. An elaborately carved English cupboard holds collections of silver and brass and a treasured Russian samovar. For entertaining, Reecie mixes old-fashioned lace-edged linens with floral-motif china, Irish crystal, and antique silver, then raids her garden for the fragrant makings of an abundant centerpiece bouquet.

From the polished formality of the living room and tradition-minded dining room, the design tempo shifts into a more casual gear for the everyday living areas. By imaginatively combining a breezeway and garage with a new addition, the Mestmans created a rustic contemporary family room with an informal dining spot (pages 266 and 267) for relaxing with the children and with friends. Sandblasting stripped paint from the exposed brick walls that now add rugged texture and earthy color to the rich organic backdrop. The ceiling is paneled in hardwood, and the floor is a coarse-grained oak.

When Reecie spotted the seating's simmering chili-powder red fabric in a textiles shop, it was love at first sight. "I liked the colors, and I thought it was somewhat dramatic, yet comfortable and wearable—we spend a lot of time in here," Reecie says. The fabric's pattern fits the family room's geometric theme, linking furnishings such as the coffee table's base and the clean angles of the faux-stone console table.

The casual dining spot serves up hospitality in a European country flavor, with a contemporary dash or two. Working the design magic here is an interplay of textures—porcelain, mellow antique woods, a brass chandelier, a slick glass-topped table, and rugged accents, such as aged basketry and an earthenware olive jar. Floral fabric insets, backing the pine Welsh cupboard's shelves, enhance the lively blues of the porcelain on display. A wash of white highlights carved flower basket motifs on the backs of a quartet of old chairs, spiffed up in ebony paint.

▲
Tangy colors in wall covering and scalloped valances add a fresh twist to tradition in the elegant dining room. Queen Anne chairs edge the mahogany table, set in Battenberg lace and heirloom tableware. A sentimental sideboard, the English cupboard with leaded-glass doors was one of the couple's first "finds" as newlyweds.

From screened porch to ▶ sophisticated season-spanning living space, the relaxed sunroom made the transition with its airy appeal beautifully intact. Against a cool neutral backdrop, antique wicker seating is refreshed with teal blue paint and cushioned in the same soft-hued cabana-stripes as the tailored Roman shades.

268

STYLE STRATEGIES
PURELY PERSONAL

Delightful juxtaposition of unexpected elements is the hallmark of a successful eclectic room, and the Mestmans' airy remodeled sun-room (page 269) is no exception. Contemporary art and a sleek glass-topped console table make an intriguing mix with porchy wicker seating, in teal blue, and a 19th-century American pine harvest table. The painted finish on the console's iron base was cued by colors in the striped accent fabric. "I wanted a dark distressed rusty look, the color of antique iron," says Reecie. Warming the sandy-hued quarry tile floor is a soft floral rug in delicate tones of mint green, violet, and blue.

What's the couple's secret to blending disparate ingredients into a high-spirited harmonious whole? "It's color, it's scale, it's texture, and mostly, it's instinct," Reecie explains. "Sometimes I think, 'Oh, that looks great!', but I don't have a reason." She candidly admits that switching from more-cluttered country to cleaned-up eclectic style demanded confidence. "Some of it was scary, but we just decided to go for it," she says. "Friends are extremely complimentary, they're very surprised . . . and pleased."

In picking perfect elements and furnishings for each room, "there have been misses, plenty of misses," she laughs. Whether it's an old favorite or a new acquisition, Reecie "auditions" each piece or accessory before deciding on placement. "I'm always moving things from one room to another. I have things that will spend six months in a room, or a week in a room, then I'll change it again," she says. "It takes on a different look, a different personality, depending on which room I put it in."

As the couple has pared furnishings to a superbly designed few, Reecie says "more and more ends up in the basement. A lot I still can't part with." The Mestmans follow a long-standing rule on major purchases, such as antiques and art: They *both* must love it. "We buy what we like, and we like things that are warm and easy to live with," she explains.

In the expanded master suite, which annexed an old porch, Reecie wanted a frankly feminine ambience, but not so frilly that it would make the gentleman-in-residence uncomfortable. English country's boisterous floral chintzes proved the lively solution, and the rich fabrics imbue the couple's very private retreat with an air of pampered luxury. The precise pattern of the Indian dhurrie rug underfoot tempers the riot of flowers. Here, as in other rooms, Reecie adds the soft, unadorned beauty of pine: a charming Welsh dressing table. "I just love the pale, sandy look of stripped pine . . . it's very versatile," Reecie says.

▲ *Charming details enhance the romance of the master suite. A dainty Welsh pine dressing table showcases family keepsakes and ornately framed photographs and stows a treasured quilt. The wall covering and fabrics wrap the room in luscious shades of raspberry.*

Swathed in a lively bouquet ▶ *of chintz, the master suite enjoys decidedly English country appeal with an old-and-new mix. The lacy reproduction iron bed has an old-world look that links it in spirit with the Victorian-era wardrobe and antique accents.*

STYLE STRATEGIES
HOME AT HEART

In romantic rose-scented rooms bedecked in linen and lace, Jennifer Quaal has staged a great escape. Her vintage-1915 bungalow, near a lake, was once a city-dweller's summer retreat. Now, with fresh cottage appeal inside and out, it spans all seasons beautifully. To recapture the cozy past, Jennifer followed her heart and design instincts. "If you surround yourself with things you love, you really make your home comfortable, tranquil, and inviting," she says.

◀ *Irresistibly romantic and richly layered, a white-on-white scheme in the bungalow's living room unifies a comfy complement of antique seating beneath snowy linen upholstery and lavish lace-edged pillows.*

Even the public face of the ▶ *reborn bungalow exudes nostalgic cottage character, with lush landscaping, window boxes brimming with blooms, and a glimpse of lace through the window.*

STYLE STRATEGIES
HOME AT HEART

Burnished woods and natural accents provide rustic counterpoint to more refined furnishings in the living room. The 1820s walnut secretary holds antique toys and family keepsakes.

◀ Warmed by sun filtering through the windows' playfully knotted lace panels, the airy solarium invites relaxing on the graceful daybed, its cushion dressed in a 1930s drawnwork tablecloth.

Treasures such as family-tree tintypes in silver frames add sentimental detail. ▼

Boasting original stained-glass windows, plaster crown moldings, and mellow oak flooring hidden for years under carpet, the bungalow's airy living room showcases Jennifer's spontaneous and sentimental decorating style and her collectible pursuits from birdcages to quilts.

A collector since childhood, Jennifer was just a teenager when she bought her first major antique: the living room's circa-1820 walnut secretary. A trip to Belgium several years ago introduced Jennifer to the intricate laces that would become not only her personal design signature, but also her livelihood as the owner of an imported lace and antiques shop. "Lace can go so many different directions," Jennifer says. "It can be crisp and clean, also ornate."

Against a pristine backdrop, the living room's beckoning mix of 19th-century seating—heirloom sofa, rocker, and chairs in wicker and wood—gathers guests for intimate talk around the fireplace. With new linen upholstery and plump lacy pillows, the diverse pieces share the same cottage spirit. The white-on-white scheme is Jennifer's canvas. "I like to be able to change fabrics and quilts. In the summer, everything is stark white. In the fall and winter months, I like to have a lot of quilts and tapestry pillows—things richer and warmer—tossed everywhere," she says.

Attention to detail nurtures the romance. New and old laces, judiciously chosen and beautifully mixed, summon a sense of grown-up luxury without being saccharine. Lavish runners soften the mantel, a drawnwork cloth drapes the coffee table, and at high tea, antique cups top wispy doily-lined saucers. Sweet scents waft from the living room alcove, where Jennifer sun-dries herbs and blends potpourri at an old pine worktable.

The solarium, off the living room, has decidedly Victorian flair, with aged wicker, clad in fresh white paint, arranged on a new parquet floor. In this sunny sitting spot, there's a more generous helping of lacy fabrics. "Each room is a little bit different," says Jennifer, who changes accents such as quilts and lacework for an everyday change of mood. When flowing panels proved too long for the solarium windows, she simply knotted each one for a charming, and shorter, new look.

STYLE STRATEGIES
HOME AT HEART

◄ Rose-toned prints and stripes link beautifully, and intentionally, mismatched seating in the convivial dining room.

The new view from the ► updated kitchen is flavored with Victorian gingerbread—fretwork that once adorned a porch.

Soft colors in richly layered accents warm the gracious dining room where Jennifer's romantic finishing-touch philosophy prevails. It's "doing those little things for yourself and your friends that used to be commonplace." The turn-of-the-century oak table might be covered in a quilt topped with Battenberg lace, or a large fabric square with corners artistically knotted, then set with an array of antique china. "None of my dishes and silverware match," Jennifer says. "I don't like that put-together look. I like to do the unexpected." The handsome circa-1860 dry sink accommodates linen storage. Because she has only two real-life doves and more than 40 old birdcages, the leftover cages become a fanciful window treatment.

Prized among her treasures are the cozy bedroom's furnishings: a hand-painted cottage pine bedroom set from the late 1800s, a style that was popular in rambling Victorian summer homes. The bedcover is a 1930s print tablecloth. Found in a forgotten crawl space in the house, the old screen was renewed with lace panels. Bandboxes, curtains, and a plush oval rug add appealing floral pattern to the restful scheme. Dolls aboard the wicker settee are from her father's childhood toy box.

Recognizing the potential of castoffs is, indeed, one of her fortes. In the renovated bath, the clean-lined pedestal sink and slat-back chair, now painted and cushioned in a pastel print, were found abandoned in an alley. Another "find" from a garage sale embellishes the kitchen windows: fretwork that once graced an old Victorian house.

◄ Embellished with painted roses and berries, a 19th-century cottage pine bed encores as a nostalgic centerpiece for the cozy bedroom.

▲ Once a dingy space with damaged walls, this bath boasts old-world appeal with new wainscoting and sponge-painted walls.

STYLE STRATEGIES
SIMPLY SERENE

▲
Custom built in the 1930s, the couple's redesigned suburban home honors architectural traditions of Federal colonial style with appealing symmetry in the tall shuttered windows.

Eras artfully mingle in the ▶ living room corner where a Louis XVI reproduction chair and marquetry table team up with contemporary art. An aged sundial and painted Italian bocci ball accent the faux marble mantel.

◀ *The elegant living room is an inspired study in contrast, with modern furnishings and a creamy backdrop playing up antiques, such as the 18th-century painted chest-turned-bar. Bibelots cluster on a sparkling glass coffee table that seems to float atop an old block-and-tackle base.*

With a broad brush of tranquil hues and a minimalist perspective, interior designer Veronique Louvet and her husband Les Miller helped their home to see the light. Once a gloomy realm, it has emerged as an elegant sun-washed oasis where East meets West, reflecting Veronique's love of spare Japanese interiors and her French roots. She describes her design style as "simplicity with soul."

STYLE STRATEGIES
SIMPLY SERENE

To create mood-soothing rooms, "we stripped every-thing—walls, floors—and painted surfaces white, and discovered a house full of light," says Veronique. Throughout, backdrops are restrained to enhance the sculptural quality and integrity of the carefully selected furnishings. Minimal window treatments accent architecture and welcome sunshine as an essential design element.

Veronique believes the void she leaves around each piece of furniture is as important as the piece itself. "I like to play with volumes, contrast, and texture, the way the Japanese do in their gardens," she says. "In designing, I use all my senses . . . I work largely on instinct."

◄ *The sleek Le Corbusier-style table and sculptural folding chairs, clad in black leather, imbue the sunny dining room with a gardenlike ambience.*

▲ *Gray glazed walls and black sisal carpet create a cozy "cocooning" effect in the family room/library.*

STYLE STRATEGIES
SIMPLY SERENE

To Veronique and Les, comfort means surrounding themselves with things they love, though their passions span centuries—from baroque and French provincial pieces to Japanese folk art and sleek contemporary furnishings. "I don't like imitations," she says. "Rather than try to create an instant heritage, I'd rather wait and buy a nice piece that has some history." This unexpected mix creates room schemes of subtle intrigue down to the smallest detail, such as tablescapes with antique bocci balls and favorite decorative objects gleaned from the couple's world travels.

◀ *Creamy colors soothe the master suite anchored by a bed, set directly on the floor, Japanese-style. An ornate antique mirror delivers elegant counterpoint.*

Softly draped with an unhemmed fabric square tied at the edges, the bedroom's leggy iron garden table is the perfect stage for an artistic composition of sentimental treasures.
▼

STYLE STRATEGIES
AN ECLECTIC MIX

▲
Its straightforward architecture typical of Midwest "pattern book" houses, the renovated 1870 home dons original shutters and new paint.

Soft backdrops, mush- ▶
room wall color and crisp white paint on shutters and trim link the living room and front parlor featuring the home's original coal-burning fireplace with cement surround feather-grained to mimic marble.

◀ *A free-spirited mix of furnishings and mirthful accents heighten the congenial mood of the living room. Atop the antique rug, simply styled seating is updated with contemporary white slipcovers. Aged woods and well-chosen collectibles add contrast.*

For collectors Margot and Jim Ladwig, coming home was the journey of a century, from a slick city high rise to an 1870 Midwest classic that offered inherent character, but posed the challenge of major renovation. With design vision, a respect for their home's historical mien, and a delightful and unpredictable amalgam of treasures, the couple created these warmly personal rooms.

STYLE STRATEGIES
AN ECLECTIC MIX

Beyond crumbling plaster and old-house wrinkles, the Ladwigs saw an appealing early rendition of today's open-plan interiors in the home's somewhat small rooms that flow easily together through broad entryways. So, with restoration architect Stephen Knutson, the Ladwigs polished when possible and rebuilt when necessary, taking great care to preserve the home's integral features.

"We wanted the permanent things in the house to be pure," says Margot. "We felt it was important to really respect the house and do it the way it was done originally. But, with things that can be removed, well, we had fun!"

For the interior stage, aged maple floors were refinished, original mullioned windows were painstakingly restored, and walls were replaced. A subtle color connection—wall colors in four shades on a gray-beige theme—visually links the free-flowing spaces, with the lightest hue in the front parlor and living room, the deepest debuting in breakfast room and kitchen at the back. Crisp white adds striking definition to old woodwork and new shutters.

Attuned to the Ladwigs' easy-living style and informal entertaining area, the living room and front parlor (pages 284 and 285), by design, seem to merge into one gracious space set with lovingly blended elements. Margot dressed the rooms' soft seating in summer whites, but likes the look so much she leaves the slipcovers on year-round as contrast to more rustic chairs and folksy accents. The living room coffee table is a small-space solution: custom-cut glass on metal-base balls. Once separated from the living room by a door, the front parlor enjoys splendid focus—the old coal-burning fireplace—and new function with open-shelved cabinetry.

From antique toys and textiles to contemporary folk art, simplicity and whimsy mark the collections the couple began as newlyweds, when a shoestring budget taught them to be creative. Whatever strikes their fancy just might be carted home. A case in point: the portrait above the living room's drop-leaf table. "We don't like old paintings, but we liked her. We thought we didn't have any ancestral paintings, so we adopted one," laughs Margot.

A twist on tradition, the dining room, with elegant chairs, starkly modern table, and homey accents, exudes the essence of "Ladwig style"—a confidence in combining disparate design elements for impact and personality. The extraordinary dining table—a 6-foot round glass disk on a shiny-metal photo lab print-drying drum—is perfect in this small setting because its reflective surfaces play to the light, visually expanding the space.

Because skimpy kitchens were typical of Victorian homes, the Ladwigs' newly spacious breakfast room and kitchen annexed a pantry and stairway to the old cookroom. Rustic furnishings and seasonal amenities make this inviting space a popular family gathering spot. The compact kitchen and eating area function together as a great room, giving the Ladwigs the best of both worlds.

◀ *Whether it's coffee and croissants or a casual buffet supper, the airy breakfast room and kitchen carved from the old cookroom, pantry, and back stairs enjoy newfound function and style.*

▲ *Subtly traditional, the dining room gathers graceful Chippendale-style chairs around a table made by topping a photo lab print-drying drum with a huge glass disk cushioned on cork.*

STYLE STRATEGIES
AN ECLECTIC MIX

◀ *Against a tranquil-hued backdrop, the master bedroom is simply set to soothe, with the bed sumptuously dressed in a down-filled duvet. Native American textiles and a bevy of baskets add color and textural interest.*

Tiny but talented, the cozy library is a family favorite for reading and entertainment, with requisite electronic gear tucked among books and artifacts displayed in custom cabinetry. ▼

▲
Once a small bedroom, the bath emerges with vintage character, thanks to the pedestal sink and tile floor.

Change is an important tenet of the Ladwigs' fluid welcome-home decorating style. Against the rooms' showcaselike backdrops, art, accents, and furnishings are on the move, shifting positions easily and beautifully, without upsetting a scheme. For example, in the breakfast room, the small sofa might change places with the hearthside table, or, in the parlor, collectibles might emerge any moment in a new and eye-catching mix. Because the Ladwigs' motto is "live your art," expect the unexpected in unlikely places.

"I could never own a house that was left the way the previous owners had done it," says Margot. "I have this great need to make it my own. It's the doing that I love. It's always in a state of change."

In the home's new library, change was definitely in order. Once a small bedroom, "This was just a simple straightforward room with the plaster falling off the walls!" Margot laughs. To cozy-up the library, where the family gathers for entertainment and quiet evenings together, carpet warms the floor, and the deepest mushroom shades the walls. With access to a new full bath, the library is also a suite set for overnight guests. The simple-lined sofa is clad in black fabric, and the chairs are resale-shop finds. As in other rooms, accents are a carefully chosen mix: an old Navajo rug, a toy plane, Peruvian dolls, poster art, and an antique Amazon walking stick. Here, as in other rooms, recessed lighting makes the wise small-space choice because it illuminates unobtrusively.

Today, the master bedroom is an airy, restful retreat accented with the American handcrafted textiles and collectibles the Ladwigs love. But, its metamorphosis has been dramatic. Initially, the space was a large antiquated bathroom, a hallway, and "a very mean back stairway. We had to take a deep breath and deal with it," Knutson recalls. Because the ceilings are lower here in the back part of the house, the Ladwigs step down into the new master bedroom. "This worked out to be a very nice advantage, making for a very romantic suite," Knutson says. Even in rooms redone from scratch, such as an upstairs bedroom-turned-bathroom, materials and accents were chosen to imbue each new space with nostalgic character.

STYLE STRATEGIES
NEW TRADITIONS

A new sun-welcoming wrap of pretty-paned windows hints compellingly that, inside, Chris and Elizabeth Williams' suburban bungalow has changed its attitude. Sharing a savvy sense of design and inspired by a love of rich colors and antiques, the Williamses have imprinted their own elegantly timeless style on the updated 1917 home.

▲
Tucked along a tree-lined suburban street, the modest bungalow found its place in the sun after a dark enclosed porch was opened up with wraparound windows that flood the interior with light.

◄ *Extending a dramatic welcome, the striking black-and-white tiled entry succeeds in the unimpeded flow of space and sunlight. Custom fretwork echoes the design of Chippendale-style chairs set for relaxing.*

A deft mix of heirloom ▶ furnishings, fresh chintz, and vibrant color imbues the living room with easy elegance. Gathered on the dhurrie rug are an Italian-style sofa, club chairs, and a Victorian armchair.

STYLE STRATEGIES
NEW TRADITIONS

Just across the threshold, the Williamses' home makes a stunning first impression as visitors step into an "entry atrium" (page 290), tiled in black and white and railed in Chinese-style fretwork. A quest for light-drenched interiors led to the creation of this all-season sun-catcher, once a dark enclosed porch walled off from the living room.

But the entry is simply Act I. With the garden-theme fabrics of an English country house, the living room (pages 290-291) exemplifies Elizabeth's flair for dramatic color. Here, the backdrop is warmed in a lively shade of coral, echoed in the comfy upholstered pieces, sofa accents, and window treatment. "I think the color of the walls makes the room," she says. Coordinated chintz fabric, in a mix of contemporary patterns, blends the varied-vintage seating. Elizabeth feels that "when you put a bright chintz on an older piece of furniture, it makes it young again."

With its traditional elegance and easy attitude, the living room "has a nice feeling for entertaining." Combining furnishings without regard to period or pedigree makes a room more interesting, she says. "I don't like a room to look like a showroom. I think it works better to mix different styles."

Symmetry of warm color and timeless furnishings links the living room and formal dining room, anchored by an heirloom table that long ago held trophies at a North Carolina hunt club. With the deletion of a wall, the two rooms now constitute a single gracious space, but new columns visually define their separate functions and add architectural interest. Pastel-patterned dhurrie rugs soften the rooms' oak flooring, stained antique brown.

Throughout, collectibles and treasured art have been pared for impact. In the living room, the garden-theme painting above the antique English chest was inspired by colors in a fabric swatch. Fanciful accents come from Elizabeth's menagerie: porcelain and hand-painted rabbits she attributes to her "bunny mania" that began in college.

In the informal dining area and kitchen, bold color, including lavender-blue on the walls, light-look furnishings, and mellow oak flooring join in a more contemporary scheme. This high-function space was once a small bedroom and a "very primitive" kitchen with five entrances.

Covered in chintz, Victorian and Louis XV chairs share a sun-washed sitting spot.

Luscious colors, rich-hued ▶ wood, and sparkling white furnishings set a contemporary mood in the casual dining area off the kitchen. The laminated Parsons table is a practical choice for this well-used space.

A wall tumbled and graceful columns rose to create a visually exciting grand entrance to the gracious formal dining room that flows from the living room and echoes the same lively color and floral theme.
▼

STYLE STRATEGIES
NEW TRADITIONS

When Chris and Elizabeth were house-hunting and visited their bungalow-to-be, Elizabeth recalls that, though it seemed short on family-size spaces, she liked its inherent cozy feeling. The couple called in architect Paul Konstant to redefine the spaces to fit their life-style. A two-story addition was added to the back of the house, and the roofline was extended. The home's second floor originally offered only one tiny bedroom and an attic, but, by combining new and old spaces, the home gained two generous-size bedrooms plus a bath and a half-bath.

Skylights keep the inviting master bedroom on the bright side by day and offer a glimpse of the stars by night. A wedding gift from Elizabeth's parents, the bed is embellished with wheat-motif carvings. Softly regal colors and exquisite linens and laces imbue the retreat with a feeling of luxury. "Everything in the room is really traditional, except for the room itself," says Elizabeth. Accents include antique plates and cherished photos in the hand-painted frames Elizabeth has been collecting for years.

Lovingly decorated and waiting to welcome the Williamses' new daughter, Elizabeth Anne, the nursery draws its tranquillity from a gentle pastel palette, white wicker furnishings, and flowered fabric accents. Balloon shades add the perfect soft touch to new windows. The fabrics' tiny-flower pattern repeats in the wall border, hand-painted porcelain lamp, and basket atop the chest.

◄ *A lighthearted pattern of pink garlands bowed in baby-blue ribbons ties together soft fabrics and sweet accents in the airy under-the-eaves nursery. The windows provide sunny exposure and new architectural interest.*

A true-to-tradition retreat ► nestled into the home's new contemporary-style addition, the master bedroom tempts loungers and sleepyheads with a grand old four-poster, elegantly outfitted in gossamer laces and linens. A few choice furnishings and accents enhance the timeless appeal.

LIVING SPACES

A home's major public spaces—living room, family room, great room, and den—deserve thoughtful attention. Living spaces, even the most elegant and formally furnished, should make family and friends feel welcome. Here, adults and children alike seek put-your-feet-up, let-your-hair-down comfort and ease. Furnishings in these spaces should be stylish yet functional, and never stifling to fun. If your house lacks a separate space for casual, carefree times, then by all means loosen up your living room to fulfill this very important function. In this chapter you'll find a selection of welcoming living spaces to suit any life-style.

LIVING SPACES
PERSONAL PREFERENCES

Designing welcome-home living spaces with plenty of living potential means, first, defining their roles in your family's life and style. Lacking obvious bedroom or dining room duties, living spaces are more flexible, prime for customized comfort and function. Ultimately, how well they serve and soothe depends upon your planning and decorating ingenuity.

To maximize livability, create appealing ambience, and make astute furnishings choices, consider how your living room or family room works. Is it a bustling everyday hub, or the company-only equivalent of yesterday's "front parlor"? Is entertaining there formal or casual? What family activities are on tap—hearthside conversation, home entertainment, hobbies, games with the children? Do you also want private spots for reading and relaxing?

In your decorating plan, look at the living space's relationship to other rooms and its architectural amenities—an elegant fireplace, carved moldings, built-in bookcases, or symmetrically balanced windows—that may dictate furniture arrangement, and even inspire a formal or informal mood. Is there an entry hall or foyer, or is the living space the first stop and first impression for guests? Could you reroute traffic around the main conversation area simply by rearranging furniture? Do you want to link living and dining areas in the same decorative spirit?

Today's homes may be smaller, but there is an increasing demand on living spaces to serve multiple roles. With dual-purpose furniture and a clever hand with design elements, less, indeed, can be more. Modulars or a stylish sleep sofa helps your living space moonlight as a guest room. A drop-leaf sofa table rises to the occasional dinner party. Or, visually stretch a diminutive living space with a splash of white paint, recessed lighting, and a ban on clutter.

An antique Swedish painted ▶
cupboard cues the fresh palette
and timelessly elegant mood of a
flower lover's living room. Rich
fabrics grant restyled sofas and
old chairs a new lease on life.

LIVING SPACES
ELEGANT EXPRESSIONS

Whether traditional flair or casual elegance suits your living space, let design elements set a formal or informal mood. Symmetrically balanced furniture groups are more formal than random ones, mahogany pieces more formal than scrubbed pine, and silk and damask more formal than rough-textured fabrics.

• Formal elements include walls in fabric, pastel colors, and historic papers such as documentary prints or florals; Oriental rugs and broadloom carpet; swag-and-jabot window treatments, cornices, and draperies.

• Informal elements encompass homey textures, bright colors, and accents with a handmade look, such as brick or natural wood walls; dhurrie, sisal, or Berber carpets; and windows with blinds, shutters, shades, cafés, or curtains.

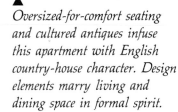

▲
Oversized-for-comfort seating and cultured antiques infuse this apartment with English country-house character. Design elements marry living and dining space in formal spirit.

◄ *A collector's well-edited living room casts an ornate Victorian fireplace as the focus for conversation. A lacquered Chinese-motif screen adds dramatic contrast to the pristine backdrop.*

Rich garnet walls, clusters ▶ of keepsakes, and a mix of settle-back seating enhance the cozy appeal of this library. The glass-topped table is file cabinets topped with plywood and fitted with a tailored skirt.

LIVING SPACES
ROOMS BY DESIGN

▲
Carved out of newly liberated space, an at-ease living room tempts with a spirited mix of new and old. Accent fabrics and an Oriental rug warm up the cool white scheme.

◄ *Soaring windows and spectacular alpine vistas grant focus to this room, a blend of restful colors, natural textures, and set-for-comfort seating.*

The quilt-inspired ► geometry of a custom-crafted rug sets the stage in this airy family oasis, wrapped in soothing neutrals. Mellow woods and wicker add textural intrigue.

Successful living spaces turn on the right mix of comfort components, with ample seating topping the list. A sofa or two is standard, but a pair of love seats may fit better. Versatile modular seating adapts to varying arrangements and can maximize floor space. Complete this primary furniture grouping with at least two lounge chairs, plus supporting players such as seat-side tables, coffee table, lamps, and ottomans. Gather conversation-area seating around a focal point—a view, a fireplace, bookshelves, a wall of art, a media center, or a tall armoire for vertical interest and storage. For visual balance and added function, plan secondary activity centers for work, casual dining, or out-of-the-mainstream pursuits such as reading. Spotlight your decorating with overall mood lighting and specific tabletop task lighting for reading, writing, and games. Floor lamps and recessed and track lighting are practical space savers.

LIVING SPACES
FIRESIDE STORIES

Most impressive among a living room's architectural assets is the fireplace, a natural focus for family activities and decorating. Consider it a major piece of furniture, and, as the focal point for seating, its character should complement furnishings. Warm a country room with a natural-wood mantel and antique fireplace accessories. In a traditional scheme, try carved wood paneling, or tile or marble facing. Stone, set-in mirrors, or simple brick works well for contemporary settings. Magnify fireplace impact, flanking it with shelves for books and collectibles. During off-duty months, pile the hearth with fresh flowers or greenery. Adding a built-in fireplace is expensive, but today's freestanding fireplaces provide a quick and economical alternative, offering versatility in style.

▲
Rich watercolor fabrics bridge the gap between the rustic backdrop and refined antiques in this easygoing living room. Random-width paneling and a cargo of Chinese porcelain enhance the hearth's appeal. Laminated linen gives today's coffee table a formal finish.

◄ *A sophisticated mix of accents, soft color, and an antique-look wall covering give a once stark-white living room new warmth and casual elegance. Peachy damask dresses a restyled sofa trio, and crisp trim and contemporary art add focus to the fireplace wall.*

◀ *Topped by an 18th-century fireboard that recalls the era of great clipper ships, the fireplace is a magnet for comfy seating and intriguing collectibles that make this an inviting spot for relaxing.*

Bold-patterned fabric rescued the paired armless chairs rounding out hearthside seating in this live-in library. Creamy walls play up the patina of the room's burnished woods. Eclectic art, colorful books, and collectibles parade across the mantel. ▼

LIVING SPACES
REVIVAL TECHNIQUES

Redecorating rallies a wear-weary room's style, improves its function, and sparks new personality. Here are some savvy redo ideas that also are easy on the budget:

• Create a start-to-finish decorating plan, in phases scheduled as time and money allow. Research new products and decorating ideas before adding new furnishings.

• Analyze your room's obvious flaws, and target priorities. Fresh paint, color accents, upholstery, or refinished furniture and floors make a quick difference. Simply rearranging furniture delivers a visual lift without the expense of redecorating. Buy fabric for a whole project at once, because dye lots vary and patterns may be discontinued.

• Rethink room and furniture function before buying new pieces. With children grown, is the family room now a Mom-and-Pop retreat? Could an armoire corral electronics gear, a treasured trunk turn coffee table, or a gateleg table serve as sofa table?

• Make thoughtful choices in personality accents, gradually adding favorite collectibles and art.

◀ *Comfort rules in a garden-inspired living room, where aged wicker, clad in fresh fabrics, tempts lingering for a look at fanciful collectibles.*

Serene sans clutter, this wood-warmed living room invites an old sofa and chairs into the new scheme under creamy canvas covers. ▼

White paint, graphic wallpaper, cotton-candy-pink canvas upholstery, and a bevy of homespun accents deliver a personality pickup.

A crisped-up backdrop and lively tartan-cued colors coax a classic family room/library into a modern mood. ▼

LIVING SPACES
COMFORT ZONES

Turning up the comfort level in living rooms, family rooms, or all-purpose living spaces doesn't mean you must sacrifice style. Literally relax your decorating scheme with good-looking durable furnishings and easy-care accents. Then your hardworking family center will still mind its company manners. Today's fabrics are elegant but tough, thanks to technology, and fabric finishes help upholstery and slipcovers repel soils and stains. Even synthetic suedes easily wipe clean. Give floors the no-fuss treatment with plush stain-resistant carpet, stylish no-wax and resilient flooring, quarry tile, or mellow-grained wood protected with coats of polyurethane. For walls, consider vinyl wall coverings, easy-to-clean painted finishes, or treated wood paneling. Special furniture finishes provide a worry-free option, and timeworn woods that don't fret over scratches add appealing character.

Put-your-feet-up comfort comes first in this rustic-flavored family room. A pine armoire stows entertainment gear, and casual dining is at hearthside. ▼

Mellow woods and hardy ▶ fabrics ensure easy living. The bay encourages child's play at a pint-size table. Folk art accents abound.

LIVING SPACES
COMFORT ZONES

Graceful old wicker, gussied up in rosy florals and crisp plaid, romances a sun-filled all-season porch turned family retreat. ▼

Sunny sidecar to a new ▶ *kitchen, this family room relaxes with a mix of overstuffed seating and garden accents.*

Creating a just-for-the-family room, apart from the living room, begins with the search for space. Then, turn your attention to activities-centered decorating to customize its function. Remodeling a basement, attic, attached garage, or enclosed porch into a family room is less expensive than a new addition. With multifunctional furnishings, a rarely used formal dining room or spare bedroom can play a dual role. Or, bring back the conviviality of yesterday's keeping room by adding a cozy sitting spot to a large kitchen.

Even though you may be spiffing up old furniture for the new space, gear the seating arrangement and amenities to family activities. For music lovers, consider the room's acoustics in choosing ceiling, wall, and floor coverings. Organize entertainment equipment in wall systems that free up floor space and expand storage. Designate creative zones, such as an artist's work space by a sunny window, or a children's play area, wrapped in easy-care materials.

Artfully tucked into media-wall niches, a complement of home electronics gets organized in the contemporary family hub. Soft sculptural chairs treat viewers to front-row seats. ▼

An on-the-bias area rug anchors this casual family room, lightened up with fresh paint, slipcovers, and miniblinds. The cut-down coffee table came from the kitchen. ▶

LIVING SPACES
COMFORT ZONES

Consider family-living spaces your canvas, a chance to artfully express your clan's personality and showcase favorite pursuits. Your reward is warm one-of-a-kind style, and your room is destined to become an inviting gathering spot for family and friends. Give the collector room to display cherished finds, and provide gallery space for the family's painter, weaver, or photographer. Let particular passions, such as whimsical folk art or Native American textiles, set the mood and cue the palette. Celebrate family talents and interests by turning handcrafts, hobby projects, and travel treasures into decorating accents. For the bookish set, create cozy library ambience with wall shelving stacked with colorful volumes.

This cozy family room is one for the books, capitalizing on traditional library trappings, classic furnishings, and warm barn-red color to set the mood. ▼

With space-stretching neutrals, modular seating, and sleek built-ins for desk work, display, and storage, a retreat-for-two got organized. ▶

DINING ROOMS

The very words imply hospitality: dining room. A place apart from the hustle and bustle of busy, often hectic, lives; a place to enjoy the good things that come when we gather to dine with family or friends. Never mind if your dining room isn't formal, or if it's not a self-contained room. A corner in the living room, an ell, a hallway, or any sliver of space will do. The important word here is "dining," not eating on the run, but savoring—at leisure—both the food and the people it's shared with. This chapter is designed to whet your appetite with a smorgasbord of delectable dining ideas.

DINING ROOMS
DINING IN STYLE

An antidote to fast food and fast-paced living, the dining room has foiled the occasional predictions of home-space planners that it is headed for extinction. It has not only survived, it is thriving, emerging in dazzling style and enjoying new importance as an at-home oasis for nourishing body and spirit. There's a welcome revival of the dinner hour, that busy-day time-out for meals and conversation with the family. For many, it's a welcome chance to show off culinary skills. And sharing good food with good friends tops any home-entertainment list.

Dining-in style begins with ambience, creating the right mood to make meals, from family-style to party-fancy, special occasions. So, consider your at-home entertaining and dining-out preferences. Are dinner parties usually casual fare, the table set with old pottery atop a bandanna-print cloth? Is dining strictly a formal affair calling for your best china, crystal, and heirloom silver? Or is your style family-style, and your dining room busy between meals as an everyday living space? Is your favorite restaurant cozy colonial, starkly contemporary, or elegantly upscale in design? Your decorating scheme should also complement your home's overall style, especially if the dining space is visible from other rooms.

Let this ambience guide choices in furniture and design elements that, together, define your personal style. You'll find a smorgasbord of dining room furniture on the market, from traditional, country, and contemporary, to art deco, neoclassic, and Scandinavian. Set a stage with era-evoking antiques, or go with a gracious amalgam of collectibles. Whether you dine in a formal space, or an imaginatively improvised setting, these dining rooms are packed with design ideas to inspire you.

Comfort tops the spirited ▶
design menu in this two-way
dining room set with curvy easy
chairs at the ebonized oak table.
For entertaining, the grouping
moves to room center, and
another chair is added.

DINING ROOMS
DINING IN STYLE

Like prized recipes that win acclaim for the cook, delightful dining rooms succeed on the ingredients, and how you blend them for mood and function. Your room's staging may be striking, but if diners are cramped elbow-to-elbow at a too-small table, or the lighting is too bright, or the chairs are uncomfortable, your production may falter long before dessert.

To create a dining room as functional as it is appealing, consider these basics on space planning, furnishings, and design elements:

● First, plan your room with entertaining and everyday meals in mind. Measure the room's dimensions carefully, and draw a detailed floor plan. Factor in traffic patterns, and space and placement for dining furniture, tableware and linen storage, additional seating, and serving extras such as tea carts and buffets. Plan a minimum of three feet of extra space around the table for easy seating and serving. If possible, site the dining area near the kitchen for the host's convenience.

● Table-and-chair options are myriad in shape, style, size, and materials. Before buying a table, consider the maximum number of diners most frequently served, because each diner should have ample elbow and leg room. Before combining mismatched dining pieces, measure the height of the table and the chair arms to make sure the seats can slip under the table. For small-space dining rooms, try fold-away tables and chairs. If the table is used for homework or children's projects, look at plastic laminates, impervious to wear, or tabletops with special surface protection.

● Choose upholstery fabrics and materials, such as flooring and wall coverings, for durability and easy care if the dining room is a mainstream family living space. Forgo the sleek glass-top table or the suede chairs if you have young children in your household.

● Nothing sparks dining room drama and romance like candlelight. But, for function, also add overhead illumination, such as on-track down-lighting, or a ceiling-hung fixture suspended about 34 to 36 inches above the table. Install a dimmer switch to control the mood, because overly bright lighting is unflattering to faces, food, and furnishings. The lighting plan should be versatile, making the room look as good at brunch as it does for midnight supper. Large dining rooms need secondary light sources, such as decorative wall sconces.

● In picking the room's palette, consider the time of day it is most frequently used. Depending on your lighting plan, wall color in a bold apple-green may be dramatic for dinner, but overbearing at brunch. Pretty by day, soft pastels may wash out by night.

▲
Set against a striped backdrop, this dining space melds old and new for formal flair—Regency-style chairs with a sleek table, and an antique mirror with contemporary sconces.

An unexpected dash of ▶ sunny yellow on chair cushions stirs excitement in an elegant dining room. For serving and storage, a 12-foot-long buffet tucks into the tableside niche.

DINING ROOMS
DINING IN STYLE

Call it personal style, call it serendipity, but, today, there's more mix than match in dining room furnishings. Even table settings can be a beautiful, and intentional, mismatch. Eclectic design and an enduring passion for country-style decorating inspire wonderfully personalized one-of-a-kind dining rooms, studded with collectible treasures, geared to comfort, and unrivaled in hospitality.

Inherently functional, dining tables and chairs need not come in matched suites anymore. For example, anchor your room with an old pine table, then choose seating in wicker or Windsor, or invite in odd-couple chairs of golden oak. To unify a seating mix, add cushions of like fabric, or pick fabrics with a common denominator color, and upholster each seat in a different pattern.

Taken out of context, individual pieces of furniture can add visual spice to any dining room, and provide focal points for schemes. Instead of a traditional breakfront or hutch, an old painted armoire adds character and color, while earning its keep as a cache for linens and tableware. As a buffet, consider a French baker's rack, an antique commode or dresser, or double-duty bookshelves.

◀ *A showstopping painted armoire inspired the soft palette of this rustic-yet-refined dining room. As useful as it is beautiful, the 18th-century Swedish cupboard stores linens and china. Atop the dhurrie rug, an old tailor's worktable teams up with reproduction Windsor chairs.*

French country prints ▶ and natural textures relax this sun-washed dining room. Dressed in new cushions, off-the-porch wicker invites diners to dally at the old pine table. Accents include Chinese porcelain platters, a French chandelier, and modern art.

DINING ROOMS
DINING IN STYLE

Apartment dwellers have long known the secret of living well in compact spaces, and today's smaller homes have prompted a closer look at how they do it. Individual dining rooms are often a luxury, but you needn't forgo the fun of entertaining just because you're shy on square footage. A variety of ingenious now-you-see-it, now-you-don't dining tables that slip into a sliver of space or stage a disappearing act when the party's over are on the market. Handsome wood consoles hold pullout tables to seat 10 diners comfortably. Flip-top tables turn over a new leaf to double their size at dinnertime. Such flexible furnishings make the anywhere-dining room a success. For seating, add stackable or folding chairs. For a nostalgic mood, install a Shaker-style peg rack to hang chairs on the wall. Even lounge chairs or mismatched wooden seats, gleaned from other rooms and cushioned in coordinated fabrics, report smartly for table duty.

▲ *A medley of elegant painted finishes—salmon walls, creamy white chairs, and a deep blue floor spattered with pastels— enrich a small dining room.*

◀ *Luxurious silk fabrics and exquisite Oriental motifs in accents and the hand-painted wall covering make everyday dining in a foyer a special occasion.*

Whatever the occasion, ▶ *this dining room offers café ambience with tables and banquettes in spirited fabrics. Off duty, it's a sitting spot for coffee and conversation.*

DINING ROOMS
DINING IN STYLE

If your dining room stands idly by between dinner parties, or you yearn for a gracious dining spot but can't find the space, rethink function, then rewrite the design script. Clever casting of rooms in new dual roles enhances a home's livability, and welcomes underused or single-purpose spaces into everyday family life.

Look beyond the room's "dining" label, and discover its natural resources. The table is simply a spacious work surface for many activities, not just the children's homework. You already have chairs there to accommodate the clan, working on family projects or relaxing between meals. Even small additions can help the dining room achieve new potential. Create a reading nook with a window seat and bookshelves that double as buffet serving ledges for entertaining. Or, ensconce an antique daybed in a cozy corner for a sitting spot plus guest bedroom.

Without an "official" dining room, you can still dish up memorable hospitality by creating dining spots in unexpected places, such as the living room, den, solarium, foyer, or even a hallway. Disguise the dining table as a game, sofa, library, or cocktail table, then, when guests are due, dress it in colorful linens and tableware. Off-duty dining chairs can double as occasional chairs in other rooms. If you lack the space to leave the table up, take a cue from diminutive dining rooms, and consider cabinet-type foldaway tables, or drop-leaf tables that unobtrusively hug the wall.

Such double-duty arrangements require imagination and a thoughtful approach to the basics. Placing the table off-center, instead of in the middle of the room, liberates floor space and eases traffic flow. Between meals, keep the table at its smallest size, ample for games and desk work. Adequate and convenient storage for the accoutrements of lovely table settings is, perhaps, the biggest problem when dining spots sprout in unlikely places. In a dining ell, where space flows from the living room, consider a low divider with storage behind sliding doors and buffet space on top. If you transform an entryway into a dining area, use a nearby guest closet for storage, or use a rolling cart to transport tableware from kitchen or pantry storage to the dining area.

Sharing space and fabrics with the living room, the dining spot dresses a glass-top table in chintz and chairs in moiré.

Plumped with pillows and treated to a view, an antique daybed turns this dining room into a reading nook, sitting spot, and overnight guest room.

Colorful books and collectibles ▶ spice up the eclectic dining room/library with an English Regency settee for relaxed reading or extra-guest seating.

324

BEDROOMS

"Options" is the big word in bedrooms these days. From beds to decorative embellishments, from lighting to lavish linens, from fancy entertainment units to high-tech exercise equipment, there are countless possibilities to consider. Indeed, space limitations excepted, you'll find no end to the amenities you can include in a bedroom. Comfort is the first consideration, in both adults' and children's bedrooms. But beyond the bed and requisite storage pieces, you can fashion the room to function any way you want on a round-the-clock basis. Are your bedrooms living up to their potential? This chapter will help you master the possibilities.

BEDROOMS
SLEEP STYLES

The home quest for space, function, and truly personal design has redefined the bedroom's job description. It's no longer just a sleeper, but often a haven for television viewing, listening to music, catching up on work and hobbies, relaxing, and snoozing. In decorating your private quarters, choose design elements and furnishings for physical and psychological comfort. Paint the walls rise-and-shine red, if you want. Wrap the room in chintz and lace to recapture a bygone era. Or, create a bright-white sleep gallery filled with favorite art. Above all, incorporate the things you enjoy most into your bedroom's decor.

Comfort begins with the bed. There's a range of sleep surfaces on the market, from king-size innerspring mattresses to water beds and Japanese futons, but check the construction and warranty carefully, and test any mattress before you buy. If you yearn for a nostalgic look, today's reproductions and adaptations make it easy to find your dream bed, be it a traditional four-poster or a brass reprise of a century-old pattern. When buying an antique bed, try to purchase the original frame, because tailoring an eccentric old bed to a new frame can be costly.

Also essential are quietude, mood, and privacy. Use plush carpet and rugs, upholstered furniture and walls, and layered window treatments as sound baffles. Add ample task lighting for reading and work, plus a dimmer to soften the scene.

Freed from convention, the bedroom welcomes a mix of furnishings. Living-room-comfy seating, porch-friendly wicker, antique woods, and sleek office-size desks can customize style and function. Stretch storage with old chests and trunks, or stackable modulars. Tuck the television into an armoire. Then embellish your retreat with collectible treasures—family photos, old toys and textiles, today's pottery, or framed art.

Dramatically draped curtains ▶ and canopy in crisp taupe stripes transform a four-poster into a dreamy oasis. Rattan chairs and sisal floor covering add textural interest.

BEDROOMS
SLEEP STYLES

Nothing wakes up a weary bedroom like fabric. Today's easy-care bed linens, coordinated with accessories from curtains and table covers to lampshades, deliver a fresh new look in no time, without breaking the budget. To unify a bedroom with color and pattern, fashion sheets into canopies, bed curtains, duvet covers, wall treatments, dust ruffles, slipcovers, and accent pillows. In sheets, thread count and cotton content indicate quality; the best all-cotton percales count 200 to 250 threads per square inch. Layering new and old linens is an especially appealing way to dress your bed in luxury. Antique patchworks make charming bedcovers, but also consider old lace or linen tablecloths and lightweight kilims as toppers. Accent with pillows covered in aged lace hankies or quilt blocks.

In this sleeping loft, a lacquered wooden bed dressed in lacy linens and a plump armchair make breezy bedfellows. ▼

Star of this haven is a brass ▶ *bed featuring home-sewn linens. With ruffles reversed, Priscilla curtains are soft, not fussy.*

▲
Tranquil blue hues, romantic accessories, and a beautiful mismatch of spiffed-up antiques imbue this beckoning bower with English country flavor.

Cotton-candy colors link the ▶ *spirited mix of furnishings in this eclectic retreat. The bed exudes yesterday's charm; the soft seating, today's comfort.*

BEDROOMS
SLEEP STYLES

Granting the bed beautiful focus is the headboard's decorative duty. Treat a plain sleeper sans headboard to heads-up appeal with creatively combined accents or visual sleight-of-hand. Unusual sources yield intriguing headboard candidates, such as old iron gates and carved or gilded dresser mirrors. Capitalize on your room's architectural elements by backing the bed up to a bookcase or into a shallow alcove. Textiles such as wall-hung quilts and tapestries always add drama and spirited color as head-of-the-bed treatments, as do collages of framed art and oversize posters. With do-it-yourself skill, conjure a headboard effect with wall covering applied canopy-style to wall and ceiling, or with fabric shirred on wall-mounted rods. And, try paint-on wall art, topping a bed with simple stenciling, block-printed patchwork designs, or even a trompe l'oeil masterpiece.

Against a sunny peach ▶ *backdrop, an Italian-style platform bed and sleek accents—faux marble vanity, metal-trimmed armchair, and torchère—play to the pleasingly spare philosophy of this suite.*

An architectural ceiling trough, studded with skylights, boosts the spirits of this sleep space. Framed prints above a boxy unit create the metal bed's appealing headboard. ▼

▲
Eras mingle in a short-on-storage bedroom that got organized with an old wardrobe and clean-lined modular units. Eyelet-edged curtains add headboard interest.

BEDROOMS
SLEEP STYLES

A grand legacy of the practical past, when bed curtains, not central heating, checked chilly night drafts, the four-poster imparts star quality to any decorating scheme, from elegant traditional to rustic country and eclectic contemporary. Dress the bed in soft drapes and fabric canopy to weave color and pattern into a room, or leave it beautifully bare. Lacking the real thing, create a four-poster effect with bed curtains hung from ceiling-mounted drapery rods. In a small room, drape only the head of the bed.

Reflecting a passion for finely detailed bed linens, this four-poster is outfitted in scarlet-trimmed piqué. ▼

Romantic floral-print fabric ▶ *and mellow antiques imbue this room with English country ambience.*

▲ *Unlined white linen edged in blue gingham gives this master suite a snappy yet sophisticated aura. Deep blue walls and a braided rug add to the mood.*

Serenely spare to highlight ▶ *architectural elements, this bedroom embraces warm Southwest style with a rustic four-poster and painted tables.*

334

BEDROOMS
GREAT FOR GUESTS

Welcoming guest quarters succeed on comfort and privacy, whether yours is a reservations-only spare room or a sleep-sofa in the den. So when it comes to extending overnighters hospitality, the how-to is more important than the where-to. Today's multitalented furnishings eliminate guest work, turning everyday spaces into set-for-company retreats. Sleek sleep-sofas fit stylishly anywhere, modular seating draws together for slumber, and Murphy-type beds hide in high-function wall systems for instant pull-down guest rooms. In skimpy space, try a Japanese futon, the cotton floor mattress that, by day, folds into an S-shape chair or drapes over a seating frame.

◀ *Twin sleepers are tucked away in a space-saving wall-storage system until guests are due.*

A restful blue-and-white ▶ *palette, pillow-plumped chaise, and abundant accents prove irresistible. A wicker laundry basket turns bedside table with a new glass top.*

An old hooked rug's folksy motifs inspired this homey hideaway, with cannonball beds dressed in quilts.
▼

BEDROOMS
DREAM SUITES

Much more than a mere sleeping spot, today's master suite is a luxurious 24-hour retreat, embracing an exciting array of personalized amenities to relax and refresh. It's the perfect place to let your design fantasies take flight, no matter how elaborate they may be. Do your suite dreams take you to an antiques-filled château boudoir, to an elegant Victorian chamber dressed in fine linens, or to a contemporary sleep space packed with high-tech extras?

Decorating alone can make those dreams come true, but space and function also enhance the master suite's role as a true in-home getaway. If remodeling or a new addition is on your agenda, consider creating an adjoining bath, exercise spa, dressing room, or sitting room and library. Add access to a sundeck or private patio just off the bedroom. A media center, tucked into a handsome armoire or built-in wall system, is a popular bedroom perk, as is a fireplace or mini-refrigerator and bar. The industrious two-career couple might even enjoy an en suite computer center for his-and-hers homework. Finding the space for expansion isn't always easy, but look to adjacent underused rooms to annex or bump out for at least a cozy bedroom sitting area. If your suite includes more than a bedroom, merge the whole in the same palette and decorating theme.

Take advantage of the master suite's private status in choosing furnishings and design elements. Antique furniture and collectibles, which might be in jeopardy in busy family areas, add immeasurable personality in the safer confines of an adults-only suite. For example, the addition of an heirloom writing desk, charming painted pieces, or displays of your prized porcelain fares beautifully in the bedroom, granting it a special-space air. Treat the bed, too, with antique linens, flowing curtains, or a dramatic headboard effect. In such multifunction spaces, define seating, sleep, and work areas by furniture groupings.

A hand-painted fireplace, exercise spa, bath, and outdoor terrace share this teal-toned "fantasy" master suite.
▼

Diaphanous voile shirred ▶ *into a canopy brings high drama to this bed, resplendent in lacy antique linens and a headboard covered in floral fabric.*

▲ *Luxury soars to new heights in a sun-washed master suite, after remodeling opened it to the roofline. The old low ceiling in the windowed bay creates a cozy zone for sumptuous seating, and the serene color scheme mixes textures for visual effect.*

◀ *Monochromatic color links a sleep space to an en suite dressing area and bath with whirlpool tub, marble-topped vanity, and built-in seating. Window shades invite light, but allow privacy.*

BEDROOMS
YOUTHFUL LIVING

Far more than just a sleep space, a child's room should, by design, be a special realm that stimulates creativity and encourages play. So, in decorating for the small-fry, let the imagination soar and factor in fun.

Is your child a bookworm, music lover, collector, sports enthusiast, computer whiz, or aspiring artist? Does the room include cozy spots for entertaining friends, working on hobbies, playing games, and pursuing solitary activities? What are your child's favorite colors and fantasy characters? By taking cues from your child's interests and by inviting your child to participate, you can create a delightfully personalized environment.

Because spilled finger paints, crayon graffiti, and rambunctious play are inevitable in a child's room, make safe, sturdy, and no-fuss furnishings the rule. Such versatile hardworking basics—accessible storage; easy-to-clean furniture, fabrics, and surfaces; durable worktops, ample display space, and warm, bright color schemes—can contribute positively to a child's development, comfort, and enjoyment.

Just for fun, transform your child's room into a fantasy land with a paint-it-yourself wall-size mural in, for example, a storybook theme. Or, on the ceiling, brush on a "sky" of fluffy clouds or a galaxy of stars. Cover a wall with an oversize blackboard or blackboard paint, and let your budding artist create an original.

Children are, by nature, collectors, and their rooms are home to an abundance of precious paraphernalia that can add decorative punch, but requires adequate storage space. Oversize bulletin boards and walls covered with pegboard or cork are perfect for tackable treasures, such as posters and artwork. Adjustable open shelving corrals toys, model cars and airplanes, books, sports gear, audio/-video equipment, and art supplies within easy reach.

Toys and treasures abound ▶ in a child-style sleep space ready for creative play. Nursery stackables have grown up into bureaus, and a wall spice rack stows art supplies.

BEDROOMS
YOUTHFUL LIVING

Children's rooms, like their on-the-grow residents, are works in progress, demanding adaptable furnishings and decorating schemes that keep pace with changing needs and interests. From the nursery-planning stage, design for the future, and with only a few modifications a room can take a child happily from infant to teen.

From the start, make safety a priority. Federal standards for new cribs require slats, spindles, crib rods, and corner posts no more than 2⅜ inches apart. They require drop-sides that are of adequate height even when lowered and that cannot be released by a child, and a mattress that fits snugly, leaving no dangerous gaps. Unless it meets these standards and is sturdy with all hardware intact, don't use a hand-me-down crib. Between crib and full-size bed, one option is a small-scale youth bed with removable guard-rails, but it isn't a necessity. Children's furniture should not tip easily and should have no protruding sharp edges or knobs. Adjustable shelves and modular units to be stacked later make good choices here, because they allow a small child access to toys and clothing without the need for climbing and the risk of falling.

For the nursery-with-a-future, choose simple, functional pieces in laminates or sealed wood. Let accents, such as charming artwork and soft rugs, set the mood. Always include more storage than initially needed. Easy care is the key to child-style decorating. Durable carpet, washable nonskid rugs, resilient flooring, and scrubbable wall coverings all add color and pattern to a room, but resist baby-ish motifs your child will quickly outgrow.

Nursery lighting should be soft and diffused, gentle on baby's eyes. Add task lighting over the changing table, and later, in hobby and homework areas. At the windows, blinds and shutters are a good nonfrilly option for monitoring light, drafts, and ventilation.

▲
Today's sunny nursery looks to the future with adjustable add-on shelves, sturdy carpet, and an easy-to-redo white-walled scheme.

Bright primary colors and a ▶ bicycle theme perk up the bedroom-playroom of a busy youngster. Open shelves keep toys and art supplies handy.

Vertical storage and a ▶ celestial motif treat a preteen's "dream room" to delightful style and lasting function. A custom-made bed with roomy drawers elevates the sleep spot.

BEDROOMS
YOUTHFUL LIVING

Children delight in bright, cozy rooms filled with nostalgic character and timeworn furnishings. But, decorate such special spaces with the young occupant's needs and activities in mind, because museumlike settings and don't-touch antiques are definitely not kid stuff. Choose pieces that are functional, sturdy, and flexible to meet changing interests. Always use lead-free paint on children's furniture. These bedrooms mix yesterday's furnishings with today's easy-care fabrics to charm girls of any age.

A budding collector shows off her treasures in a sentimental scheme anchored by an iron bed brushed in white paint. ▼

Abloom with fresh fabrics, ▶ *a cozy bedroom with four-poster and Victorian lady's chair is home to a child's menagerie.*

▲
Pretty in pink, an English daybed doubles as sitting spot and sleeper, with a footstool to boost short legs aboard.

Periwinkle blue links a bevy ▶ *of sprightly elements in this fancifully feminine bedroom with antique sofa and bed clad in country plaid.*

BEDROOMS
YOUTHFUL LIVING/SHARING

When the bedroom equation adds two or more children to one room, the solution to peaceful coexistence is multiplying functions. Although pint-size roommates will undoubtedly enjoy common play areas, each child also needs privacy—a separate and well-defined area for sleep and solitary pursuits such as homework and hobbies. If you're scouting for space to share, look at idle attics or underused rooms to redo into cheery child-styled suites. You needn't undertake a costly makeover, however; there are creative ways to pack separate-but-equal functions into a single room. To define personal spaces, use wall-attached accordion dividers that open and shut, a handy two-sided storage unit with closed and see-through shelving, or even a ceiling-to-floor venetian blind. When such dividers aren't feasible, locate individual sleep and study areas on opposite sides of the room, facing them away from each other.

◄ *Architectural wizardry divided a large room into thirds and conquered the privacy problem for an 11-year-old brother and his 7-year-old sister sharing space. Each child enjoys a tree-house-size duplex—his at left and hers above—with a cozy lookout loft bed, a roomy play and study area, and plenty of built-in storage.*

346

Visually stretch the shared room by brushing the backdrop in bright white, neutrals, or cool colors, and keeping furnishings simple. Children love color, so liven things up with bold-hued furniture, flooring, and accents. In the interest of harmony, color-code each child's possessions. Because beds, desks, and play gear in duplicate and triplicate are a tight squeeze for even a spacious room, maximize storage with vertical shelving, under-bed drawers, and stackable modular units that combine desktops and shelves. Going vertical is also a good option for multiple sleep spaces when floor space is at a premium. For example, consider sturdy freestanding or built-in bunkbeds. If your budget allows architectural changes, look at built-in lofts that elevate sleepers above play-and-study areas.

▲
This nautical bunk room nestles under attic eaves. Beaded paneling covers the walls and the partitions separating cabin-style quarters, each with under-bunk drawers for storage.

A large divider, with storage inside and gallery outside, transformed a room into a suite for two. Sporty motifs zoom from wall border to bedspreads, and the carpet is kid-proof.
▼

KITCHENS

The word *kitchen* barely suffices these days. Having catapulted prematurely into the 21st century, today's kitchens are amazingly ahead of their time. The best among them are spacious culinary showplaces offering the utmost in style, easy care, and convenience. But more than this, the kitchen of the 1990s is apt to be an expanded "living center," where families gravitate to cook, dine, lounge, watch television, use the computer, or work on hobbies or homework. Sophistication and multifunction aside, the kitchen is a place for sharing home-style amenities. Take a look at this chapter to find out what's cooking in today's kitchens.

KITCHENS
THE BASICS

Whether you're remodeling to the studs or sprucing up an existing space, wise and thorough planning will help you get the most out of your kitchen. Workrooms and social hubs, kitchens must function for cooking, baking, cleaning up, and storage—and often for dining and entertaining, as well. It takes planning to make all those tasks coexist happily and with a personality that's yours alone.

Your goal is to design an appealing, high-performance kitchen that works for you and your family. So consider function first: What are the kitchen's roles? Is it a one-cook center or does a the-more-the-merrier philosophy prevail? Is the kitchen where your family gathers? Are you a serious baker, a specialty cook, an active host? Is a kitchen planning center a priority? These factors help determine the features that make sense for you.

Launch your kitchen redo with research, gathering ideas from magazines, books, model homes, and building supply centers. Don't be swayed by status amenities you won't use or decorating styles that don't fit your family.

A GREAT FLOOR PLAN

Remodeling a kitchen should yield more than just decorative improvements. In fact, your *first* priority should be a layout that maximizes the efficiency of the space you have. Here are some of the most common plans:
- The U-shape kitchen is ideal, with three walls of work space plus a dead-end to limit through traffic. Even if the kitchen is large, keep the work core compact.
- The L-shape kitchen is an easy layout for a small area. Keep the work core near the corner.
- The corridor kitchen is prone to through traffic. Place the sink and refrigerator on the wall opposite the range. Try for extra-wide aisles.
- The island kitchen adds an island to a U- or L-shape layout. In an oversize kitchen, locate work centers in the island to keep the central work core compact and efficient; working islands can often double as eating counters, too.
- The peninsula kitchen employs an angular peninsula to stretch space. This layout is flexible, defines traffic flow, and is a good option where wall space is limited.

- The single-wall kitchen is a last resort. Center the sink, with the range and refrigerator at opposite ends.

The best way to plan a kitchen is on paper, with scale floor plans. Think in terms of work centers, such as mixing, cooking, or cleanup centers. Before you start sketching, do a mental walk-through of how each center will function. Remember that mechanical matters, such as the location of plumbing lines, influence what goes where. Because of plumbing, for example, the sink is the most expensive element to relocate.

A good starting point for planning is the work triangle, a formula used to site the refrigerator, sink, and range in an efficient, triangular design. First position your sink, then:
- Place the refrigerator 4 to 7 feet from the sink.
- Place the range 4 to 6 feet from the sink.
- Place the range 4 to 9 feet from the refrigerator.

The distance among the major trio should be at least 12 feet, and no more than 22. Try to route traffic patterns around the triangle, so you can work uninterrupted.

PLANNING TIPS

Keep these tips in mind in planning a new kitchen:
- Allow adequate aisle space—a minimum of 4 feet opposite work areas, and 3 feet elsewhere.
- Plan for "hidden" space users, such as appliance doors that swing open and chairs that must be pulled out for comfortable use. Note these on your plan.
- Allow counter space for work centers: to 42 inches for a mixing center, 12 inches on each side of an island cooktop, and 18 to 24 inches flanking the range or counter cooktop.
- For two cooks, consider duplicating some functions, such as adding a small vegetable sink to a kitchen island.
- Before you commit to a material, consider its suitability for kitchen use and its maintenance needs.
- Plan adequate lighting. The "Lighting" chapter has specific recommendations.

KITCHENS
PERSONALITY KITCHENS

A truly successful kitchen does more than function well: It has personality. Gathering spot, cooks' oasis, mission control for a busy family, a kitchen is a full-fledged living space deserving of its own memorable style.

Individuality is the earmark of a room with personality. So, in composing the elements of a kitchen style, trust your own instincts and nudge your imagination into action. Are you a clean-counter type or do you love to show off cherished collectibles? Do you yearn to re-create an era of Victorian elegance or colonial simplicity? Are you soothed by the spirit of a homey country kitchen, or do you prefer the electricity of the eclectic? The mood of your kitchen should make you and your family happy. If your kitchen is open to other living spaces, it should complement the style of those rooms, as well.

Whatever your style, call on design elements such as color, fabric, surface materials, lighting, art, and one-of-a-kind accents to create the personal touch.

◀ *Taking cues from original heart-of-pine flooring, this charming kitchen reflects the historic mien of the 19th-century home it serves.*

▲
Open to living areas, this kitchen needed show-off stature. A dramatic pairing of darks and lights imbues the setting with elegance.

Unique antiques, imported accents, and up-to-date amenities impart a formal-yet-fun style to this striking kitchen makeover. The rich cherry cabinets set the tone; French floor tile and snowy counters add sophisticated contrast to the dark cabinetry and hunter green wall covering.

Sun-washed by a sky-light, this contemporary kitchen redo summons fluid forms, natural textures, and soft color to warm its state-of-the-art design. Curves abound in the oval dining table, storage wall, domed lighting, and soaring ceiling. A terra-cotta tile floor and dashes of blue unite kitchen and seating area.

KITCHENS
PERSONALITY KITCHENS

Kitchen personality doesn't come prepackaged: you have to build it in yourself. But sometimes, all the options seem overwhelming. If you're planning a redo, a professional may be able to help you bring your ideas to life.

An architect can tell you what changes are structurally feasible—but, then, so can most competent contractors. More importantly, a good architect is ingenious in solving problems and can design spaces of uncommon character. Interior designers have a strong background in all aspects of design; they can advise you on floor plan, help you choose cabinetry and materials, and suggest wall and window treatments. Kitchen designers, often affiliated with a kitchen supply dealer, may have a general design background. Some are certified by the National Kitchen and Bath Association, based on their expertise in kitchen design and construction.

Good communication is essential in working with a design specialist. Share your likes and dislikes about the soon-to-be-remodeled space; tell the specialist how your family lives; discuss budget; show pictures of kitchens you like. Analyze a professional's recommendations with care. Most importantly, ask yourself: Does this plan solve my kitchen problem—or just disguise it in new cabinets and surfaces? Don't settle for less than what you want in a final plan.

▲
When a wall came down, this kitchen gained room for a cozy corner dining spot.

Hand-painted tiles give heart to old-style cabinets and lighting fixtures.

◀ *A rustic roofline calls for country character—but not clichés. Green-painted cabinets and softly colored walls gentrify this farmhouse. Antiques impart an English flavor.*

Blush-pink laminate ▶ cabinetry tempers the slickness of this orderly Japanese-style kitchen. Nature's accents include a pale oak floor and gleaming black granite countertops.

KITCHENS
COSMETIC FACE-LIFTS

Easy-on-the-budget spruce-ups grant kitchens past their prime futures that are bright and beautiful. For a kitchen that is basically efficient but mired in the decorating doldrums, fresh paint, a cabinet face-lift, and an update of design elements guarantee major impact. Consider these strategies for new kitchen style:

• **Work magic with paint.** Nothing renews a kitchen faster than a wash of color. For a light, crisp look, brush white paint overall—walls, woodwork, cabinets, ceiling, even the floor—then punctuate with colorful accents such as framed art or cookware on display. Vibrant colors and pastels are also at home in the kitchen; just prepare surfaces meticulously before you paint so the look will be as fresh as the color.

• **Replace cabinet doors.** Professionals can outfit your cabinet frames with new doors and drawer fronts in wood or laminates, then cover the rails and boxes in matching materials. (A highly skilled do-it-yourselfer may be able to handle the job at home.) One caveat: Don't invest in new doors if your cabinet frames are of poor quality, or are inefficiently arranged.

• **Revive cabinets.** Sanding and refinishing can yield handsome results. To lighten dark wood, consider stripping and whitewashing it. You can whitewash cabinets with a mix of equal parts white alkyd enamel and paint thinner; you brush the mix into the wood, let it set no more than 15 minutes, and rub off the excess. When the cabinet is dry, apply a protective sealer. To paint cabinets, use a gloss or semigloss alkyd paint; you may want to embellish them with stenciled or hand-painted designs.

You also can dress up cabinets with door insets of leaded, beveled, or etched glass or simple panes. Stock molding, applied to plain-front cabinet doors, adds traditional flair. Treat updated cupboards to new hinges, handles, and decorative pulls.

• **Bring appliances** into the new color scheme with spray-on enamel paints or, for some models, with snap-in color panels. An automotive painter also can paint appliances.

• **Renew kitchen surfaces.** State-of-the-art materials such as heat- and scratch-resistant countertops, no-wax flooring, and wipe-clean vinyl wall coverings are low-maintenance and budget-wise additions. If you long for hand-painted tile on backsplashes, but your budget won't permit it, try a tile-patterned wall covering. The good ones look astonishingly real.

• **Remember the little things.** Small accents and design elements can rescue an OK, but drab, kitchen. New window treatments, lighting fixtures, cookware racks, shelves for kitchen collectibles, or even colorful linens can pay off in personality and style.

▲
Stripped of varnish and whitewashed, knotty-pine cupboards assume a fresh country air. Dashes of blue, in fabric and the sink's inset of ceramic tile, accent this kitchen's pale pine scheme.

Blue-and-white porcelain ▶ inspired this kitchen update with dramatic results. Cabinets clad in glossy white paint pair up with a blue-striped wall covering for a crisp, classic look. The counters are wood laminate, a modern-day complement to the old, 250-pound butcher block.

The owners of this kitchen traded peeling paint and cracked linoleum for colonial style. The wall covering gives a chair rail effect to white walls, hand-stenciled at the top. Accents are homespun and primitive.
▼

A cabinet face-lift changed the tune of this 1970s kitchen. Bright white paint and new, oak-trimmed doors updated the cabinetry. Appliances got a spray of white; the floor, a sheet of vinyl; and counters, new laminate. Miniblinds and the wall covering add red-hot accents.
▼

KITCHENS
SMALL-SPACE STRATEGIES

Often, the best kitchen designs come in compact spaces. Though packing necessities—appliances, work centers, and storage—into limited floor area sometimes seems impossible, careful planning can make it work. In fact, because undersize kitchens demand attention to detail, small kitchen redos often emerge with singular efficiency.

Today's appliances that match high function to smaller scale are ideal for compact kitchens. New refrigerators fit flush with cabinets or under counters, washers and dryers come stackable, and small appliances install under cabinets to free countertops. Some ovens combine cooking functions; there even are dishwashers designed to go directly underneath a sink.

Illusion can work magic in limited spaces. Here are some strategies for visually expanding space:
- Direct the eye upward with vertical lines in cabinetry and wall treatments or above-cabinet lighting.
- Keep upper walls open by replacing cabinets with open shelving, or by adding glass-fronted doors to cupboards.
- Eliminate clutter, real and visual. Keep counters clean and shelves orderly; use simple patterns in surface materials such as tile and flooring.
- Keep colors simple. Use a light palette and limit it to two or three tones; match cabinets, counters, and walls. Or, make a wall recede with dark cabinets or wall treatment.

If your budget permits, you'll find that even moderate structural changes can pay big dividends in ambience:
- Add a ready-made greenhouse window to invite light and impart depth to a wall.
- Gain counter space and an open look by replacing a wall with a peninsula.
- Reclaim underused space in closets, pantries, or porches beyond the kitchen perimeter; even a bump-out into the garage can create an appliance niche or laundry center.

▲
The sleek star of this kitchen spells ultimate utility—sink, range, and dishwasher in one unit. The color-wise scheme mixes black, for depth; white to brighten; and red, for punch.

Architectural trellises define ▶ this black-and-white galley, a sliver of space with high-style efficiency. The open wall gives breathing room; a black counter offers dining for two.

A from-scratch remodeling produced this compact classic, timeless in beauty and function. The neutral, tone-on-tone color scheme gains spark from granite countertops; extra-high kick plates add depth and avoid low storage. A recess at the top of the cabinets achieves the effect of molding and draws the eye upward.

A slim working-and-eating ▶ counter solved the deep-window dilemma of this modest kitchen. To maintain the room's sunny disposition—while putting the end wall to work—an oak-and-laminate counter strip was stretched across the windows. Flip-up counters, roll-out tables, and pullout cutting boards also can expand work surfaces.

KITCHENS
KITCHEN STORAGE

Whether your kitchen is a tiny galley or spacious enough for a crew of cooks, selecting storage is often the biggest challenge. But, making every storage inch count always yields high-efficiency rewards.

Well-planned kitchen storage takes into consideration convenience, the cooks' specific needs, kitchen style, and your tolerance for clutter and cleaning. The right gear at the right place at the right time hastens kitchen chores. So the cardinal rule of convenience is: Store it close to where you use it—bakeware near ovens, cutlery near the chopping block, pots and pans near the cooktop, and tableware near the dishwasher.

Open and closed storage have devotees and disadvantages. If you like clean counters and minimal clutter, closed or cabinet storage that stows gear and protects it from everyday grime is a good choice. But, if you like the decorative appeal of colorful kitchenware on display, opt for open shelving and overhead or wall-hung racks. Open storage has an airy look and visually enlarges a room, making it an astute choice for the small-space kitchen. To minimize cleaning, store in the open only the kitchenware you use—and usually scrub—daily.

With a bit of ingenuity, you can easily maximize the space you have with buyable storage accessories. Customize drawers and cabinets with vinyl-clad wire bins, shelves, cutlery trays, stemware racks, and cup hooks. Consider adding specialty storage units, such as partitioned drawers, corner lazy Susans, spice cabinets, pull-out pantry shelves and breadboards, and a small-appliance garage tucked between the countertop and upper cabinets. Don't overlook the backs of cabinet and closet doors that can be outfitted with custom-use racks.

In your storage quest, consider windows and walls as prime candidates for open storage. Put a no-view window to work by installing wooden shelves across the front. If you want to savor the view, too, add glass shelving across the window for storing colorful glassware, then watch it sparkle in the sun. Walls can be outfitted easily with space-making wall systems, perforated hardboard, or a gridwork of dowels secured by screws. Add cuphooks and S-hooks for storing cookware and kitchen gadgetry.

▲
This hardworking appliance center has it all: a strip of electric plugs, a pull-out work surface, and storage shelves aplenty. Close the doors, and it blends into the background.

A step- and timesaver, this convenient laundry center and utility closet were tucked into the kitchen's pantry-type storage. Ample shelving keeps cleaning supplies handy.
▼

▲

A tiny section of unused wall was plenty for a planning and message center. Wall-hung shelves provide space for cookbooks; cubbyholes corral clutter and messages.

▲

To get more from the small pantry, vinyl-coated racks were fitted inside the doors. Easy to clean and install, such shelving is less costly than custom-built storage remedies.

▲

Taking advantage of a tight space, this custom cabinet keeps bakeware organized and accessible. Shelves, a mere one-pot wide, adjust vertically to handle kitchen gear.

▲

In space too narrow for a walk-in and too deep for shelves, these twin pantry towers offer a roll-out solution. The units slide on heavy-duty casters and are guided by track hardware.

◄ *Around a kitchen island, open storage adds visual appeal and keeps essentials at hand. The overhead rack displays a battery of copperware; shelving holds tableware.*

▲

An island of efficiency, this work center stores small appliances on pop-up shelves for easy access. Outlets are inside the cabinetry.

BATHS

Yesterday a stand-in and today a star! Once, the bathroom was relegated to second-class status on the decorating scene. No longer. Today's bath is a sybaritic center designed to refresh both body and soul. Many modern bathrooms are veritable storehouses of personal care implements. The most lavish contain saunas, exercise equipment, whirlpool baths, bidets, built-in hair dryers, even flotation tanks. Some baths are as big as the bedrooms they adjoin. But, of course, most baths are far less extravagant in terms of size or appointments. The ideas presented here are food for thought when you're seeking ways to give your bath top billing.

BATHS
PERSONALITY BATHS

Once a Spartan space defined by necessity, the bathroom has stepped into the home design spotlight. Infused with sensational style and luxurious function, it now stars as a truly personalized living, relaxing, and grooming center— a revolution as exciting as the advent of indoor plumbing and central heating that long ago set the stage.

If your old bathroom is cramped, cluttered, and filled with aging eccentric fixtures, it may be ripe for the revolt. Whether you wage a full-scale remodeling coup led by professionals or opt for a do-it-yourself bathroom face-lift, thoughtful planning with a realistic eye on the budget comes first.

Beyond well-mannered plumbing, how do you want your new-and-improved bathroom to feel and function? Would twin sinks ease the family's morning rush hour? Does a lounging spot, exercise space, hot tub, laundry nook, or dressing room top your luxury list?

What mood do you want design elements to create? Even minor changes—a brush of fresh color, a vintage fixture, a stretch of soft carpet, or the visual punch of art and collectibles—can make a big splash. Let your answers guide your redesign plans.

Choosing to remodel, bump out, or add on for a more spacious bathroom can be an expensive proposition if it involves relocating plumbing and major fixtures. So hire an architect or contractor to at least look over your plans. Putting pros on your remodeling project, especially for electrical wiring and plumbing, can prevent costly, even dangerous, do-it-yourself mistakes. Leave plumbing lines right where they are and design around them, or watch budget dollars go down the drain.

On an hourly-fee basis, professional interior designers will consult on myriad project details, such as choosing color palettes, floor plans, materials sources, and custom fixtures. Or, they will oversee your project from the idea stage to the ribbon-cutting.

Find the right pro for your dream-bath team through local chapters of national professional associations such as the American Institute of Architects or the American Society of Interior Designers.

▲ *Awash in soothing pastels and natural light, this easy-living bath grew to luxuriant proportions when an addition doubled its size and linked it to an outdoor deck. Contrasting textures create beautiful balance with wicker, wood, and an Oriental rug.*

Undeniably sophisticated in ▶ a bold black-and-white scheme, this master bath hints at the homeowners' humor in its self-effacing accents: a pair of charming Bavarian dolls. High windows in the curved storage wall "stretch" sunlight from the adjacent bedroom.

BATHS
PERSONALITY BATHS

Whether you take the remodeling plunge or simply primp walls with fresh paint, consider these bath basics and ideas for a successful makeover.

● Fixtures are foremost. If toilets, sinks, and tubs are worn and stained, new ones offer a rainbow of color options, streamlined shapes, and hot-water-saving features. Tubs range from standard size to mini-swimming-pool size, the result of the bathroom's emergence as a rejuvenating spa, and even average-size tubs come with soothing water-massage. If walls are less than sturdy, choose a pedestal sink. Epoxy paint, in dramatic colors, brightens old fixtures but requires careful application for a smooth, durable finish.

● Walls look new in no time with paint, vinyl wall covering, laminate or wood paneling, mirrored tile, or super-size fog-resistant mirrors. Coat wood with protective polyurethane, and in high-spatter areas, use sealer on vinyl wall covering. For tired tile walls, try epoxy paint or new, easy-to-apply tile that layers over the old.

● Underfoot options range from expensive marble floor tile to ceramic tile, to moderately priced tile, to inexpensive marble-look vinyl. Carpet always spells luxury, but its backing should suit bathroom use.

● Lighting brightens the outlook, and with a dimmer, sets a mood. Banish freestanding lights that could be knocked over easily, eliminating shock potential. Surround grooming mirrors with localized no-shadow lighting such as warm white fluorescents that flatter morning reflections. And, if you read in the tub, make sure the light is right.

● Thwart steamy-room mildew problems with a fan vented outside, or an extractor fan designed for windowless internal bathrooms.

● Take storage cues from the kitchen. Vinyl-coated racks and bins corral clutter, cabinets double as vanities, and wall units add a vertical option.

● Make "safety first" a bathroom rule. Child-proof cupboards for medications and cleaners. Install tub and shower grab-bars for elderly or handicapped family members. Choose nonskid floor tile and rugs.

▲
Dazzling and invitingly luxurious, the red whirlpool tub ignites high spirits in this small bath. Mirrors expand the space and bounce bold primary color to every corner.

◄ This elegant master bath was created by merging two small rooms. The sunken whirlpool and pastel-tiled vanity are angled to save space. Tubside windows afford a woodsy view, but pull-up Roman shades guard privacy. Lush plants and botanical prints invite the outdoors in.

Though harbored in a new home, this master bath is warmed with tradition and sunlight. Topped by a soft Roman shade, the charmingly paned window indulges the bather with a garden vista.

▼

▲
Modest remodeling restored vintage character to this master bath. A ceramic-tile surround camouflages the tub's worn exterior.

BATHS
PERSONALITY BATHS

Traditionally, style stopped at the bathroom's intimate threshold, but the bathroom's new role in leisurely pursuits demands a personalized design touch to inspire the right mood, be it lively or mellow.

Dip into history and collectible treasures to set an era-evoking theme. Splash on color to rev up or cool down the bath's visual thermostat. Or, embrace your private spa in the sleek scheme of your home's other living areas.

Depending on space and the bathroom's amenities, furnishings can be grouped for appealing comfort or go solo for impact. Adding plump-pillowed seating in an alcove, or chaise longues or a desk by a sunny window invites you to linger longer and relax. Even the small bath is pampered by adding a wicker stool, boudoir chair, or cushioned window seat.

If your bathroom is in a nostalgic mood, antique pieces add fetching focus. Outfitted with a wash-basin inset, a vintage sideboard or dry sink, for example, does double duty as vanity-plus-storage. A pie safe makes a rustic bathroom cache perfect for fresh towels and linens. Opt for an old wall-hung cupboard as a medicine chest in countrified schemes.

Nothing punches a bath with personality like collectibles and art. Whatever you fancy—from Victorian crystal atomizers, lacy antique linens, or aged brass lanterns to prized ceramic pigs born yesterday—invite in your favorite accents for eye appeal and color. Framed botanical prints summon natural serenity, sepia-toned photos set Edwardian elegance, and bold poster art adds a graphic contemporary touch. But reserve your framed finest for less tropical regions of the home.

To keep the bath on the sunny yet private side, pull-up Roman shades, curtains, and shutters with fabric panels handle privacy and add to the sprightly mix of color and pattern in the room's fabric accents. Stained glass or glass-block window inserts guard privacy without elaborate window treatments.

From Oriental rugs underfoot to crystal chandeliers overhead, almost any design element plays beautifully in the bath. For lush natural accents, capitalize on the bath's greenhouse effect, in which plants flourish.

▲
Tucked into a rehabbed Victorian townhouse, this bath echoes the home's spare black-and-white scheme. Clean curves on the mirrored basin soften the sweeping grid of blue-gray tile.

▲
Shower lovers designed this small but efficient bath with flair: pedestal sinks, wicker vanity, and brass accents.

▲
Taking its cue from the marble sinks of great deco-era luxury liners, the leggy vanity is open to view in a loft redo. Its sculptural faucet and shiny chromed-steel underpinnings add architectural appeal and the cross-bar keeps towels handy.

◄ *Elegant design elements shimmer a dramatic bath makeover. Custom cut from blue-pearl granite, the vanity has an off-center bowl allowing towel space on the apron. Alabaster sconces glow in soft contrast to the slick surfaces.*

369

BATHS
OOMPH FOR OLD BATHS

For the bathroom hardly aging gracefully, with peeling tile, cold cavernous spaces, and odd old fixtures, a costly redo isn't necessarily the savvy solution. If the plumbing works perfectly, try design sleight of hand with color, fabric, wall and floor coverings, and accessories to coax inherent character and charm.

Accent the positive: the room's vintage pluses. Highlight aged wainscoting and moldings with glossy white paint for crisp contrast to bold color or pattern on the walls. Freshen the backdrop, and that old pedestal sink and claw-foot relic of a tub once again share top billing. Add a piece of the past—a marble-topped chest for storage or a flower-filled English lavabo—just for fun.

Design tricks can cozy up an oversize bath and disguise too-high ceilings and large windows. Tame a soaring ceiling with dark color or patterned wall covering overhead. Unify a sprawling space with coordinated fabric in accents and window treatments, or add a warm-hued carpet.

◀ *Lilac-blossomed bed linens weave magic in a tiny under-eaves bath. Beribboned shams top the window.*

▲
Casting a vintage pine dresser with inset brass basin as powder-room star sets a casual country mood, with accents following suit.

▲
Scrubbed pine, fragrant accents, and lacy heirloom linens at the window and sink romance a pint-size powder room.

◀ *From boring to bold, this bath made the transition with an infusion of vivid red wall covering and fabric, elegant accents, and white contrasts.*

▲
Nostalgia reigns in this red-and-white bath granted fabulous focus by a pedestal sink. Towels and a rug keep the look lively; moldings and accents add a country touch.

371

BATHS
LUXURY BATHS

Today's universal yen for healthy bodies and tranquil spirits has transformed the humble bathroom into a luxurious retreat. Fundamental plumbing has gone glamorous. And a tempting array of suite amenities—whirlpool baths, saunas, fireplaces, fitness gear, comfy seating, libraries, and audiovisual equipment—lets you create a sumptuous home-spa even the ancient Romans would envy.

Luxury is defined in a very personal and very private way. What makes you feel pampered? Is it splashing in an oversize tub beneath a star-studded skylight? Is it a bath-side bookshelf, television, or telephone? Is it a sink-in chaise for post-ablutions reading?

Essential for the deluxe bathroom is grand-scale space for the requisite complement of indulgent fixtures and furnishings. The true sybarite forages for annexable space such as a small adjacent room, then deletes walls for a new super-size master bath. If it's architecturally feasible, bump out your present bathroom to gain not only space but also light by adding a windowed bay or a skylight. Before launching a quest for square footage, remember that drastic plumbing changes can be expensive. So try to find extra space near present plumbing lines.

For unrivaled spa appeal, merge a bathroom with a master bedroom, solarium, or study, or indulge it with a panoramic view or access to a sundeck. Then pack it with high-function perks for soothing away cares of the day. Details such as heated towel bars or exercise bars that double as towel bars, heat lamps, special grooming mirrors, and mood-setting accents and lighting enhance the pampering effect.

In choosing bath fixtures, consider size, quality, and site. An extra inch or two in lavatory size is well worth the cost. Vitreous china lavatories are more durable than those of enameled cast iron or enameled steel. The standard bathtub is a less-than-lavish 5 feet long, but some models come with a whirlpool-type feature. The sunken splendor of an oversize tub requires adequate floor space for the tub and its environment, often "landscaped" in multilevels softly carpeted or slicked with marble or ceramic tile.

▲
Count hearthside bathing and lounging among the pampering perks in this spa. Sleek marble, mellow oak, and sparkling mirrors spell deluxe.

▲
Bumped out into a sun-
drenched bay, this verdant
sanctuary enjoys luxury on tap:
a sunken whirlpool tub for
soaking.

Sherbet-hued marble and ▶
Midas-touched faucets and
accents summon elegance to this
pristine bath.

GLOSSARY

Accent colors: Contrast colors used to enliven room schemes.

Adaptations: Furnishings that capture the flavor of the original, but are not authentic in detail or construction.

Analogous colors: Any series of colors that are adjacent on the color wheel, such as blue, blue-violet, and violet.

Antique: Any object that is 100 or more years old.

Antiquing: A technique whereby paint, varnish, or glaze is applied to a surface and then blotted off with a cloth to suggest the appearance of age.

Armoire: A tall, free-standing wardrobe devised by the French in the 17th century; originally used to store armor; now used for storage of clothes and other items.

Art Deco: A style of architectural and furnishings decoration popular in the 1920s and 1930s; characteristics include streamlined, geometric motifs expressed in materials such as glass, plastic, and chrome.

Art Nouveau: The forerunner of Art Deco; a style of decoration between 1890 and 1910 characterized by flowing lines, sinuous curves, and stylized forms derived from nature.

Austrian shade: An elegant curtain that is shirred in scalloped panels and pulled up like a window shade.

Balance: A state of equilibrium that can be either symmetrical (formal) or asymmetrical (informal).

Balloon shade: A poufed fabric shade that forms soft, billowy folds when raised.

Banquette: A long, benchlike seat, often upholstered, and generally built into or placed along the wall.

Barcelona chair: An armless leather chair with an x-shaped chrome base; designed by Mies van der Rohe in 1929.

Bauhaus: A German school of art and design that operated from 1919 to 1932, and stressed a doctrine of functionalism; the school's influence on design and architecture was profound, and much of what we refer to as "contemporary" today can be traced to Bauhaus beginnings.

Bay window: A series of windows (usually three or more) set at an angle to each other in a recessed area.

Bergère: An armchair with upholstered back, seat, and sides, with an exposed wood frame.

Bow window: A circular or curved version of a bay window.

Breakfront: A large cabinet with a center section that protrudes beyond the sections at each side.

Cabriole: A style of furniture leg where the top curves out, the center curves in, and the foot curves out.

Café curtains: Curtains that cover the lower half of a window.

Celadon: A pale green color.

Chair rail: A molding, usually of wood, running along a wall at the height of chair backs; originally used to protect walls from scratches; now used mainly for decorative effect.

Chaise longue: Pronounced *shez long;* literally, a "long chair," suitable for reclining; *not* a lounge chair.

Chinoiserie: Furnishings, fabrics, and objects inspired by Chinese design.

Chintz: Printed cotton fabric, often "polished" or glazed.

Chippendale: Name applied to the elegant 18th-century furniture designs of Thomas Chippendale; the upholstered wing chair and camelback sofa are two of his classics.

Combing: A decorative paint technique whereby a comb (often made of heavy cardboard) is pulled across wet paint to create a striped or wavy pattern.

Commode: French word for a low chest of drawers, often with a bowed front; in Victorian times, it referred to a nightstand that concealed a chamber pot.

Complementary colors: Colors that are opposite one another on the color wheel, such as blue and orange.

Console: A rectangular table usually set against a wall in a foyer or dining room; also, a bracketed shelf attached to a wall.

Cornice: A horizontal molding at the top of a wall, often used to conceal drapery fixtures.

Credenza: A sideboard or buffet.

Custom-made: Any product made to specification of size, color, shape, and material.

Dado: The lower section of a wall, often paneled or decoratively treated to contrast with a wallpapered or painted top section.

Decoupage: Cutouts of paper or other materials applied to various surfaces, then varnished for permanence.

Dhurrie: A traditional Indian woven carpet of cotton or silk.

Dimmer switch: A type of light switch (also known as a rheostat) that allows light levels to be controlled at various gradations, from dim to bright.

Documentary pattern: An adaptation or exact copy of a wallpaper or fabric design from a past era.

Down: The fine, soft fluff from the breasts of geese or ducks; considered the most luxurious filling for seat cushions and bed pillows.

Downlight: A type of spotlight that is recessed or attached to the ceiling and casts light downward.

Drop-leaf table: A table with hinged leaves that can be folded down.

Eames chair: A classic lounge chair and ottoman made of molded plywood and fitted with down-filled leather cushions; designed by Charles Eames in 1956.

Eclecticism: A style of decoration characterized by furnishings and accessories of various styles and periods that are deftly and harmoniously combined; *not* a hodgepodge of just anything.

Étagère: An open-shelved stand used for display of decorative objects.

F–J

Fauteuil: A French-style chair with open arms, upholstered back and seat, and small upholstered pads for resting the elbows.

Faux: A term to describe anything that is simulated to look like something it's not.

Faux bois: French for simulated wood.

Fiddleback: A chair with a center splat shaped like a fiddle.

Flocked wallpaper: Wallpaper with a raised surface that looks and feels somewhat like velvet.

Fluorescent: A type of cool, glareless light produced by the fluorescence of gas.

French Provincial: Not a period but a term to describe countrified versions of formal French furnishings of the 17th and 18th centuries.

Futon: A Japanese-style mattress that is placed on the floor and used for either sleeping or seating.

Gate-leg table: Similar to a drop-leaf table, but with two sets of legs that swing out like gates to support the raised leaves.

Gilding: A technique for applying gold to furniture and other surfaces.

Gimp: Decorative braid used to conceal tacks and nails on upholstered furniture.

Glazing: A decorative paint technique whereby a film of color is applied to a painted surface to create a semitransparent effect.

Gloss: A type of oil-based paint that dries to a high sheen.

Gold leaf: Wafer-thin sheets of gold used in gilding mirrors, picture frames, and other decorative objects.

Graining: A decorative paint technique whereby feathers or sticks are dragged through wet glaze to create the effect of wood graining.

Grandfather clock: A wood-encased pendulum clock that measures 6½ to 7 feet high; shorter versions are called grandmother clocks.

Graphics: A broad term for reproductions of artworks such as lithographs, serigraphs, and engravings.

Grass cloth: A type of wall covering made of woven reeds and dried grasses that are glued to paper or fabric.

Halogen: A fairly new type of incandescent light source that uses metal halides in compact, highly efficient bulbs, tubes, or reflectors; special fixtures are required for their use.

Heading: The top part of a curtain or drapery extending above the rod.

Highboy: A tall chest of drawers, sometimes mounted on legs.

High tech: A design style employing materials and articles usually found in industrial settings.

Hitchcock chair: A black-painted chair with a stenciled design on the backrest; named after its originator, an American cabinetmaker.

Hue: The name of a color, such as red, blue, or yellow.

Hutch: A two-part case piece that usually has a two-doored cabinet below and open shelves above.

Incandescent light: The kind of light that emanates from standard light bulbs.

Indirect light: Light directed toward, then reflected from, a surface such as a wall or ceiling.

Jabot: Vertical fabric sections in a swag drapery treatment.

Jardinere: An ornamental stand or tub for holding large plants.

K–Q

Kilim: A woven carpet or rug without a pile.

Lacquer: A hard varnish that is applied in many layers then polished to a high sheen.

Ladder-back: A chair with horizontal slats between upright supports.

Lining paper: A plain, thin wall covering designed to provide a smooth surface for wallpaper or paint.

Malachite: A green-colored mineral used for ornamental objects.

Marbling: A decorative paint technique used to create the veined, streaked look of real marble.

Marquetry: Inlaid decorative detail on furniture and other surfaces using wood, metal, or other materials.

Matt: A flat paint finish with no shine or luster.

Modular furniture: Versatile units of furniture that can be stacked or placed side by side in various arrangements.

Moiré: Fabric, usually silk, with a rippled, wavy pattern that gives a watered appearance.

Molding: Strips of wood, plaster, or other materials applied to walls for decorative effect or to conceal structural elements.

Monochromatic scheme: A color scheme whereby one color, in various tones, is used throughout.

Occasional furniture: Small items such as coffee tables, lamp tables, or tea carts that are used as accent pieces.

Oriental rug: Handwoven or hand-knotted rugs native to the Middle or Far East.

Palette: Term used by artists and decorators to describe a range of colors.

Parquet: Inlaid geometric patterns of wood; used primarily in flooring.

Parsons table: An unadorned square or rectangular straight-legged table in various sizes; named for the Parsons School of Design.

Patina: The natural finish on a wood surface that results from age and polishing.

Pedestal table: A table supported by a center base rather than four legs.

Pembroke table: A versatile occasional table with hinged leaves at the sides; usually fitted with a small drawer; one of Thomas Sheraton's most famous designs.

Pickled finish: The result of rubbing white paint into previously stained and finished wood.

Picture light: A shaded metal light fixture, usually oblong, that projects over a picture to light it.

Picture rail: A molding placed high on a wall as a means for suspending artwork.

Plissé: Fabric with a puckered look similar to seersucker.

Primary colors: The three colors—red, blue, and yellow—from which all other colors are derived.

Primitives: Paintings and art of an unsophisticated culture.

R–S

Ragging: A textured effect produced by passing a crumpled rag over wet paint or glaze.

Refectory table: A long, narrow dining table; originally used in monasteries for community dining.

Reproduction: An exact, or nearly exact, copy of an original design.

Restoration: Anything that has been brought back to its original condition through reconstruction or replacement of missing parts.

Rococo: A highly elaborate form of decoration and architecture dating from the early 18th century in France.

Roman shade: A flat fabric shade that folds into neat horizontal pleats when raised.

Rya rug: A shaggy, hand-knotted area rug made in Scandinavia.

Scale: A term refering to the size of objects in relation to each other and the human body; in decorating, good scale is the result of an eye-pleasing relationship between furnishings and other objects, and the space in which they are used.

Secondary colors: Colors produced by mixing two primary colors, such as yellow and blue to form green.

Shaker design: Furniture made by a religious sect of the same name; noted for its functional simplicity and austere beauty.

Shoji screens: Japanese-style room partitions or sliding panels usually made of translucent rice paper framed in black lacquered wood.

Slipcovers: Removable fabric covers for upholstered furniture.

Spattering: A decorative paint effect produced by tapping or flicking a loaded paintbrush onto a plain background.

Sponging: A paint technique involving the application layer after layer of opaque and translucent paint colors with a sponge.

T–Z

Terrazzo: A hard-surface flooring material consisting of small chips of highly polished marble or stone.

Ticking: A striped cotton or linen fabric used for mattress covers, slipcovers, and curtains.

Tieback: A fastener made of fabric, ribbon, or braid that is attached to the sides of a window and is used to hold back curtains or draperies.

Tint: The lighter values of a particular color obtained by mixing the color with white.

Tole: Paint-decorated metal, usually tin.

Tone: The darkness or lightness of a color; different colors may be of the same tone.

Trompe l'oeil: French for "fool the eye"; a two-dimensional painting designed to appear three-dimensional when it is actually flat.

Turn-of-the-century: Anything that was made around 1900.

Uplight: A light fixture that directs light toward the ceiling; can be freestanding or wall-mounted.

Valance: An overdrapery treatment made of fabric or wood; designed to conceal hardware and fixtures while providing a decorative touch.

Veneer: A thin layer of wood, usually of fine quality, that is bonded to a heavier, lesser quality, wood surface. Most new furniture is made of veneer construction.

Wainscot: Wood paneling that is applied to walls from the baseboard up to the desired height; a wall covering is used above.

Wallwasher: A type of spotlight that bathes a wall in ambient light.

Welsh cupboard: A large cupboard with open, wood-backed shelves on top and a cabinet base; generally used in dining rooms for the display of china.

ACKNOWLEDGMENTS

Interior Designers And Architects

Pages 18–19
Marjorie C. Penny
Interiors
Pages 22–23
Michael Hoffmann
Lawrence Grays Inc.
Pages 26–27
Michael Edlin
Page 28
Top: Kathy Niemi
Bottom: Handman
Associates
Page 29
J. Barron Kidd Associates
Pages 30–31
J. Barron Kidd Associates
Page 33
Dianne Josephs
Pages 34–35
Patricia E. Payne, ASID
Page 36
Top right: Carolynn Harder
Bottom left: Corky Wolk of
Carol Wolk Interiors
Pages 37–39
Gary McBournie of R.
FitzGerald & Co.
Page 42
Dianne Josephs
Page 43
Bottom: Paper White, Ltd.
Pages 44–45
Handman Associates
*McBride & Kelley
Architects, Ltd.*
Page 46
Top right: Timothy
Macdonald Incorporated
Bottom left: Handman
Associates
*McBride & Kelley
Architects, Ltd.*

Page 47
J. Barron Kidd Associates
Page 80
Jeff Peck
Page 88
Top: Richard FitzGerald of
R. FitzGerald & Co.
Bottom: Beverly Mager,
Interiors
Page 89
Carolynn Harder
Page 91
Michael Edlin
Page 94
Marsha Sewell, ASID, of
Sewell and Company
Page 96
J. Barron Kidd Associates,
Interior Design
Page 97
Dale Carol Anderson
of Dale Carol Anderson
Ltd.
Page 98
Top: Barbara Inbody
Bottom: Linda Carbutt of
Now & Then
*The Office of Michael
Rosenfeld, Inc.*
Page 99
Michael Hofmann
Page 102
Right: Joseph P. Horan,
ASID
Page 105
Suzie King
Pages 106–107
Phyllis Nickel of
Livingston, Nickel
& Notkins
Page 111
Michael Valvo Design

Page 123
Larry N. Deutsch, ASID,
of Larry N. Deutsch
Interiors, Ltd.
Allan J. Grant, AIA
Page 128
Deby Heumann of Intra
Design
Page 129
Bottom: Marsha Sewell,
ASID, of Sewell and
Company
Page 131
Linda Matthews
*Bokal, Kelley-Markham
Architects*
Page 132
Susan Thorn, ASID
Page 133
Carolynn Harder
Page 144
Karen Levering
Page 145
Top middle: Now & Then
Top right: Joseph P. Horan,
ASID
Page 147
Bottom: Carol Knott, ASID
Page 148
Top: Carol Siegmeister of
Taylor-Siegmeister
Associates
Page 163
Bottom: Now & Then
Page 171
William Hodgins, Inc.
Page 172
Top: Nancy Geisler Grimes
Bottom: J. Barron Kidd
Associates
Page 174
Bill Bigel of
H. Chambers Co.
Page 175
William Hodgins, Inc.

Page 176
Susan Kroeger
Page 184
Top right: Jeff Peck
Pages 188–189
M.J. Berries/Boston
Page 192
Right: Wendy Reynolds of
Cheever House
Page 193
Carolynn Harder
Page 194
Dianne Josephs
Page 195
Bottom: Beverly Mager,
Interiors
Page 196
Top: Beverly Mager,
Interiors
Bottom: Gary McBournie of
R. FitzGerald & Co.
Page 197
Nancy Geisler Grimes
Page 199
Handman Associates
*McBride & Kelley
Architects, Ltd.*
Page 201
Marsha Sewell, ASID, of
Sewell and Company
Page 208
Lyle Skinner of Lyle
Skinner Inc.
Page 213
Lyle Skinner of Lyle
Skinner Inc.
Page 221
J. Barron Kidd Associates
Page 224
Top right: Taylor-
Siegmeister Associates

Regional Editors

Estelle Bond Guralnick
Sharon Haven
Mary Anne Thomson
Jessie Walker Associates
Barbara Cathcart
Joan Dektar
Eileen A. Deymier
Carolyn Fleig
Margaret Ann Fowler
Helen Heitkamp
Cathy Howard
Linda Magazzine
Bonnie Maharam
Trish Maharam
Ruth Reiter
Maxine Schweiker
Bonnie Warren

Illustrators

Robert Dittmer
Mike Henry

Photographers

Alan Abramowitz
Laurie Black
Kim Brun
Stephen Cridland
Mark Darley
George de Gennaro
Mike Dieter
Timothy Fields
D. Randolph Foulds
Ted Fullerton
Susan Gilmore
Ed Gohlich
Jay Graham
Gayle Renfro-Harden
Hedrich-Blessing Studio
William Hopkins
Bill Hopkins, Jr.
George Jardine
Mike Jensen
Jenifer Jordan
Maris/Semel
Maxwell Mackenzie
Barbara Martin
Mike Moreland
Mary E. Nichols
John Rogers
Rick Rusing
Bill Stites
Perry L. Struse, Jr.
Rick Taylor
Al Teufen Photography
John Vaughan
Jessie Walker
D. Zanzinger

Photo Credits

Page 50
Trestle table: From the collections of Henry Ford Museum & Greenfield Village.

Page 50 *(continued)*
Queen Anne lowboy: Photographs © Chun Y. Lai/ESTO. All rights reserved.

Page 51
Banister-back armchair and Queen Anne card table: The Museum of Fine Arts, Houston, The Bayou Bend Collection, Gift of Miss Ima Hogg.
Queen Anne vase-splat side chair: Courtesy of The Henry Francis duPont Winterthur Museum.
Queen Anne tea table: Courtesy of Christie's New York.
William and Mary gateleg table: Photographs © Chun Y. Lai/ESTO. All rights reserved.
Queen Anne wing chair: The Metropolitan Museum of Art, Gift of Mrs. J. Insley Blair, 1950.

Page 52
Pembroke table: Courtesy of Mr. and Mrs. George M. Kaufman.
Tall-case clock: The Museum of Fine Arts, Houston, The Bayou Bend Collection, Gift of Miss Ima Hogg.
Tilt-top table: Courtesy of Israel Sack, Inc., N.Y.C.

Page 53
Windsor settee and bow-back Windsor chair: Old Sturbridge Village Photo.

Page 53 *(continued)*
Comb-back Windsor chair: Photographs © Chun Y. Lai/ESTO. All rights reserved.
Chippendale side chair and chest-on-chest: Courtesy of The Henry Francis duPont Winterthur Museum.
Chinese Chippendale settee: Colonial Williamsburg Foundation.
Camelback sofa: The Metropolitan Museum of Art, Purchase, Gift of Mrs. Louise Guerineau Myers, in memory of her husband, by exchange, 1972.

Page 54
Louis XVI armchair: The Metropolitan Museum of Art, Anonymous Gift, 1944
Bombé commode: Courtesy of the National Gallery of Art, Washington, D.C., Widener Collection.

Page 55
Bergère: The Metropolitan Museum of Art, The Jack and Belle Linsky Collection, 1982.
Fauteuil: The Metropolitan Museum of Art, The Jack and Belle Linsky Collection, 1982.
Provincial armchair: The Montreal Museum of Fine Arts.

Page 55 *(continued)*
Guéridon: Courtesy of Christie's New York.
Armoire: Courtesy of the French Connection, Inc. and Mr. and Mrs. John B. Lavin
Lady's desk: Courtesy of the National Gallery of Art, Washington, D.C., Widener Collection.

Page 56
Hepplewhite sideboard: Courtesy of Museum of Art, Iowa City, Iowa.
Tambour desk: Courtesy of Mr. and Mrs. George M. Kaufman.

Page 57
Shield-back chair and Grecian couch: Courtesy of The Henry Francis duPont Winterthur Museum.
Lolling chair: Courtesy of Mr. and Mrs. George M. Kaufman.
Bow-front chest of drawers: Photographs © Chun Y. Lai/ESTO. All rights reserved.
Lyre-base table and square-back sofa: The Museum of Fine Arts, Houston, The Bayou Bend Collection, Gift of Miss Ima Hogg.

Page 58
Dower chest: Courtesy of The Henry Francis duPont Winterthur Museum.
Chair table: Photographs © Chun Y. Lai/ESTO. All rights reserved.

Page 59
Hitchcock-style chair: Old Sturbridge Village Photo.
Shaker rocker: Collection of The United Society of Shakers, Sabbathday Lake, Maine.
Cupboard, Federal drop-leaf table, and grain-painted blanket chest: Photographs © Chun Y.Lai/ESTO. All rights reserved.
Schrank: Courtesy of Philadelphia Museum of Art: Purchased.

Page 60
Thonet bentwood armchair: Courtesy of Thonet Industries.
Wiener Werkstätte chair: Courtesy of ICF.

Page 61
Belter center table: Courtesy of The Henry Francis duPont Winterthur Museum.
Rococo Revival armchair, cottage chest of drawers, and Eastlake settee: Photographs © Chun Y.Lai/ESTO. All rights reserved.
Herter secretary: The Metropolitan Museum of Art, Gift of Paul Martini, 1969

Page 62
Noguchi coffee table: Courtesy of Herman Miller, Inc.

Page 62 *(continued)*
Paimio armchair: Collection, the Museum of Modern Art, New York, Gift of Edgar Kaufmann, Jr.
Cesca armchair: Courtesy of Knoll International.

Page 63
Wassily chair, Barcelona chair, and Barcelona sofa: Courtesy of Knoll International.
Art deco club chair: Courtesy of Christie's New York.
Eames lounge and ottoman: Courtesy of Herman Miller, Inc.
Le Corbusier chaise: Collection, the Museum of Modern Art, New York, Gift of Thonet Brothers, Inc.

Sources

Pages 202–207
Carpet and rug information: Carpet and Rug Institute Box 2048 Dalton, GA 30722

Page 205
Carpet: Armstrong World Industries, Inc. P.O. Box 3001 Lancaster, PA 17604

Pages 210–211
Rugs: Stark Carpet Corp. 1 Design Center Place Boston, MA 02210

Page 215
Wood flooring: Bruce Hardwood Floors 16803 Dallas Pkwy. Dallas, TX 75248

Page 218
Solid vinyl flooring: Azrock Industries Inc. P.O. Box 34030 San Antonio, TX 78265

Page 219
Rubber floor tile: Flexco Company P.O. Box 553 Tuscumbia, AL 35674
Vinyl sheets: Armstrong World Industries, Inc. P.O. Box 3001 Lancaster, PA 17604
Inlaid vinyl and *solid/inlaid vinyl:* Azrock Industries Inc. (see above)

Page 222
Marble: American Olean Tile Company Lansdale, PA 19446-0271
Terrazzo: PermaGrain Products Inc. 13 West Third St. Media, PA 19063

Page 223
Ceramic tile information: Tile Council of America
Mosaic, glazed, unglazed, and *quarry tile:* American Olean Tile Company (see above)

Page 223 *(continued)*
Bricks: Midland Brick & Tile Co. 1 Ashworth Rd. West Des Moines, IA 50265

Page 234
Torchère and ginger jar (brass): George Kovacs Lighting, Inc. 24 West 40th St. New York, NY 10018

Page 235
Floor canister, pharmacy lamp, cylinder light, and *halogen balance:* George Kovacs Lighting, Inc. (see above)

Page 236
Chandelier: Trend Lighting 2700 Sidney St. St. Louis, MO 63104

Page 237
Track lighting and recessed lighting: Halo Lighting 400 Busse Rd. Elk Grove Village, IL 60007

Undershelf: Halo Lighting (see above)
Reading and study: George Kovacs Lighting, Inc. (see above)

Page 239
Pendant light: Trend Lighting (see above)

INDEX